HERE
TO
HELP

HERE
TO
HELP

NGOs Combating
Poverty in
Latin America

Robyn Eversole
Editor

M.E.Sharpe
Armonk, New York
London, England

Library of Congress Cataloging-in-Publication Data

Here to help : NGOs combating poverty in Latin America / edited by Robyn Eversole.
     p. cm.
Includes bibliographical references (p.) and index.
ISBN 0-7656-1106-6 (alk. paper) — ISBN 0-7656-1107-4 (pbk.: alk. paper)
   1. Non-governmental organizations—Latin America—Case studies. 2. Economic
assistance—Latin America—Case studies. 3. Poverty—Latin America. I. Eversole,
Robyn Harbert.

HC125 .H45 2003
362.5′576′098—dc21

                                                                    2002029206

Printed in the United States of America

BM (c)   10   9   8   7   6   5   4   3   2   1
BM (p)   10   9   8   7   6   5   4   3   2   1

Contents

Tables and Map

Tables

Map

Here to Help

NGO Meets Community—And What Happens Next?

Robyn Eversole

> Poverty is the denial of the opportunity for people to have
> a decent standard of living, useful work, and to participate
> in decisions that affect their lives.
>
> —*UNDP 1998*

What role can nongovernmental organizations (NGOs) really play in combating poverty? Worldwide, over $6 billion in development assistance is funneled annually through NGOs,[1] yet the nature of NGOs' relationships with communities, and the real impact of their work, are little understood.

As Linn Hammergren writes,

> In an era when development assistance may be in crisis, it becomes necessary
> to re-examine the premises informing it, to reassess its accomplishments and
> failures, and to attempt more constructive engagement among those concerned
> that such assistance has too often missed the mark. (1999, 181)

In a review of some of the key literature on Latin American development efforts in the 1990s, Hammergren highlights common threads of agreement about the state of affairs in the region: that the economic decline since the 1980s has impacted the poor most, while the proffered cure—structural adjustment programs—has tended to make inequalities worse; that globalization "is having profound effects on national economies" and that democracies have often failed to give the poor majority a voice. At the same time, external assistance strategies have been unable to make a significant difference. As for Latin American NGOs, they "have assumed a greater role" yet "the rhetoric surrounding them obscures important variations in their performance and may overstate their real and potential contributions" (Hammergren 1999, 81).

This book is about analyzing the real and potential contributions of NGOs in one key area: reducing poverty. The book brings together academics and practitioners from inside and outside the region to discuss, critically and thoughtfully, their on-the-ground experiences with NGOs in Latin America. The perspective is local: how NGOs' work directly affects the communities where poor people live. Many of the articles focus specifically on projects. They show NGOs actively involved in local communities to accomplish specific antipoverty goals: increasing household food production, training artisans, developing local businesses. Yet amid the local scene, regional, national, and international forces continually emerge. What roles can NGOs play, and what complex relationships emerge when NGOs join forces with local communities to seek out solutions to a problem called poverty?

The following chapters offer a space for dialogue between North ("developed") and South ("underdeveloped" countries), between NGOs and communities, and between practitioners and academics (who, as Hammergren observed, tend to hold "notoriously jaundiced views" of each other). The contributing authors present specific case studies to explore the central question, *What can NGOs really do about poverty?* These chapters analyze the implications of the work of NGOs in poor communities, exploring the perspectives of both NGOs and community members about how NGOs are perceived, and what roles they play. Complex interactions emerge among NGOs, local people, and other actors (such as donors, local governments, and tourists), interactions which directly affect the success of antipoverty work— including how *success* itself is defined. As a whole, this collection takes a hard look at the social contexts, the political forces, and the cultural understandings that underlie NGO–community relationships, and how these impact NGOs' ability to fight poverty.

Insiders, Outsiders, and Intervention

NGO, or nongovernmental organization, is used here in its common colloquial sense to refer to nonprofit private organizations working in the area of "development"—organizations with a social mission. Carrie Meyer defines NGOs as "independent organizations that receive outside funding to support either staff, programs, or both," and are "engaged in activities related to sustainable development" (1999, 2). This book focuses on these kinds of funded social-development organizations, which often employ at least some professional or technical staff. Yet grassroots, self-funded organizations such as neighborhood associations, community kitchens, and so forth can be defined as NGOs as well, and such organizations often play key social development roles in the lives of poor people.

NGOs working in Latin America may be based in the country where they work or elsewhere (see e.g., Meyer 1999, 3). Among in-country NGOs, a further distinction is often made between grassroots organizations (GROs), based in local communities, and grassroots support organizations (GRSOs), based outside the communities they assist (Fisher 1998, 4). Both international NGOs working in Latin America and national GRSOs are essentially outsider organizations, separate from the client population they serve. They may be organizations for the poor, but they are not organizations *of* the poor.

"Outsider" NGOs arrive to help, and a process of relationship building with local communities begins. These NGOs may act in local communities as catalysts, organizers, educators, solidarity workers, or bearers of money, supplies, and information. As concerned outsiders, NGOs may offer considerable resources, but they also bring along outside biases and interests. Outsider organizations will generally have a different culture from the locals: different attitudes toward what is important, and different understandings of how things get done. Their goals may be very different from community goals. Mistrust must be overcome, and common ground established, before any sort of productive relationship can take place. Even then, communication may be clouded and often incomplete.

A common assumption underlies NGOs' entry (or "intervention") into communities—whether these communities are halfway around the world, or in the slum next door. The assumption is that something is wrong. Something needs fixing, or improving. And very often, something *is* wrong. Children are sick. Babies are dying. People are hungry. Fathers and mothers have to leave home to find work. Neighborhoods aren't safe. Working conditions are bad. The particular catalogue of social and economic ills varies from place to place, but local problems often form the starting point, the common ground for the NGO–community relationship. Vastly different cultures and value systems may unite under some common banner: agreeing that more food is better than less, that healthy children are better than sick ones, and that it is worthwhile joining forces to try to find a way to make things better.

Economies, in the broadest sense, are the contexts of exchange in which people act: social, cultural, economic, and political. They include what Amartya Sen (1981) has called "entitlements"—the various relationships people use to access the resources they need. Seldom, around the world, do local economies work really well; seldom do they provide opportunities—

and safety nets—for everyone to access resources fairly and sustainably. But in some places, local economies seem to work particularly badly: they do not provide many resources for most of the people living in them. These are the "poor communities," where human development statistics are generally low and quality of life suffers from lack of resources. Here, poverty is both more prevalent and more acute than elsewhere. Outsiders are moved to help. NGOs enter to effect a repair job.

Their strategies vary considerably. Many NGOs address poverty through market relationships, trying to improve local people's access to outside income. While recognizing that poverty is not just about money, they know that many resources, from education to housing, can be purchased in the cash economy. Thus, finding ways to increase poor people's access to cash is often a priority in antipoverty efforts. In this collection, Patrick Wilson (chapter 5) and Ana Mayta (chapter 6) consider two very different cases in which NGOs stimulate local craft production to generate income, in Ecuador and Bolivia, respectively. Frank Hutchins (chapter 9) examines ecotourism as another NGO strategy for drawing income into indigenous communities, while Makonen Getu (chapter 7) looks at urban microenterprise in Honduras and the role NGOs can play in improving income levels for self-employed people.

Other NGOs are hesitant to promote links to often volatile market economies, and choose instead to focus their efforts on expanding the resources that communities can produce and consume themselves. The generation of "subsistence" resources need not imply stagnation at survival level—the goal is generally for local consumption to increase and for people's well-being to improve. It does mean, however, that many resources available through larger market relationships will remain out of reach. Laurie Occhipinti (chapter 4) and Jeanne Simonelli and Duncan Earle (chapter 10) present cases of NGOs that have oriented their programs toward increasing local production (primarily food) for local consumption. The case presented by James Keese (chapter 1) shows that market articulation and subsistence-oriented production are not mutually exclusive strategies, and NGOs may promote both; improving local agricultural productivity may mean more food to eat—and more food to sell.

Other strategies for poverty reduction may not involve any income-generating component whatever, whether in cash or in kind. Rather, strategies may focus on building up a range of key nonmonetary resources. Thus, NGOs that work in areas such as the environment, education, literacy, health care, and so forth may have an antipoverty focus as they seek to improve poor communities' access to resources, both in the short and long terms. Many NGOs work to strengthen local community organizations as key social and political resources in the development process (Keese, chapter 1), recognizing that:

The foundation of poverty reduction is self-organization of the poor at the community level. Such self-organization is the best antidote to powerlessness, a central source of poverty. Organized, the poor can influence local government and help hold it accountable. They can form coalitions with other social forces and build broader organizations to influence regional and national policy-making. (United Nations Development Program 2000b, 72)

NGOs' roles as organizers, and their promotion of organization among the poor as a way to alter existing power structures, has long been a hallmark of their work; as Michael Cernea has written:

[NGOs] organize people to make better use of their own local productive resources, to create new resources and services, to promote equity and alleviate poverty, to influence government actions toward these same objectives and to establish new institutional frameworks that will sustain people-centred or actor-centred development. (1988, 8)

Yet both Keese and Ana María Condori (chapter 8) critique NGOs' tendency to impose organizations on poor people while ignoring their existing organizational forms.

The personal development (or "empowerment") of poor people—individuals as well as groups—is one route NGOs take to build social resources for change. Paolo Freire's (1974) consciousness-raising and related forms of popular education are strategies to build these sorts of resources. Recognizing that initiatives for change should come from poor people themselves, the following chapters explore how NGOs may act as "catalyst agents" (Esman and Uphoff 1984) encouraging people to make change happen. In chapter 8, using the metaphor of awakening for both herself as an Aymara woman and for her NGO, Condori considers the need for poor people to reflect on their situations and seek their own solutions to problems. This parallels Hutchins's view in chapter 9 that the development of perspectives about the world is a key goal for development work in poor communities. "Perspectives" imply not only knowledge about the world, but an understanding of oneself and one's own place in the world; the transformation of poverty, according to Getu (chapter 7), is internal as well as external.

Yet the question remains: what role can outside organizations really play in combating poverty? Are development NGOs able to provide information, networks, empowerment, financing, skills, and other ingredients to local people in a way that will help create sustainable solutions to poverty? Or are the problems too big, the vested interests too powerful—and the NGOs' own blinders too effective—for real cooperation to happen?

Poverty and Power

In Latin America, greater political stability in recent years has not marked the end of widespread poverty. Despite the relative prosperity of the region when compared with Africa or much of Asia, Latin America is still the most inequitable region in the world (IADB 1999). In its isolated rural communities and urban squatter settlements, local people struggle to improve their livelihoods and gain access to resources.

> Governments in Latin America [have] worked hard to achieve macro-economic stability, but they have yet to report convincing progress for the poor. Inflation rates have come under control, and public sector deficits have been nearly erased. Market reforms have encouraged growth, but the growth rates are disappointing given the magnitude of reforms. The recovery in real wages has been modest and the poverty rate still hovers around 35 percent. (IADB 1997; quoted in Meyer 1999, 20)

Poverty has often been defined according to economic measures:

> In the World Bank document *World Development Report 1990* the lack of economic growth was seen as the major cause of poverty. Increased economic growth on a global scale along with some limited public spending on basic education and health services were recommended as necessary to reduce income poverty. Today the Bank acknowledges that the results were dismal. Poverty figures from the South, however defined, remain ludicrous. (Oyen 2000, 7)

Recent writings (e.g., World Bank 2000; Ziccardi 2001; Sen 1999; Maxwell 1999) have emphasized that poverty is more than a lack of economic resources. Amartya Sen (1999, 14) writes that "a major issue in conceptualising development" is the gap between "an exclusive concentration on economic wealth and a broader focus on the lives we can lead." Poverty, according to Simon Maxwell (1999, 1) goes by many definitions, including income or consumption poverty, human (under)development, ill-being, vulnerability, lack of basic needs, relative deprivation, livelihood unsustainability, and social exclusion. Each term throws slightly different light on the question of what poverty is, and how it can be measured.

The 2000 Human Development Report defines poverty as "deprivation in four basic dimensions of human life—a long and healthy life, knowledge, economic provisioning, and social inclusion" (UNDP 2000a, 150). The World Bank report *Attacking Poverty* states:

[The poor] often lack adequate food and shelter, education and health, deprivations that keep them from leading the kind of life that everyone values. They also face extreme vulnerability to ill health, economic dislocation, and natural disasters. And they are often exposed to ill treatment by institutions of the state and society and are powerless to influence key decisions affecting their lives. These are all dimensions of poverty. (2000, 1)

Whatever the specific definition used, it quickly becomes clear that at heart poverty is about power and access to resources. These resources may be economic (such as assets or income); they may also be noneconomic (such as education, social networks, or spheres of influence). Understandings of poverty thus leave the exclusive realm of balance sheets and enter the realms of rights, resources, and relationships (see e.g., Maxwell and Kenway 2000).

At the same time, the economic balance sheet still has its role: Some resources can, after all, be bought. The role of economic growth in poverty reduction is still a topic of debate. Tony Killick writes:

Poverty rarely declines in stagnant economies but it usually diminishes in rapidly growing economies. Moreover, the evidence suggests, surprisingly, that the poorest groups also usually participate in the benefits of growth. (1999, 2)

The World Bank's *Attacking Poverty* report, not surprisingly, stresses that economic growth leads to poverty reduction. Yet, as Else Oyen (2000, 7) points out, "the fact that economic growth also creates poverty is played down." This bears emphasizing: Economic growth does not automatically equal poverty reduction. Why should it? Human relationships influence how resources are accessed and distributed. If the poor are socially excluded, deprived of resources and rights, they may lack the tools with which to reap the fruits of growth. As Patricia Feliu writes in chapter 3, in Argentina,

Economic growth has shown itself only through the concentration of wealth, because this growth is not built upon a model of social equity. Growth has thus led to the progressive implementation of mechanisms of exclusion. (62)

Growth creates opportunities and incentives, which some people may be well equipped to seize—perhaps at the expense of others. Thus, a development program that focuses on economic growth must concern itself not only that growth occurs but that it occurs in a way that its benefits are accessible to the poor, and its drawbacks (economic, environmental, or social) are not borne by them.

Rights, resources, and relationships: these are key ingredients influencing whether economic growth can decrease poverty. Even the World Bank, whose very identity is linked to economic definitions of growth, recognizes that poverty depends upon noneconomic factors, including politics:

> Poverty is the result of economic, political, and social processes that interact with each other and frequently reinforce each other in ways that exacerbate the deprivation in which poor people live. (World Bank 2000, 1)

In practice, these "processes" often result from the concrete actions of powerful individuals and groups working to safeguard their own access to resources. Self-interest may be expressed through conscious actions, or it may be unconscious: hidden in layers of social institutions and cultural assumptions. Whichever the case, the balance of power can be very difficult to shift; as Killick (1999, 1) writes, "Policies based on the existing distribution of power often cannot easily be changed because those who benefit are often influential enough to block reform."

If poverty is understood as a lack of power to affect resource distribution, then the role of development organizations working within existing power structures is called into question. Knut Nustad writes:

> If the problem, poverty, is seen as a political problem and the specific instance as a part of a much wider network of power relationships, then the potential developer has already defined him or herself away as the provider of a possible solution. (2000, 4)

The sharp critiques of development voiced by writers such as Escobar (1995) and Ferguson (1990) come from their understanding of how the *development process* itself can serve to remove power from the poor and transfer it to the organizations charged to help them.

Yet NGOs have often been seen as an alternative to existing power relationships, a sort of grassroots option.[2] Many NGOs, for instance, played a key role in the transition process from authoritarian to democratic regimes in Latin America (Meyer 1999, 17). A main NGO strength has long been seen as their local focus: capacity to reach the rural and remote poor, to promote community participation and local control of programs (Cernea 1988, 17). In the past decade, NGOs' increasing participation in international fora would seem to herald opportunities for a grassroots voice to reach into high levels of policy making. Yet it is important to realize that many NGOs—even those of local origin —are not particularly grassroots in nature. And none are exempt from questioning their role in existing power structures.

In this collection, NGOs and their observers take a hard look at the role of NGOs in local communities, and their position as brokers between the communities and outside interests. How do NGOs challenge the power structures that disadvantage the poor? Many of the NGOs in this volume are working to give poor communities the tools to gain power within existing structures. This may involve assisting communities to access government services (Keese, chapter 1), building coalitions to influence national and international policy (Grugel, chapter 2), or helping local producers to gain market knowledge and market power (Mayta, chapter 6). Yet as NGOs begin to question and attempt to address the power structures surrounding and reinforcing poverty, they are also led to question their own positions within these power structures. NGOs work for change—but whose change is it? The relationship between NGOs and local communities has been defined by poor people themselves as "often one of unequal partners" (Narayan et al. 1999). NGOs hold the greater power: resources, status, and veto rights on project decisions. Given this, how can NGOs ensure that their work does not impose inappropriate "solutions" on poor communities? How can NGOs be sure that their actions, fueled by their own assumptions, do not unintentionally reinforce the power structures that perpetuate disadvantage?

This collection provides an opportunity for NGOs and their observers to probe the assumptions underlying their work with poor communities and the power structures that inform these relationships. Over and over, in widely varied settings, the themes of participation, community empowerment, and community resistance emerge—as NGOs explore the boundaries of "participation" and come face to face with their own biases. The result is not a mere critique of NGOs, but a learning process for them—*consciousness-raising* for NGOs themselves.

The NGOs in this book work with communities to improve the well-being of local people who are poor. These NGOs all value participation: "working with" rather than merely "working for" the local community. Several speak eloquently on the dangers of paternalism, and the importance of local people taking charge of their own development. Yet the following chapters reveal contrary tendencies that disempower local people, often deeply imbedded in project design, and rooted in the assumptions that underpin an NGO's work. NGO staff may be unable to "hear" what local people are saying if their own culture throws out too much static. As Mexican NGO director Claudia Duran Duran expressed it, her experience running an NGO became, "an intense reflection concerning our work with indigenous women, as designed and implemented by mestiza women" (181).

Even for NGOs that have a strong rhetoric of "participatory development," *participation* is often limited to what Keese calls "a predetermined set of ideas, methods, and project activities" imported by NGOs into communities: "fast-food menus" of options that Simonelli and Earle have dubbed "McDevelopment." Yet, as Occhipinti writes, "communities have their own agenda for change." Local people respond to projects according to their own priorities and may even transform projects to meet their needs—if they have the power to do so. Simonelli and Earle repeatedly discover in their adventures with the Chiapas community of Cerro Verde that local people's project priorities differ markedly from those of outsiders. Even the terminology— such as "ecology" and "culture" in the ecotourism projects discussed by Hutchins—can mean completely different things to community members than to NGOs. Yet locals may be loathe to directly express their viewpoints and preferences, even when given the space. They are only too aware that NGOs hold the power in the "unequal partnership."

When NGOs move away from fast-food models of development to ensure local communities greater voice in project design, the problems are still by no means solved. An issue that surfaces repeatedly in the following chapters is that what communities want—and what they imagine NGOs can provide— is tinged with local people's own assumptions about the role of outsiders who come to help. Thus, in light of their prior experiences with *patrones*, governments, and/or paternalistic NGOs, community members ask for (and expect) giveaways, large capital goods—or, as Occhipinti observes for the Wichí of Argentina, any project at all as long as it provides employment. When NGOs and communities build a relationship, it is not only the NGO's assumptions about the community, but the community's assumptions about the NGO, that can impede communication and collaboration. As Hutchins states, dialogue is key in defining the "terms of development."

Another obstacle facing NGOs that attempt to challenge existing power structures is their own reliance on donors for resources. While empowering communities to create their own development, most NGOs are faced with the need to design projects that meet donor requirements—requirements designed far from poor communities. The vast majority of NGOs in developing countries are funded by international donors (Fowler 1997). As a result:

> To stay in business, NGOs need to satisfy the clients—the donors who pay the bills and demand the services. Thus the essential role of NGOs funded by foreign donors is to serve the international community—they provide international public goods. (Meyer 1999, 60–61)

But are these the same goods local people demand? As John Cameron (2000, 635) writes, NGOs may experience "pressures . . . to modify behaviour in ways that do not necessarily seem in the best interest of their target groups."

Such pressures may be direct and financial; Simonelli and Earle observe that when the NGO they studied traded "women-focused" development for the whole-of-community focus that local people wanted, their international funding disappeared. Philosophies of development may differ markedly; as Patricia Feliu observes in chapter 3 (54), many NGOs in Argentina "are concerned about the lack of freedom to create projects based on local needs, feeling themselves pressured by emerging trends from abroad."

Combating poverty may be the goal of both international donors and local community members—but their understandings of what poverty is, and how it should be fought, are not necessarily the same. Thus, a key challenge faced by NGOs is the bridging of cultures. NGOs must find commonalities and forge communication between themselves, the communities where they work, and external funders—as well as work with governments, markets, and other key players. Patricia Feliu offers a thoughtful exploration of the differing "perceptions" about NGOs and their roles: from the viewpoints of NGOs themselves, of international donors, of governments, and of people in poor communities. These perceptions differ, and reveal the tenuous lines of communication connecting poor communities with those who claim to help them. The following pages do present evidence of successes crafted jointly between community outsiders and community insiders. But they also offer a strong caution. NGOs dare not remain ignorant of the cultural assumptions that inform their relationships with local communities: the assumptions they make about communities, and the assumptions community members make about them.

Finally, it is vital that NGOs not overlook the implications of the power they hold relative to the community members with whom they work. Risk is a key issue, particularly when dealing with people who are poor and thus by definition *vulnerable*. NGOs' antipoverty projects generally involve commitment from community members, a commitment based on trust and implying some level of risk. Project failure is always a possibility: who will bear the cost? Patrick Wilson (chapter 5) discovers that a failed project in Ecuador had limited impact on the NGO itself, but a much stronger negative impact on the female community members who were supposed to benefit from it. Community members had invested no money in the project—so a superficial analysis might conclude that only the NGO stood to lose. But for women involved in the project, time, labor, household subsistence, personal reputations—and even personal safety—went on the line. Project failure was unfortunate for the NGO; for several poor community members, it was devastating. Outsiders can go home; it is the community that is left to pick up the pieces.

An intuitive truth is that outsiders can only do so much, that they can be trusted only so far. They are not, after all, invested in the local community.

Their knowledge of the people, politics, culture, and history tends to be superficial. Outsiders can bring valuable resources, but seldom achieve a really complete understanding of local needs—or of the local obstacles to meeting these needs. As Deepa Narayan et al. have written:

> To develop effective poverty reduction strategies, we must understand poverty from the perspective of the poor and explore the interlocked barriers poor women and men have to overcome, many of which have to do with social norms, values and institutional roles and rules beyond their individual control. (1999, 7)

Taking time to understand, in depth, the complexity of the local scene is one strategy that can help NGOs increase the effectiveness of their antipoverty work. James Keese (chapter 1) writes that, "detailed local knowledge and study [are] necessary to truly understand the NGO-induced changes on the local culture, economy, and environment" (3). Simonelli and Earle argue for the important role ethnography can play in helping outsider NGOs understand the inner workings of local communities—and avoid costly errors. Nor does the learning process move in one direction only; as Ana Mayta writes of her long pre-project conversations with local people, "We got to know the community, and they got to know us" (114). Similarly, Occhipinti describes how two Catholic NGOs "negotiate" development with indigenous communities in northwestern Argentina. Such two-way relationships are key to bridging the divides that keep poor people from accessing resources. Yet the power dynamics that underlie these relationships remind us that our communication is often incomplete, our assumptions seldom safe—and our motives always subject to question.

NGOs and Their Roles

NGOs have been part of the Latin American scene for the past fifty years, but have emerged in much greater numbers in the past twenty. Carrie Meyer (1999) traces the beginnings of NGOs in Latin America from as early as the Great Depression in some countries, when Catholic church charities were established to assist the poor. In the mid-1950s "private voluntary organizations" or PVOs from the United States entered Latin America. In the 1960s, the Alliance for Progress, funded by the United States Agency for International Development (USAID), helped to organize peasant groups, and in the early 1970s the U.S. Inter-American Foundation (IAF) also began supporting Latin American NGOs. More funding from European and Canadian donors arrived in the 1970s, and "the repressive military regimes of the late

1960s and 1970s encouraged increased funding of NGOs that provided alternative visions of economic development." USAID began to fund NGOs in the 1980s; since that time, NGOs have gone on to occupy a much more central role with multilateral donors and a variety of other development partners (Meyer 1999, 23–24).

NGOs' original mission was, according to Anthony Bebbington, to challenge the "dominant exclusionary, top-down, and often repressive forms of development" prevalent in the sixties and seventies (Bebbington 1997, 117). Key was NGOs' emphasis on the grassroots. In the mid-1970s, the Washington, D.C.–based IAF highlighted the relative novelty of the thought that local "grassroots" people would know how to solve their own problems:

> The people with whom we have come into contact in Latin America have shown over and over again that they know how to identify and resolve their own development problems. To do so, they need, not direction and technical assistance from outsiders, but additional resources, in most cases modest amounts of capital. (IAF 1977, ix)

In practice, the "people" that the IAF have funded over the years have been primarily Latin American NGOs. Whether local grassroots organizations or intermediary support organizations, these NGOs have been seen to hold local knowledge obviously lacking from the repertoires of international technocrats. Yet the mystique of "local knowledge" has been applied to even international NGOs. According to Bebbington, international NGOs have been known for focusing on small farmers, rural communities, and other grassroots groups; on building civil societies, and on working on behalf of the poor and oppressed—ultimately, for believing that "development" should be a participatory process.

These days, NGOs are well-known actors, key players in both Latin American civil society and in international arenas. Carrie Meyer writes on the "enormous diversity of objectives and political viewpoints" now represented by Latin American NGOs:

> Some are powerful advocates for the right, the left, the poor or the environment; others are efficiently providing public services; others both advocate and efficiently provide public services. Some NGOs are close to grassroots groups, and others are close to powerful elites. Some NGOs are accused of opportunism, illegitimacy and commercialism; others are attributed greater indigenous authenticity. (1999, 46)

The NGOs in this book are ones that implement projects in and with local Latin American communities, toward the goal of reducing poverty. Nearly all work with grassroots groups; some have facilitated the formation of such groups. In the previous section, we saw that the relationship between the NGO and the communities is key. But how are these relationships structured? What roles do NGOs—particularly outsider NGOs—take in local communities?

Many NGOs arriving from outside have felt a need to organize local communities, to better equip local people to take charge of their own development. Part of the rationale behind this has been to give local communities more political leverage—and thus, the power to demand resources. However, as Bebbington writes:

> The withering away of the state seems to make somewhat obsolescent the NGO approaches that aimed almost exclusively at building campesino capacity to make claims on the state (rather than on the market or other actors). (1997, 124)

Community organizing thus moves beyond developing a capacity to demand, and into developing a capacity to create. Community organizing can be used as a base to build "vibrant" communities of the sort promoted in community development literature: communities with positive vision and community pride, with strong community capacity in the form of knowledge and skills, with organizational arrangements that foster participation, and with strong community leadership (Lackey et al. 1987).

NGOs that work to help poor communities create their own change would recognize themselves in the role of "community development facilitator." As defined by Kenyon and Black (2001, 2), community development facilitators perform the following roles:

- *Energizer:* creating an atmosphere of energy, excitement, optimism, and positiveness;
- *Broker:* linking communities to experiences, methodologies, tools, networks, information, and resources that may be relevant to their needs and aspirations;
- *Coach:* optimizing the knowledge, confidence, and experience of community participants by demystifying concepts, processes, and strategies; facilitating group discussions; and helping to overcome stumbling blocks and conflict;
- *Champion:* promoting the community and its efforts to the wider world.

The energizer role includes acting as a catalyst for change: this may include catalyzing the formation of local grassroots organizations. Catalyst agents can play a key role in facilitating the emergence of local organizations where these have not emerged on their own; however, it is important to distinguish between local organizations catalyzed by outsiders and organizations that are directly *imposed* by outside aid organizations (see Esman and Uphoff 1984; Hirschman 1984). Imposed organizations, as Keese observes in chapter 1, tend to simply disband at the end of the project. Here lies the challenge for NGOs attempting to energize communities and act as catalysts for change: poor communities are more accustomed to receiving "development" than creating it, and catalysts must resist the pressure to put outsiders in the driving seat.

Part of an NGO's broker role generally includes attracting funding for local projects, but their role is much broader than that. NGOs may act as brokers for technical knowledge, market contacts, and information of all kinds. They may broker relationships with governments, international bodies, or other communities and organizations. At the most basic level, as Occhipinti explores, NGOs can act as cultural brokers: helping outsiders to understand communities, and communities to understand and navigate advantageously through outside institutions and organizations. The broker is a bridge, and such a bridge "between poor . . . populations and the dominant society" as the NGO Fundapaz has expressed it, can be key to establishing relationships where poor people can participate and access resources on more equal footing.

The coach and champion roles in community development facilitation can also be used to describe NGOs' work. As coach, NGOs may help the community to understand and implement the knowledge and resources obtained through brokering; NGOs may also facilitate internal communication and assist with conflict resolution. The champion role tends to be an extension of the broker role: the NGO "communicates" the local community to outsiders—and more important, provides community members with the tools and contacts to communicate themselves.

Relationships are key to accessing resources, so the bridging function played by NGOs can be vital. As Narayan et al. write:

> There is usually no direct connection between the informal networks or organizations of poor people and formal institutions. Typically they work quite independently of each other, which means that unlike the rich, poor people's organizations have little access to or influence on the resources of the state. This is precisely why the work of many NGOs and now government agencies is to reach out to poor people's groups to build these bridging connections. (1999, 13)

Poor people in communities where NGOs work often recognize the importance of having an advocate and broker who is knowledgeable and skilled at moving through the complex institutions of governments, markets, and international bodies. Laurie Occhipinti quotes a community member addressing an Argentinean NGO: "We don't know much about the outside world—but you do. . . . There are many things we need" (69).

The bridging function of NGOs can also be understood in terms of reducing transaction costs for community members. Cameron (2000) suggests that NGOs can lower the transaction costs poor people and communities face when attempting to access resources. Poor people face high levels of uncertainty and insecurity, and they are disadvantaged actors in society's institutions. NGOs can work to equip them with tools to deal with institutions—such as markets and governments—from a more advantageous position. Yet by definition, this implies a change in the local culture: different ways of thinking, different ways of working, to fit with the more powerful and dominant institutions which control access to resources.

Clearly, there are dangers here. Keese expresses the implications of the change process clearly: "What the NGOs are really trying to do is change local culture, and they typically want to do it in three to five years" (22). Yet, how much should poor people themselves be expected to change? And how much do outside institutions need to change to accommodate them? Whose mold are poor people expected to conform to when they "learn," "build capacity," "produce," and "participate"—all of those typical project objectives? If people are expected to homogenize—to trade their own meanings, values, and priorities for those of the outsiders who hold the power—what social alternatives are being discounted, devalued, and ultimately lost? As Narayan et al. warn:

> In any environment, it is easy for well-intentioned, more powerful and articulate outsiders to take over local processes, and thereby diminish the very local level processes they want to support. (1999, 226)

"Combating poverty" requires a vision of the future and actions (such as projects) that can achieve that vision. For some NGOs, a relatively simple picture, such as "market success for poor farmers" or "healthy, confident, articulate women," becomes their driving vision. For others, the vision is deeper, and takes into account the ways that many different aspects of community life interlink. Opportunity International's concept of transformational development (Getu, chapter 7), for instance, is based on a Christian vision of values and relationships, involving "a deeply rooted change in people's economic, social, political, spiritual, and behavioral conditions" (120).

Vision is not a luxury, it is a necessity: *Any* decision to create change is necessarily vision-driven. What does this change look like? A vision of change—such as *combating poverty*—is informed by values and ideals, whether conscious or simply assumed. It implies a transition from what *is* to what ought to be. And someone defines *what ought to be*. As Hutchins (chapter 9) under-lines, development interventions are always moral issues: they imply value judgments as to what ought to be, and what ought not to be.

NGOs' role in the change process is a delicate one. There is a fine but infinitely important line between *sharing* a vision and *imposing* it. NGOs arriving from outside a community can offer ideas, resources, and possibili-ties. They can share their vision and knowledge with community members, without using their power to impose—and community members can do like-wise. By retooling the notion of NGO "intervention" to one of relationship-building, a better scenario appears on the horizon. The change process becomes a dialogue, a "bridge upon which ideas are allowed to travel in both directions" (66) as the Argentinean NGO Fundapaz has expressed it. Here, the NGO recognizes and values community members' own visions—even when these differ from the NGO's ideas of how things should be. For col-laboration to happen, NGO and community must identify common ground —that is, a shared vision. In creating and pursuing this vision, community members will likely change. NGOs will change too.

Mapping a Path for Change

This book is a dialogue, charting the tension between NGO practice and NGO critique. This tension is real, with basic practical consequences. It is, at heart, the struggle between the desire to do good and the desire to do no harm. Many NGOs want to fight poverty, and their existence is based on the belief that they can. Yet most are aware that they play a dangerous game. They may fail to make things better. They may even make things worse.

Poverty is a fact; the poor are with us, and in astonishing numbers. Pov-erty is also a relationship. The relationship between laborer and landowner, farmer and intermediary, artisan and market, and citizen and state, illuminate poverty: here, we see the breakdown or blockage of poor people's access to resources. Poverty is the fruit of disadvantageous relationships: a vicious circle in which people lack not only *endowments* in Sen's (1981) terminol-ogy, but also *entitlements*—the relationships necessary to obtain these.

So what, in the end, can NGOs really do about poverty? The following chapters suggest a partial answer, by looking closely at NGOs as they work in local communities across Latin America. These NGOs are on the front lines of the fight against poverty. They have direct relationships with poor people in poor communities. The case studies in the following chapters show how these relationships themselves can be vital tools against poverty. Relationships between poor communities and outsider NGOs can help breach the blockages and bridge the chasms that separate poor people from resources: knowledge, information, personal contacts, services, money, ideas, and so forth. Relationships can also be resources in their own right; for people accustomed to exclusion and invisibility, experiencing the respect of NGO staff, with opportunities for self-expression and equal dialogue, and having the opportunity to build trust and friendship with outsiders, can be of immeasurable value.

Yet while reflecting on local-level experiences, it is important to emphasize that not all problems can be solved locally. Poverty is situated in much more complex and wide-reaching networks of relationships. Even as NGOs catch glimpses of real change in one or two communities, they are still faced with the longstanding problem of scale: As Narayan et al. (1999, 8) write: "Given the scale of poverty, NGOs touch relatively few lives." How appropriate, how effective, is community-level work, when poor people themselves observe that NGOs' work is appreciated but "NGOs are not as present as often believed" and "even the most successful large NGOs do not reach the majority of poor households" (1999, 8).

In 1987, Sheldon Annis asked the core question of scale: How can small-scale development be converted into large-scale policy? His question was based on the realization that the local level alone is not enough; not only do local-level interventions reach few people, but, as Alice O'Connor has observed: "even the most effective community-based initiatives cannot, by themselves, reverse the interacting economic, social, and political trends that have generated growing inequality" (1995, n.p.). The authors in this book observe how factors beyond the control of individual communities—things like national macroeconomic policies, state social policies, entrenched social attitudes, international trade barriers, and so forth—impact NGOs' and communities' ability to fight poverty locally.

Annis's discussion of the links between NGOs, their networks, and government, pointed to the key antipoverty roles NGOs can play in higher-level arenas. NGOs can strengthen civil society, creating stronger links between people and their governments, and so stimulate policy change (Fisher 1998). As educators and advocates with growing presence and voice in national and international fora, NGOs can work to shift policy in a way that favors the poor. This role is vital. In chapter 2, Jean Grugel explores the interface between NGOs' direct project-based work with poor communities and advocacy coalition building that aims to influence policy in favor of poor people's interests.

The latter is essentially founded on the former. Effective advocacy on behalf of the poor must be grounded in a true knowledge of poor people and their issues. It is often assumed that NGOs possess this knowledge, because of their close work with poor communities and grassroots groups. The following chapters, however, raise questions about how close NGOs necessarily are to understanding the real goals and priorities of the people with whom they work, or the complexity of the obstacles facing them. NGOs' ability to be effective at combating poverty at a higher level hinges upon their actual knowledge of reality at the grassroots—and a clear understanding of how local and macrolevel institutions interact. Relationships with poor communities are vital.

These relationships can help NGOs understand poverty while helping poor communities gain access to resources. Or, alternatively, NGO–community relationships can help NGOs perpetuate myths about poverty and the poor while continuing to block poor communities' access to resources. As Narayan et al. observe: "Poor people often report that besides being rude and forceful, NGO staff are poor listeners" (1999, 8).

Poor listeners seldom build effective relationships. The key question for NGOs is what kind of relationships they will build—and how they will build them, given the contexts and constraints under which NGOs themselves must work.

The experiences of the following authors and NGOs, taken as a whole, provide sound guidance on the art of relationship building. Each chapter explores how different NGOs approach antipoverty work with local communities in different parts of Latin America. Despite great differences among NGOs, communities, and contexts, from the Andes to the *selva* and from Mexico to Argentina, key themes emerge to guide NGOs' work:

1. Understanding local culture is vital. "Culture" goes beyond a surface knowledge of ritual and language. It involves an in-depth knowledge of the local institutional context: "The rules of the game" (North 1990).
2. NGOs must also understand their own culture. They need to be willing to question their own assumptions, listen, exchange, and find the delicate balance between fulfilling their own mission and responding to local needs. The same goes for organizations that fund NGOs.
3. NGOs do have vital roles to play within local communities. Their roles as broker and bridge to outside resources can be of immense value.
4. The heart of success is grounded in the relationship between the NGO and the local community. "Best practice" can provide a guide for structuring specific kinds of projects, but it is secondary to NGOs' core relationships with the communities. Do NGOs listen, or do they impose? Do local people feel free to express their views, and are they willing to do so? Does the relationship with the NGO truly serve to "build up" local people?

We don't have money saved up in the bank, but we have Cesar, we have Augustine, we have other colleagues in the communities who now will help you plan, who now will push you, who now will criticize you, who now will question you—who in general help us to generate ideas, to improve things. (Hutchins, 172–73)

When local economies are "broken"—when they don't provide for people's well-being—it is usually the relationships that need mending. When poor people can forge relationships with people and institutions and deal with them on equal footing to access the resources they need, they cease to be poor. Obtaining an identity card, tapping into a lucrative market for handicrafts, gaining access to new technology, lobbying government for better services, joining with neighboring communities to staff a health clinic, sending a child to college—all depend upon relationships, and all generate new relationships in turn. The problems occur when these relationships are blocked, when the poor can't deal on equal footing, when key resources remain at higher levels, out of reach.

This book explores how NGOs and communities work to overcome these blockages—with views of successes and failures, encouragement and disappointment. The first two case studies present international NGOs in their on-the-ground work with poor Latin American communities. Geographer James Keese provides case studies of international NGOs CARE and PLAN at work in highland Ecuadorian farming communities, and considers the long-term impacts of their projects. In chapter 2, political scientist Jean Grugel then explores the philosophies of poverty and change of several major British NGOs in Latin America, and how these NGOs work with local NGOs in both community-based antipoverty projects and higher-level advocacy.

Patricia Feliu continues the conceptual discussion of NGOs' work and the interplay between local, national, and international forces, examining the role of NGOs in Argentina from multiple perspectives. Laurie Occhipinti then offers a view of how NGO–community relationships in Argentina play out at a local scale, in a comparative case study of two Argentinean NGOs at work with indigenous communities. Patrick Wilson presents an Ecuadorian NGO's struggle to establish an income-generating handicrafts project in a lowland Quechua community and analyzes the reasons for project failure from the perspectives of community members, the NGO, and the market.

In chapter 6, Ana Mayta offers a contrasting experience of a more successful handicrafts project coordinated by a Bolivian NGO, highlighting the importance of market relationships and the role NGOs can play in mediating these relationships for microenterprises. Makonen Getu continues the focus on microenterprise, from the perspective of Opportunity International's microenterprise credit programs. He explores how for this NGO, facilitating enterprise development is only one ingredient in a larger vision of "transformational development" and demonstrates how this vision is reflected in case studies of successful local microfinance clients in Honduras.

Chapter 8 continues to develop the theme of transforming poverty into well-being, through an Aymara woman's perspective. As director of an NGO that works closely with indigenous grassroots organizations, Ana María Condori speaks from her own experience as both a cultural "insider" and a facilitator of development initiatives. The interface between grassroots indigenous groups and outside NGOs is also a focus of Frank Hutchins's case study in chapter 9, as he explores the implications of ecotourism projects in the Amazon that generate income while redefining local places in new ways. Finally, in chapter 10, anthropologists Jeanne Simonelli and Duncan Earle draw on the experiences of an indigenous community in Chiapas, Mexico, to describe the transition from common NGO-driven models of antipoverty work, to a community-driven approach to change.

In the following dialogue, throughout these ten chapters, a range of voices emerges: indigenous peoples, foreign academics, urban professionals, community leaders, poor women and men, NGO directors, governments, international funders, development theoreticians, and local NGO staff. They all talk about poverty: what it is, and what NGOs can do about it. The thoughtful reader will listen carefully to all of them: What do they say? What do they mean? Most important, what do they do, and why? The thoughtful reader will watch for the relationships. Poverty lies in the relationships. So do its solutions.

HERE
TO
HELP

1

Smallholder Agriculture and Poverty Alleviation in Indigenous Communities

James Keese

This chapter focuses on the work of two international NGOs, Plan International and CARE, with indigenous smallholder agriculturalists in highland Ecuador. On a global scale, these two NGOs alone spend well over half a billion dollars annually on development assistance in sixty countries. They are central actors in transferring ideas, methodologies, and resources from more developed to less developed regions. With this transfer comes the ability to influence patterns of production, resource management, culture, community organization, and policy that affect the daily lives of millions of the world's poor. Given this power, it is essential to know what the NGOs actually do in the field, and the results obtained. This chapter provides an in-depth, empirically based, community-level analysis of the agricultural and other poverty alleviation projects of Plan and CARE.

A "before and after" methodology is the outstanding feature of this study. Initial field data were collected over a nine-month period ending in 1995. A follow-up visit was made in 2001 to determine what had happened to the NGOs' projects after the withdrawal of assistance. With these comparisons, I have been able to draw conclusions about the success and failure of certain aspects of the NGO projects. Also, I actually lived in the communities and spent an extended period in the study region when I gathered the initial data. This type of detailed local knowledge and study is necessary to truly understand the NGO-induced changes on the local culture, economy, and environment.

Research in cultural and political ecology provides an appropriate conceptual framework for analyzing the impact of NGOs on rural areas in Latin

America. Much work in cultural ecology has focused on traditional agricultural systems and the adaptive strategies used by local peoples in response to change (i.e., Knapp 1991; Mathewson 1984; Nietschsmann 1973; Turner 1989). Work in political ecology has emphasized the need to link traditional resource-management strategies of peasant communities with the larger context of open and changing political economies (Bebbington 1993; Peet and Watts 1993; Zimmerer 1991). As a geographer and a political ecologist, I understand that traditional communities, and the work that NGOs do in them, are influenced by a complex and interconnected set of local, national, and global processes.

This chapter begins with an examination of the changing rural conditions in highland Ecuador. I attempt to place the NGOs' work and the study communities within a larger and rapidly changing national and global context. This section is followed by a review of the methodological principals that have influenced NGO work, especially in agriculture. Then, I present field data that describe the projects of Plan and CARE, during and after the NGO intervention. I conclude with a discussion that explains how the actions of the NGOs, and importantly, the larger contextual variables, contributed to what happened after the NGOs stopped working in the communities.

The Changing Rural Context in Highland Ecuador

Ecuador, an Andean country with a population of 12.9 million people (PRB 2001), is commonly divided into three geographic regions. From west to east, the three regions are the Pacific coastal lowlands (*costa*), the Andean highland region (*sierra*), and the lowland territory in the Amazon basin (*oriente*). The densely populated intermontane basin area in the sierra, or *callejón andino*, is home to most of Ecuador's approximately one and a half million Quichua-speaking indigenous people. Over the past forty years, Ecuador's population has tripled resulting in intense land pressure, invasion and degradation of marginal lands, and colonization of the less populated zones in the costa and oriente.

Ecuador's rural areas exhibit patterns of uneven development that are characterized by noticeable historic, economic, and social differences. Historically, the sierra was dominated by extensive estates (*haciendas*), where landlords maintained high levels of social and political control over the indigenous peasants. In contrast, the costa is dominated by commercial banana, rice, sugar cane, and shrimp farms using modern capitalist production techniques and employing wage labor. Within this structure are thousands of small, marginalized, highly fragmented holdings, or *minifundios* (Brown, Brea, and Goetz 1988; Redclift and Preston 1980). The minifundios are holdings of less than ten hectares and are worked by peasant farmers (*campesinos*) who eke out a living by cultivating traditional crops and obtaining temporary off-farm work. The traditional economy of the highlands involves farming of potatoes, corn, beans, barley, and wheat in combination with the raising of cattle, sheep, pigs, and a variety of small animals. Smallholder production in the sierra is mostly for subsistence or the domestic market, but is hindered by resource constraints and has suffered from stagnation.

Over the past four decades or so, Ecuador's rural areas have been dramatically transformed. During the 1960s and 1970s, land reform was carried out in order to free up dependent hacienda labor and to modernize production, primarily for the purpose of meeting growing demand for food in the cities and the demands of foreign markets and producers. Agriculture on farms of all sizes became more commercialized (Commander and Peek 1986). However, government agricultural policies have had uneven spatial and sectoral impacts (Lawson 1988). Large producers, the export sector on the coast, and urban consumers were the primary beneficiaries of import substitution industrialization policies and agricultural subsidies. Meanwhile, the small farm sector and highland indigenous communities have generally been neglected, resulting in marginalization.

Urbanization, agricultural modernization, and economic change also have contributed to a transformation of labor utilization patterns in Ecuador, resulting in high rates of temporary labor circulation and permanent out-migration. Seasonal migration, primarily to urban areas and the commercial farms in the costa, and temporary off-farm wage labor are common. In the 1980s and 1990s, international migration, especially to the New York area, eclipsed domestic migration as a dominant force for culture change (Jokisch 2001). As many as 400,000 Ecuadorians, many from the region addressed in this chapter, live in the United States, sending approximately $1.4 billion annually to Ecuador in remittances. After petroleum, remittances represent the number two source of foreign earnings for Ecuador.

Beginning in the 1960s, substantial oil revenues from production in the oriente facilitated the economic and rural transformation processes in Ecuador. However, a drop in oil prices in the early 1980s led to a period of neoliberal structural adjustment and austerity that continues to the present. The late 1990s were characterized by particularly severe political and economic instability. A brief war with Peru over the southern border broke out in 1995, resulting in investment loss and budgetary problems. Between 1996 and 2000, two presidents were forced to resign because of corruption scandals. Inflation and rapid devaluation of the national currency (the sucre) ultimately led to the dollarization of the Ecuadorian economy in 2000. The adoption of the U.S. dollar as Ecuador's official currency has dramatically affected demand patterns in the national market, the incomes of smallholder agriculturalists, and even the purchasing power of the NGOs themselves.

In the 1960s and 1970s, the NGO role in Ecuadorian development was limited, mostly oriented toward the land-use transformation process and consultations regarding the spending of new oil revenues. With the onset of Ecuador's economic problems in the 1980s, the state proved itself to be incapable of addressing (or unwilling to address) the needs of all of Ecuador's citizens, especially among the poor, the indigenous people, and geographically isolated areas (ALTERNATIVA and PNUD 1992; Keese 1998; Plan Ecuador 2000). NGOs took a leading role in filling the institutional void left by reduced government budgets and lack of attention to small farmers in the highlands. Underfunded Ecuadorian government agencies have openly encouraged international NGOs to enter impoverished areas and provide development services (Torres 1994). NGOs have become important actors working in marginalized rural communities helping them to maintain themselves and adapt to the challenges presented in a rapidly changing national and international context.

NGOs and Development

Over the past two decades, NGOs' work with smallholder agriculturalists has shown a convergence of project methodologies around four concepts: *sustainable development, participatory development, agroecology,* and *the wider impact* (Keese 2001). For development professionals in Ecuador, the term sustainable development has two different meanings. First, do projects promote conservation and good management of natural resources? This meaning has an ecological focus, referring to whether human activities enhance, maintain, or degrade a resource base. The second meaning is organizational. Are project activities continued, or sustained, after the withdrawal of project assistance? While the ecological component is designed into the projects that are examined in this study, the organizational aspect is most emphasized by the Ecuadorian professionals I interviewed. If project activities are not sustained, then there is no long-term change.

Participatory development is an organizational strategy that has been developed and tried extensively by NGOs. The goal of participatory development is to teach a process by which people can take charge of their lives and develop their own agricultural and community programs (Breslin 1987; Bunch 1982). In contrast to large, centralized, top-down development programs commonly financed by governments and some multilateral aid agencies, participatory development projects are small-scale, flexible, innovative, and bottom-up, and incorporate local people, technology, and resources in the development process. The poor participate in the planning, implementation, and management of their own projects, which leads to more appropriate project activities, more interest, and better long-term maintenance of projects (Fisher 1993).

Given that poor farmers today are faced with serious challenges and resource limitations, a small financial, technical, or organizational input may sometimes be needed to jump-start the development process. However, in order to avoid problems with paternalism and dependence, the role of "outsiders" and the use of complicated technology and giveaways must be limited. Participatory development projects pay strict attention to local customs, especially in areas inhabited by native peoples, and project personnel who are farmers and community members are preferred. The participation of women is also an important issue, as NGOs focus on empowering and enhancing their productive capacities, not just on their domestic and reproductive roles (Mehra 1997).

Agroecology provides the natural resource management and farming techniques for promoting sustainable agricultural development among smallholders. Miguel Altieri (1995), D. Kaimowitz (1993), and others have outlined an integrated holistic approach to small farm development that incorporates economic, cultural, and ecological aspects of production. The starting point is "the improvement of traditional mixed farming systems in small autonomous units of production by encouraging and building on indigenous knowledge, experimentation and adaptation" (Conway and Barbier 1988, 668). However, in order to survive in today's commercial economy, modern inputs and methods are used to assist, complement, and improve upon what farmers already do well. Agroecological farming methods focus heavily on soil and slope management practices, and are generally labor and management intensive, not capital and technology intensive.

A final concern of NGOs is their ability to influence the larger context and policy environment. At the community level, the organizational methods introduced by NGOs can help local people deal more effectively with the larger society. Anthony Bebbington (1996) argues that in a rapidly changing world, indigenous communities are increasingly required to forge new market relationships, manage development of on- and off-farm techniques, and negotiate new relationships with government and other organizations. NGOs are also concerned with expanding the scale of their achievements and influencing the larger policy environment. John Clark (1991, 75) states that individual projects, no matter how successful, by themselves are "only islands of relative prosperity in a sea of misery." NGOs must work with states and donors to try to change the larger context in which they operate, thus creating better conditions for development. They act as links between governments, donors, other NGOs, and local communities to facilitate the movement of funds and information, and to influence policy. NGOs facilitate contact and the flow of ideas between what A. Brysk (2000) describes as the global village and the tribal village.

The Study Region: Upper Cañar

The study area for this research is the upper drainage of the Cañar River (commonly known as upper Cañar) in the south-central sierra of Ecuador. Upper Cañar is a topographically and agroecologically diverse region ranging from 800 to 4,500 meters above sea level. The population of the region is approximately 70,000, half of which are indigenous people who constitute a majority in the rural areas.[1] Upper Cañar faces similar changes to those that are affecting the Ecuadorian sierra in general. The traditional economy of the region is becoming more commercialized, with approximately 50 percent of traditional staple crops now being sold in local markets. Field data (from 1995) document annual per capita income in the study communities from on-farm production to be $96 (approximately 18 percent of national GDP per capita). For most families, land holdings are not sufficient to utilize all of the available labor or to generate the cash income needed to meet household needs.

Land pressure in the more densely populated zones has created a situation where campesinos are looking to the less populated but more ecologically fragile zones as a means of gaining access to more land and resources. Meanwhile, the elite-controlled, and often corrupt, Ecuadorian government has done little to limit destructive land use practices. Steep slopes are commonly deforested, plowed, and cultivated, exposing them to erosion. The deterioration of production in upper Cañar has resulted in lower yields and incomes, and increased reliance on local wage labor, seasonal migration to the costa, and more recently, international migration to the United States and Europe.

Plan International and CARE were chosen as the focus of the study because they had the largest budgets, worked in the most communities in the region, and had the most comprehensive programs. They are typical of well-funded international NGOs that engage in integrated community development. In general, the NGOs work with the poorest people in the poorest communities, noting that families owning five or more hectares of land usually do not need or want NGO assistance.

The initial fieldwork was part of my dissertation research. I spent nine months in the study area during 1994 and 1995. I returned for a fifteen-day follow-up visit in the summer of 2001 to document project results after the NGOs had ended project assistance. Data were collected using a combination of participant observation and semistructured, unstructured, and informal interviews with community members, NGO workers, government officials, and other affected interests. The focus is on a human-scale analysis. What can be observed in the field, and what does it mean to the daily lives of the people?

Plan International

Plan International, founded in 1937, is an international humanitarian, child-focused development organization that has no political or religious affiliation. Plan invests annually about $270 million in forty-three countries on health, education, housing, water, sanitation, and production enhancement projects. Plan enrolls children and then provides project assistance to their families and communities. The larger goal of Plan is to help poor children to realize their full potential, contribute to society, and be actors in their own growth and development (Plan International 2001).

In 2001, Plan Ecuador sponsored approximately 68,000 children living in 1,200 communities (Plan Ecuador 2000). Plan has identified provinces and regions for assistance based on its own national analysis of poverty. Plan determined that rural areas have the highest percentage of people living in poverty (74.4 percent of the rural population), and indigenous communities tend to be poorer and need special attention. Among the poor, pregnant women and children under five years of age are at the highest risk for illness and lack of basic services. Other factors that Plan considers are whether a community is accessible and the motivation of the community to work with Plan.

Plan has worked in Cañar province since 1982. The Plan office in Cañar has an annual budget of $220,000 (Paguay 2001), and has projects in approximately fifty communities in the study region. Plan is the largest NGO working in the province, both in the number of projects and the size of its budget.

Plan International Field Site: Sunicorral 1995

Field study of a Plan project in the indigenous community of Sunicorral San Juan was used to document Plan's methods, results, and ability to reduce poverty. Sunicorral is located at 2,960 meters above sea level, adjacent to the Pan-American highway, and near the canton seat and market center of El Tambo (pop. 3,000). Holdings are characterized as minifundio, ranging from one-quarter to seven hectares per family. Production is mixed crop and livestock. Plan provided assistance to the community over a fourteen-year period, from 1986 until 2000. Plan worked with a group of twenty-three agriculturalist families (in a community of approximately seventy-five families).

Plan placed great emphasis on community organization as essential to sustaining the development process. Rommel Carpio (1995), director of Plan Cañar's agricultural program, believed that getting people to work together was the only way to address the problems of poverty and development. Bebbington et al. (1993) have argued that strong local organization is a pre-requisite for sustainable resource management. Plan influenced the organi-zation of the community by requiring the formation of a "Plan group." The group elected a president (always a man), treasurer, and secretary. An effec-tive president was especially important to the progress of the project because a good leader is able to coordinate group work, manage money, and deal effectively with interests outside the community (e.g., government agencies, other NGOs, and banks). Plan field staff held weekly workdays with the Plan group to give instruction and work on project activities.

In addition to the larger group, Plan also sought to organize the women in the community by establishing a separate women's group. They did this in 1994. It too had its own leaders, project activities, and funds. The men of the group did not oppose this action. One of Plan's goals is to empower women by giving them more control over household production and income (Plan Ecuador 2000). Plan expects the well-being of the household (and the chil-dren) to improve along with the status and power of the women. In practice, the men and women generally worked together, regardless of which group received the aid.

The focus of Plan's assistance from 1986 to 1988 was on infrastructure-type projects. The first project activity was the construction of a potable wa-ter system. Plan helped the community work with the government to secure rights to a source of water (a spring located above the community). Plan provided the construction plan, materials, technical assistance, and hired the labor. Community members provided unskilled labor for digging ditches, gave food for the hired professionals, and paid half the cost of the water meters. Faucets and meters were installed in sixty homes (which included many nonenrolled families). A community-based administrative committee was set up to check the meters and charge nominal user fees that were to be used to maintain the system.

The second project activity, provided at the same time as the water system, was the installation of latrines. Latrines were constructed by building a cement pad, a wooden barrier, and a roof. Ceramic toilets were installed along with PVC leach lines running ten meters from the toilet into the ground. Plan gave all of the materials to sixty families. The community provided the labor.

Electrification was the next project activity. Electrification involved a tri-partite agreement among Plan, the government electric company, and the community. Plan paid for the transformers and meters. The government installed the wire and poles. The community provided labor when appropriate. Sixty homes were connected. The power came from the national grid, and the government read the meters, assessed fees, and maintained the lines.

Plan suspended project activities in Sunicorral from 1988 to 1992, stating "lack of community organization" as the reason (R. Carpio 1994). Project assistance resumed in 1993 after the election of a new community president. One might view the threat of project suspension as paternalistic. It could also be seen as a necessary push from the outside to encourage community organization and aid in the development process.

From 1993 to 2000, Plan's assistance shifted to agricultural development. This change reflected a new focus on income improvement as a means of poverty alleviation and improving child welfare. Increased agricultural production and on-farm income, it was hoped, would also reduce the need for seasonal migration to the coast. This would in turn enhance community cohesion and long-term development prospects in the highland indigenous communities.

Initially, Plan gave the project participants in Sunicorral high-yielding potato, corn, wheat, and onion seeds, along with chemical fertilizer and a truckload of chicken manure. Plan reported production gains of 15 percent in the first year (R. Carpio 1994). According to community members, yields declined quickly in the following years because families did not have sufficient income to buy the purchased inputs after Plan stopped giving them. Also, one of the families took the seeds for itself, indicating a concern for the abuse of giveaways.

Next, Plan helped the members acquire land, reasoning that more land would result in more production. During 1993 and 1994, the group purchased four plots of land within the community totaling approximately two hectares, which were to be owned and farmed communally. The group initially bought a one-half hectare plot for $500. Plan paid 50 percent of the cost ($250). In 1995, Plan families were farming the plot in traditional crops, and dividing the harvest equally. Plan then bought a quarter-hectare plot for the purpose of building a community center which was never built. In 1995, the women's group was farming this plot in traditional crops. The Plan members themselves then purchased another quarter-hectare plot for $1,300. Plan helped them get a bank loan to purchase the land. When I left the community in June 1995, the group was delinquent on the loan, and owed penalty charges. The plot was being used by the Plan extensionist as a test plot for a high-yielding variety of peas.

The most costly agricultural project component in Sunicorral was a communal pasture and irrigation project. The Plan group bought one and one-half hectares of land in the middle of the community, at a cost of $1,365, of which Plan paid 80 percent and the members paid 20 percent. Plan built a modern irrigation system utilizing a gravity flow system (with cement holding tank) and rainbird style sprinklers. The cost of the system was $6,820. The project was designed to support seven milk cows, which the members had not yet purchased in 1995. It was to be managed communally, with the milk sold at a local collection point and the income split equally. Plan also provided a course on veterinary assistance and breed improvement. Plan made arrangements with the state university in Cuenca (sixty miles from the community) to send technicians and students out to the community to teach them how to manage an irrigation system. The university people were not well received by the community, most likely because of a clash of cultures between urban *mestizo* professionals and the rural indigenous agriculturalists.

The high up-front costs of the pasture project subsidized an innovative production change, but raised questions of paternalism and dependence. Plan justified the costs and methods used because they allowed project families to achieve immediate economic benefits. They also hoped that the innovations would be copied by non-project families, thus initiating diffusion and multiplier benefits to the region (R. Carpio 1994).

Beginning in 1994, and after the completion of the pasture project, the focus of Plan assistance in Sunicorral until its withdrawal in 2000 was on the women's group. The Plan project for the women's group was referred to as the integrated farm project. The integrated farm is an agroecological approach to coordinating the household production unit. Field crops, vegetables, fruit trees, livestock, soils, and water are integrated in ways that augment and complement the productive, biological, and ecological capacities of the farming system (IIRR 1996). This project was an attempt to intensify production on existing land.

Each family constructed a ten-by-ten-meter vegetable garden adjacent to its house. Plan provided fencing material, seeds, and training. The families planted carrots, cabbage, lettuce, cauliflower, broccoli, beets, tomatoes, radishes, chard, turnips, onions, garlic, cilantro, and several other herblike plants. Vegetables, which were not part of the traditional diet, added to family nutrition, and surpluses were being sold in the nearby El Tambo market. In 1995, they were being purchased for local consumption, trucked to nearby cities and the costa, and sometimes exported (by intermediaries) to northern Peru. I concluded that given market conditions, vegetable production represented an economically viable and sustainable method of income improvement.

The families also built one-by-two meter wooden-framed holding areas for raising earthworms. Worms produce a rich organic fertilizer for the vegetables, and it can also be used to grow potatoes. The group then added *chancheras* (pigpens), with Plan giving the cement and wood. Pigs, which are part of the traditional system, provide a valuable source of income, meat, and manure. An integrated farm generally utilized one-quarter of the household production area for irrigated and cultivated pasture for dairy cattle. Beside the obvious income benefits from selling milk, pasture expansion and improvement protected the soil from erosion (assuming overgrazing did not occur) and increased the availability of manure for the other parts of the farming system.

In 1995, nine years after work began in Sunicorral, Plan made more changes in its methodology. First, Plan began using a participatory community self-diagnostic in all project communities. The diagnostic is a method of participatory development, and part of a global effort by Plan International to make its projects more grassroots oriented. In Sunicorral, all members of the community were invited to participate in a one-day facilitated workshop. The people documented and assessed historic and current conditions, defined problems and needs, and developed strategies for carrying out project activities. In addition, the diagnostic provided Plan and the community a baseline for evaluation. Plan also required project families to pay for 50 percent of the cost of purchased inputs. These methodological changes represented a shift away from a paternalistic approach that relied on giveaways and capital inputs toward an approach that focused more on education, training, and technical assistance.

In 1996 and 1997, Plan added guinea pig and chicken raising to the integrated farm project. Guinea pigs are a traditional food in the Ecuadorian Andes, as well as an important source of income. A large animal can bring up to $10 in the local market. Guinea pigs are fed grass from the cultivated pasture. Chickens are an ideal addition to the integrated farm because they will eat most of the crops in the traditional rotation. The eggs and meat are an important source of nutrition and income. Chickens sell for up to $5 each in the market, and an egg sells for ten cents. The manure from both of these animals is useful in the gardens, earthworm boxes, and in the fields. Plan provided the women of sixteen families with materials and technical support to build fully enclosed five-by-three-meter structures that were divided and shared by the guinea pigs and the chickens. Plan also gave each family high quality breeding pairs of both types of animals. Each pen could hold about a hundred guinea pigs and ten chickens. Plan paid approximately $130 per family to get the guinea pig and chicken raising projects started, which represented about 50 percent of the costs.

During the last two years of Plan's involvement in Sunicorral, no major new activities were carried out. Project assistance focused on maintaining and improving what had already been done. The project formally ended in March of 2000.

In 1995, I estimated a per capita income increase of $43 from the sale of milk, vegetables, and livestock directly related to Plan project improvements. This represented a 50 percent increase in household income and did not include potential gains from the sale of guinea pigs, chickens, and eggs. Plan personnel were pleased with the results, and referred to Sunicorral as an example of a successful Plan project.

Plan International Field Site: Sunicorral 2001

My return visit in August of 2001 involved visits and conversations with Plan directors in the national office in Quito, the regional office in Cuenca, and the field office in Cañar. I also spent three days in Sunicorral observing project changes and conversing with former project participants. Given my extensive prior knowledge of the community, it was not difficult to identify the differences. However, to the untrained eye, one probably would never have known that an NGO had worked in the community. Except for the Plan signs painted in blue on the guinea pig pens, Sunicorral looked virtually the same as any other community in the immediate area. Upon closer examination, there was some reason for hope.

The infrastructure projects fared reasonably well over time. The water system still functioned. In 2000, a main line had broken, and the community got together to fix it. The water committee was inactive, and the meters were broken, but the families still had piped water in their homes. The electricity was still functioning in all households, and had been expanded. The latrines, however, were in disrepair, with broken toilet fixtures and deteriorated siding. I suspect that most people had gone back to using the wide-open spaces, as they had always done. This seemed more convenient than having to get a bucket of water for flushing, not to mention investing money to repair a latrine.

Plan's efforts in agricultural development in Sunicorral generally were not successful. When the project assistance stopped, the Plan group disbanded. There was conflict over how to manage the group's land. All of the land was divided among the individual families. Nineteen families received parcels from the original four plots that were owned by the group. The irrigated pasture plot was divided among fourteen families, and was being farmed individually in the traditional rotation of crops. Most of the irrigation standpipes were still visible in the pasture plot, but the system did not work. In 1998, a slide had ruptured the main water line from the storage tank on the hill, and it was never replaced. The storage tank was overgrown with weeds.

None of the sixteen families were raising chickens in their pens. The animals that Plan had provided died of disease. Only one of the pens was still functioning as intended for guinea pigs. I saw two others, but people were living in them, not guinea pigs. All of the gardens except one were either gone, abandoned, or barely being used for vegetables. Apparently, a combination of disease and/or insufficient market demand worked against guinea pig raising and vegetable production. The chancheras had fared a bit better because pig raising is an integral part of the traditional production system. People need places to bed their pigs.

Of the twenty-three families that made up the core of the Plan group, only one was still maintaining the agricultural projects that were part of the integrated farm project. This family had actually expanded their garden to about three times its original size, and were selling vegetables (mostly lettuce) in the El Tambo market. They were making it in agriculture, and the head of the household was no longer migrating to the coast for seasonal work. However, they were the most dedicated family. They were innovators, hard working, community-minded, and liked working with the group. The couple functioned well as a team, and they understood the development concepts introduced by Plan. This case demonstrates that Plan's approach to agricultural development had merit when applied in a comprehensive and diligent manner.

For the rest of the Plan members, they were no longer interested in working in an NGO-based group. Apparently, Plan's organizational and communal approach did not match the way that most of the people wanted to work. They did not like all of the meetings, rules, and payments that had to be made toward group projects. This was viewed as a waste of time and money, and took away from their individual work. For them, the results did not warrant the effort. Plan's attempt to promote a participatory and sustainable form of agricultural development in Sunicorral had largely failed.

CARE—PROMUSTA

CARE, founded after World War II to deliver emergency aid, today is one of the world's largest private international relief and development organizations. Working in more than sixty developing countries, CARE's annual budget of over $400 million benefits more than 25 million people (CARE 2001). CARE no longer provides just emergency aid, but seeks to address the root causes of poverty by promoting empowerment, equity, and sustainability. Project assistance is given in the areas of health, education, economic development, and environment.

PROMUSTA (*Proyecto Manejo del Uso Sostenible de las Tierras Andinas*, or Sustainable Andean Land Use Management Project) was a CARE-Ecuador project focusing on agriculture and natural resources.[2] PROMUSTA represented a cooperative effort that consolidated CARE's Communal Forestry Project with the Ecuadorian Ministry of Agriculture and Livestock's soils division. Funded from 1988 to 1999, PROMUSTA provided assistance in eight highland provinces. PROMUSTA's national budget during the funding period was approximately $625,000 annually, 60 percent of which came from CARE (CARE 1995). The major CARE funding partner was the Dutch government. The PROMUSTA office in Cañar province worked in twenty-two communities in the study area with an annual budget of approximately $75,000.

PROMUSTA's initial objective was the promotion of grassroots development among minifundistas in the Ecuadorian sierra through the adoption of sustainable land use techniques (PROMUSTA 1995). Project activities included soil conservation, pasture improvement, livestock management, conservation agriculture, and forestry. From the beginning, PROMUSTA did not use giveaways, as it was felt that they promoted paternalism and dependence. The provincial director in Cañar believed that if participants paid for something, they were more likely to take care of it, thus contributing to sustained development (Gárate 1995). Project emphasis was on training and technical assistance. The people were expected to contribute land, time, and money for project activities.

CARE–PROMUSTA Field Site: General Morales 1995

Field study of PROMUSTA's work in seven indigenous communities located near the parochial town of General Morales (pop. 250) was used to document the NGO's methods, results, and ability to reduce poverty. General Morales is situated at 2,450 meters above sea level, in a more remote location than Sunicorral. The Pan-American highway is twenty minutes up a rutted dirt road, and the regional market center of Cañar is about an hour's drive. Landholdings range from one-half hectare to four hectares. The production of the region is based primarily on corn and volunteer pasture, with less emphasis on potatoes because of the lower elevation. High rates of seasonal migration to the costa characterized the region in 1995.

PROMUSTA provided project assistance in General Morales from 1992 until 1999. The communities are small, averaging twenty-five families. Project participation rates varied between 50 and 60 percent of the families. PROMUSTA, like Plan, required that communities get "organized" (Gárate 1995). To avoid division within a community, PROMUSTA worked through existing leadership, generally not forming its own group. However, community members had to agree to work with PROMUSTA's methodology.

Early project work focused on forestry, conservation agriculture, and livestock improvement. Trees were planted in forestry plots and along stream banks in order to protect slopes and provide wood for fuel and construction. Trees were also used in crop areas to line fields, prevent erosion, and improve soils, and as natural barriers and windbreaks. Conservation of natural forest and watershed areas was discussed, but PROMUSTA had little success in reducing deforestation in the zone because of intense pressure on the land. PROMUSTA sold *aliso* (a variety of Andean alder), pines, eucalyptus, and cypress trees to community members for about three and a half cents each. Each project family purchased 100 or more trees. PROMUSTA also helped several communities in upper Cañar establish tree nurseries.

Conservation agriculture techniques included terraces and deviation trenches to prevent erosion on steep slopes. Other practices were tested to enhance soil fertility, including crop rotation, intercropping, organic fertilizers, integrated pest management, green manure, and contour tilling. Instruction on fertilizer use, pesticide use, seed selection, and planting and harvesting methods was also given. Deviation trenches, increased crop rotation, contour plowing, composting, and the use of chicken manure as fertilizer were widely adopted by local farmers.

Livestock and pasture improvement activities emphasized improving the quality of pasture forage, silviculture (integrating trees with pasture), and irrigation. Demonstration plots showed cultivated pasture plantings with rye grass, blue grass, and clover. Livestock courses taught techniques to improve animal management and breed quality. Animal health courses (organized with cooperation from the government rural development agency) emphasized the management of either large animals (usually cattle) or small animals (guinea pigs and rabbits).

PROMUSTA was a national leader in the adoption of participatory development and agroecological farming methodologies, ideas that came from CARE International (Cadena 1995). PROMUSTA's goal was to help the poorest farmers to intensify and diversify the traditional farming system, not replace it. Until 1994, the focus was on resource management and conservation.

In 1994, PROMUSTA changed its goals. The first new goal was to improve the productive capacities of project communities and affiliated institutions. The second was to guarantee the continuance of PROMUSTA's activities after the withdrawal of project assistance (PROMUSTA 1997). The first change was a move away from a focus on conservation, toward emphasis on production gains and income improvement. Experience in the field had shown that if a project activity was not economically viable, then participants were not likely to adopt or continue the practice. The second change was toward a focus on teaching the development process and promoting community organization. PROMUSTA staff felt that local communities had to be organized and trained if they were going to sustain project achievements.

PROMUSTA developed a set of workshops that trained people to form groups, choose leaders, do community diagnostics, design and implement projects, evaluate results, and consolidate and replicate the gains. PROMUSTA tried to prepare communities to take charge of their own development once project assistance ended. The timetable for this process was three to five years. On a regional level, PROMUSTA sponsored and helped organize weekly radio talk shows that addressed community development issues. The local hosts, who were known personalities, commanded attention and interest. PROMUSTA would focus on income improvement and community organization for the final six years.

The first major income-producing project in a General Morales community was a trout breeding facility. PROMUSTA cooperated with an Ecuadorian national NGO (*Cuenca Alta del Rio Cañar*—CARC) to construct a series of four ponds that had the capacity to hold 4,000 trout. PROMUSTA provided technical assistance, while CARC purchased the materials and initial fish stock. Trout (or fish in general) are not part of the traditional diet of the rural indigenous people of the region. The ponds were first filled during the initial field study, but no fish had yet been harvested. The fish were to be sold in the weekly market in Cañar (one hour away by truck). Fish sells for ten to fifteen cents a pound.

When I left Ecuador in 1995, PROMUSTA had just introduced community vegetable gardening and earthworm growing in all project communities. Previously, vegetables were not being cultivated in the region. PROMUSTA gave training and seeds to get the gardens started, which were usually worked by groups of women and children. There were no income gains at that time.

On my return visit in 2001, I learned that from 1996 to 1999, PROMUSTA had accelerated the income-producing aspects of the project. The NGO helped three families in different communities build large *cuyeros* (guinea pig pens), similar to the Plan model, to hold 100 animals each. PROMUSTA provided technical assistance and some materials, while CARC provided materials and animals. During this period, hot houses were also introduced to promote larger-scale vegetable production. Commercial farmers throughout highland Ecuador commonly use hot houses. Vegetables and flowers are sold in domestic and international markets. Hot houses would make vegetable production more reliable and profitable in General Morales, as the area is susceptible to extreme variations in temperature, torrential rains, and high winds.

PROMUSTA helped three families build hot houses. Local hot houses vary in size, but range from ten to twenty meters in length by five to eight meters in width. They are made of wooden frames from locally milled wood, with plastic stapled on the outside. The cost of the plastic for the largest hot house was $150. PROMUSTA provided technical assistance, plastic for "demonstration" purposes, and sold seed and plants to the families. Tomatoes were the primary commercial crop, with the cultivation of carrots, beets, cabbage, and a variety of herbs being secondary. A tomato plant can produce up to twenty tomatoes, selling for five cents each in the local parochial market, and up to ten cents in larger and more distant Cañar market.

CARE–PROMUSTA Field Site: General Morales 2001

My return trip in August of 2001 involved conversations with CARE personnel in the national office in Quito and the regional office in Cuenca, and with the former director of PROMUSTA Cañar. I was able to visit four of the original seven study communities. PROMUSTA had terminated its project assistance in 1999. Therefore, a return visit two years after the withdrawal of project assistance would be a good test of the sustainability of this NGO's methods. Given that the agricultural program in Sunicorral had failed, I wondered if PROMUSTA's approach would be any more effective.

My first observation was that all of the trees were there, but they had tripled in size. I saw large plots of pine growing on reforested upper slopes in the zone, and many small forest plots of aliso, pine, and eucalyptus next to houses. All of the trees that were lining plots, crossing plots, lining creeks, and on steep slopes within the communities were still there. However, none of the campesinos I spoke with expressed an interest in the trees. They obviously help reduce erosion, and the aliso leaves provide organic material and nitrogen for the soil. However, they do not bring an economic return, which is the primary measure of project success for a campesino. No new trees had been planted. I visited a nursery site, but it was no longer operational. When the trees are large enough to be harvested for lumber, they will undoubtedly be cut.

Only remnants of the practices in conservation agriculture were still visible. Composting pits were the only component that was still in widespread use. However, this did not surprise me because the use of crop residues and manure has been part of the traditional farming system for centuries. The terraces and deviation trenches were gone, plowed over. A big change was that there was very little crop cultivation at all in the communities. About 80 percent of the land was in pasture (up from about 60 percent in 1995). In the past five years, the region has seen a dramatic out-migration to the United States, which has affected labor availability. In all of the communities, I only saw one plot of cultivated pasture. Pasture in the region was in volunteer *kikuyu*.

Only one large cuyero was still operating of the three that were introduced. It only had about twenty guinea pigs in it, which was nowhere near capacity. Apparently, the local demand was insufficient to meet the higher levels of production. No diffusion of this practice had occurred.

I found four previous sites of community gardens, but none were functioning. Back in 1995, one of the gardens had been organized by a women's group, and I thought that maybe an organized women's group could sustain the project activity, but that did not happen. One family was growing earthworms, but this was one of the most active families from before.

The hot houses failed as well. I found one of the three hot houses partially functioning. However, the previous year the plastic had ripped and was shredded by high winds, and had not been replaced. I saw the leveled area where another hot house had been built, but the only evidence that it had been there was a small piece of plastic tied to a tree and a few volunteer tomato plants. The owner told me that production was good the first year, but declined in the second year because he did not buy new tomato plants, which he was told to do. In the third year, high winds ripped the plastic on his hot house. I could not find the third one in its reported location. The income benefits of vegetable production were minimal because of very limited local demand and long distances to larger market centers. Given the lack of profitability, investments to maintain the hot houses and other garden projects were not made.

What happened to the trout ponds? The other cooperating NGO (CARC) kept them going for another year. Then, they were abandoned about six months after project assistance ended. One of the larger ponds still had some water running through it, but the others were partially filled-in and overgrown. The one pond had a couple of dozen small trout still in it. According to a neighbor, they had survived on their own.

Discussion: Why the NGOs Failed

It is clear from the follow-up visits to the Plan and PROMUSTA field sites that very little project work related to agriculture was sustained after the withdrawal of NGO assistance. So, why did Plan and PROMUSTA fail to promote long-term sustainable agricultural development in Cañar, Ecuador?

The first reason has to do with the methods of the NGOs themselves. There is a pattern of paternalistic relationships between NGOs in upper Cañar and the recipients of aid. Until 1996, Plan had a reputation as one of the most paternalistic of all NGOs. Plan gave away too many things. The irrigation project, complete with rainbird sprinklers, was too expensive and too technical. Plan's reliance on giveaways fostered a belief that outside technology and capital were required for development.

PROMUSTA, on the other hand, was a leader in the implementation of participatory development methods. So, why weren't the results of PROMUSTA different? PROMUSTA found that other NGOs, often working in the same communities, relied on giveaways. Some communities in Cañar province were so used to receiving them that they refused to work with PROMUSTA. Over time, PROMUSTA increasingly relied on giveaways, calling them demonstration projects. They had been coopted into the local giveaway culture as a consequence of conflicting NGO methodologies.

More important, J. Gárate (2001), former director of PROMUSTA Cañar, indicated that in the end they failed to implement a true participatory development model. The initiative did not come from the people. What both NGOs were doing was going to the communities with a predetermined set of ideas, methods, and project activities. Because of this, local people never really took ownership of a project. It was the NGO's project, and when things broke down, they expected the NGO to come and fix it. Leaders in two communities told me that NGOs "ruined" the people by teaching them that they could not solve their own problems. I believe that many people in Sunicorral and General Morales were only willing to work with the NGOs because they expected a handout.

This creates a dilemma for NGOs. Given local poverty and resource constraints, outside assistance is necessary and can be justified. However, a paternalistic approach hinders local development. At the other extreme, if an NGO leaves it up to the local community to determine what the project will do, they will frequently ask for expensive giveaways. I observed community members in Sunicorral asking for trucks, tractors, and cattle. Another community in the region asked for a road to get their wood and charcoal out faster, clearly a practice that does not lead to long-term sustainable development. It seems clear that Plan and PROMUSTA found it difficult to find the right balance between bottom-up and top-down development.

One must remember, however, that the NGOs are working within a context. Paternalism predates the arrival of international NGOs in Ecuador. There is a long history of subjugation of the indigenous population in Ecuador, and elsewhere in Latin America. Many haciendas in upper Cañar were not broken up until after the 1973 land reform law, and many people in Sunicorral and General Morales were *huasipungueros* (local term for peon). The paternalistic relationship of the past between landlord and huasipunguero still affects social relations today. It is easy for an NGO to fall into this pattern.

Plan and PROMUSTA also had to confront tradition as a barrier to change. It is not my intention to characterize the indigenous people of upper Cañar as custom-bound conservatives or to blame them for their own poverty. However, the local cultural context does play an important role as a filter for outside influences. NGOs are working within contexts at multiple scales. Understanding the local context is essential for the NGOs, because ultimately they are trying to change the actions of individuals who live in communities.

Development is a western concept brought to the communities by NGOs. Readers of this book generally understand (and often take for granted) ideas such as progress, change, continuing education, creativity, and empowerment. Yet, after millennia of cultural adaptation and survival, tradition is paramount to the people of upper Cañar. Agricultural innovation and conversion entails a certain level of risk. Indigenous agriculturalists are generally risk-averse because they often live at or near subsistence level. What they value most is stability, not change. Even when contemporary conditions suggest the need for new adaptive strategies, some people do things simply because that is the way they have always been done. Tradition, when combined with geographic isolation, illiteracy, and even alcoholism, present difficult challenges for NGOs.

The indigenous farmers in upper Cañar also lack a coherent perspective on resource conservation (P. Carpio 2001). There has been much discussion about the sustainability of traditional agricultural systems (see Wilken 1987). Traditional farmers, through centuries of experimentation, adaptation, practical experience, and accumulated knowledge, know how to maximize production with limited resources. However, these systems are coming under new pressures. Contact with the global economy has resulted in an increased need and desire for cash incomes, labor commodification, economic diversification, and a host of other changes. Meanwhile, current population numbers in upper Cañar are perhaps five times the preconquest numbers, thus accentuating pressure on the land. Driven by poverty and resource shortages, the assault on the fragile forests and uplands of the callejón andino continues at an alarming rate. Highland smallholders may know how to maximize production with limited resources, but the concept of resource conservation in a contemporary sense has little meaning in the rural areas of upper Cañar.

What the NGOs are really trying to do is change local culture, and they typically want to do it in three to five years. After centuries of tradition, subjugation, and marginalization, is it reasonable to expect people to empower themselves, adopt new forms of community organization, and change their production systems in such a short period of time? This is not to say that local people cannot change, or that NGOs cannot succeed. The work must be long-term, however, and the challenges are substantial.

To make matters worse, Plan and PROMUSTA were not just dealing with their own organizational challenges and with local cultural constraints. National and global processes also influenced the communities and regions where they were working. In a sense, Ecuador is a different country than it was in 1995. A series of national political and economic crises rocked the country between 1995 and 2000, profoundly impacting the context in which NGOs operate. This started with the war with Peru, which created a drain on the economy. Then, corruption scandals caused two presidents to resign and flee the country, resulting in an environment of political instability and loss of confidence in the system.

In 1998, the national banking crisis hit. In the mid-1990s, the Durán Ballén dministration implemented measures to make the Ecuadorian economy more market oriented. The banking system was deregulated. Under the loosened laws, speculative investments among bank owners and associates led to a loss of confidence in the banking system and a run on accounts. Several of the nation's largest banks went bankrupt. The political and banking crises contributed to the rapid devaluation of the sucre, the national currency of Ecuador. In 1995, the exchange rate was 2,200 sucres to the dollar. In 2000, it was 25,000 to the dollar when the Ecuadorian congress ultimately dollarized the economy.

Devaluation and dollarization eroded the purchasing power of the indigenous farmers and the urban middle class consumers that buy goods from them. As a result, the prices in local markets for most agricultural products have remained stagnant or fallen. Milk, the most important source of on-farm income, was selling for twenty-five cents a liter in 2001, the same price as in 1995. Back in 1995, vegetables were a new and expanding (and I thought sustainable) source of income. Vegetable prices also remained unchanged. The market for field crops collapsed. A 130-pound sack of potatoes averaged $10 in 1995. It was selling for around $2 in 2001. The collapse of the market for field crops further reduced the incentive of campesinos to invest in agriculture, and reinforced the perception that agriculture is not profitable.

Dollarization also reduced the purchasing power of NGOs. Money from international donors arrives in the form of dollars. NGOs used to gain in the conversion of dollars to sucres, an advantage that was lost. In dollar terms, the cost of purchased inputs and other services that NGOs require has risen (R. Carpio 2001; Cordero 2001; Gárate 2001). Both of these factors have limited the reach of NGOs' work. Furthermore, Gárate (2001) stated that PROMUSTA had the most success in communities that had some resources to invest. Otherwise, the NGO had to rely more on giveaways. The people of General Morales were the poorest among all PROMUSTA communities.

International migration is having a dramatic impact on upper Cañar, and thus on the NGOs. There is a well-established migration stream from Cañar province to the New York area. Campesinos from indigenous communities pay "coyotes" $12,000 to $14,000 (which includes interest) to deliver them to the United States. The families mortgage their land, and then pay off the debt once the migrant finds work on the other side. This migration is affecting the social context of the region. Migrant families with U.S. incomes have the means to acquire resources and improve their standard of living. Formerly poor indigenous farmers now have new two-story houses and own cars. (Remittances are sometimes used to buy land and dairy cattle as well.) Nonmigrant families are reduced to near subsistence on the farm, and increasingly rely on local off-farm wage labor. There is a mounting perception that the campesino who works in agriculture is someone who is poor, lacks esteem, and is not developed. Smallholder agriculture still serves an important function in tradition, for growing food for subsistence, and for earning a small amount of income. However, except for commercial dairying, the people do not want to invest in agriculture, and do not see it as a means of improving one's standard of living or status.

In Sunicorral, eighteen of the twenty-three head of households in the Plan group have migrated to the United States. In the General Morales area, approximately 80 percent of the heads of households have migrated in the past five years. In the community with the trout ponds, sixteen of the twenty-two families had male migrants in the United States. There is very little labor available for farm work. Migration made it extremely difficult for NGOs to organize communities, mobilize labor, and carry out projects. Group members disappear without notice. The migration phenomenon might present an opportunity for NGOs to organize the women that remain. However, they have also begun to migrate to join their husbands, leaving the children with grandparents. Those who remain eke out a living growing traditional crops, while they wait for the remittances to come so they can get their house, car, land, and cattle.

Conclusion

I return to the central question of this book. What role do nongovernmental organizations really play in fighting poverty in upper Cañar? The case study indicates that over the past forty years, the indigenous communities in highland Ecuador have faced many changes, including population growth, land degradation, commercialization, and migration, as well as external factors such as national economic and political crises and increasing global integration. NGOs have stepped in to provide development services and resources when the government and markets have failed to do so. This is especially true for the poor, indigenous, and marginalized people in rural areas. Furthermore, international NGOs provide a vital link between global-and local-scale processes. They facilitate the introduction and adaptation of new ideas, organizational structures, and productive activities that can play a positive role in helping smallholder agriculturalists maintain themselves, adapt, and improve their standard of living.

Plan's potable water and electrification projects were successful. This suggests that certain types of infrastructure projects, ones that require coordination with government and/or substantial outside resources, merit assistance by NGOs. Many poor communities do not have the organizational capacity, capital, or technical expertise to acquire these things on their own. Therefore, they need assistance from outside institutions, meaning government and NGOs. In addition, water and electricity were viewed as essential basic needs. Few people want to carry water from a far away source. Electricity is desired for night lighting, radio, and TV. Community members were willing to make efforts to maintain these systems once they were installed.

Plan and PROMUSTA did have short-term success with their agriculture projects. While they were giving aid, they demonstrated that they could successfully improve agriculture and reduce poverty. In the Plan community, I observed the results and documented the gains in income (see Keese 1998, 2001). As long as the NGOs were actively engaged in the community—showing up every week to organize, train, supervise, and give the impetus—project activities were maintained and advancements made. The people were clearly better off while there was assistance and instruction. On an important level, this should be considered a success. In the case of Sunicorral, some residual benefit has come from the ownership of more land. The NGOs helped people with their aid. This might be enough for some donors.

NGO staff believed that if project recipients were trained, then they would have the capacity to take over the projects and maintain them (Gárate 2001). The NGO could, little by little, withdraw support until the people could take charge of their own development. However, the case study shows that once the support for agriculture ended, things began to wither, until eventually, most of the project activities stopped. This raises a number of questions. Did the NGOs fail to adequately train the people? Were the project goals and methods inappropriate?

The reason for long-term failure in the agricultural projects might be as simple as the new practices were not economically viable. Had the work been profitable, the people probably would have maintained it. There is still an important role for NGOs in helping marginalized peoples overcome technical barriers or capital shortages to land use conversion. But, in the end, the work must stand on its own economically. This was not the case in upper Cañar. However, to be fair to the NGOs, what constitutes profitability is greatly influenced by the contextual factors described above. Market shifts influenced by national (and international) events can make previously profitable activities unprofitable. Also, perceptions have changed greatly because of international migration. The income from remittances can make the returns from an NGO project seem insignificant.

Despite the fact that Plan and CARE are aware of the problems associated with paternalism, both failed to implement a true participatory methodology in the study communities. The ideas are good, and the methodologies are improving; but effective implementation of participatory methodology at the grassroots level is still an elusive task. However, on another level, substantial progress has been made toward the training of in-country nationals to direct NGOs in Ecuador. There are many highly educated, trained, and experienced Ecuadorian development specialists. On the return trip, I noticed that their understanding of development issues had kept pace with the global-level debate. However, these professionals are generally urban middle-class mestizos. The next step, and apparently a far more difficult one, involves transferring this process to the campesinos. NGO work in highland Ecuador is a nexus of three cultures: Euro-American, urban Ecuadorian, and rural indigenous. It requires skillful bridging of cultural differences.

Before my return visit, I believed that the success of an NGO project rested primarily on the ideas and methods of the NGO itself. If the directors only designed and skillfully implemented appropriate project activities, then they would be successful. The case of upper Cañar demonstrates that external factors play a larger role in project outcome than I previously understood. When the macroscale influences are combined with the local cultural influences, they become formidable barriers to development with which the NGOs must contend. Given the poor long-term results, it is not surprising that both NGOs either cancelled or dramatically reduced their agricultural programs in the study area.

The experience of Plan International and CARE–PROMUSTA in upper Cañar demonstrates that context matters. Local, national, and global processes come together and play out in ways that vary from place to place. The ability of an NGO to influence these internal and external factors may be limited. Therefore, directors of NGO projects need to understand the specific cultural and ecological characteristics of local places, as situated within a rapidly changing multidimensional context. This is a political ecology framework of analysis: local knowledge in a globalizing world. With this understanding, they can make better decisions about what they can change, and how to do it.

Plan Cañar's budget was cut by 20 percent in 2001 as part of a national restructuring effort (Paguay 2001). Despite the need, Plan chose to cut funds and staff for agriculture and natural resource management (Cordero 2001). Given that the larger societal processes worked against progress in these areas, this decision is justifiable. In yet another reevaluation of assistance, resources have been shifted to education, health, and infrastructure projects. Health projects, like those in infrastructure, often require coordinated efforts, and can have recognizable benefits that would motivate people to continue the practices. In a larger sense, education helps to influence the cultural context in which NGOs operate. With education, project recipients may be more open and better able to conceptualize ideas related to development.[3] A focus on education is also a recognition that development is a longer-term process than projects.

NGOs increasingly realize that the context in which they work affects project outcomes. Both Plan and CARE have made influencing the context a major focus of their work. In the 1995–96 program year, Plan started emphasizing cooperation, coordination, and partnership with other NGOs and government. Since 1998, a national policy requires all Plan offices to work in networks. Plan now sees itself as a facilitator of development, helping to form networks of cooperation, or networks of service (Freire 2001). Plan is looking for a balance between the macro and the local, the strategic and the operative. Local plans mesh with larger goals in an integrated approach at multiple levels. Plan now coordinates its education and health programs with local municipalities. Decentralization of Ecuadorian government services, which began in the mid-1990s, has given municipalities more decision-making power. In this case, a change in national policy helped Plan.

CARE has a long history of cooperative efforts. PROMUSTA was the product of cooperation. Evidence of CARE's continuing focus on the larger context is demonstrated by its regional development effort for the three southern provinces of Ecuador. (Work in the area was made possible by the peace agreement with Peru in 1998.) This program involves work with approximately 260 institutions, including local community organizations, NGOs (national and international), corporations, government (municipal, provincial, and national), universities, and the United States Agency for International Development (USAID). Much of the assistance will be for water, sanitation, health, and road improvement.

More attention on the larger contextual framework also serves to address two critical weaknesses that have plagued NGOs. First, they have been criticized for the lack of cooperation resulting in the wasteful duplication of services—NGOs doing the same things in isolation, in essence competing with each other (Clark 1991). Today, Plan and CARE place greater emphasis on partnership, and on sharing methods, costs, and resources. Each NGO does what it does best. Some goals and methods may be in conflict, but compromise may allow the partners to deliver aid more efficiently and to more people. Second, NGOs have had difficulty translating local-level successes into larger scale social change, meaning that their wider impact is limited (Carrol 1992). Cooperative efforts with other NGOs and government, however, may result in policy changes that lead to more opportunities for the poor. Of course, NGOs could lose some of their independence if they get too close to governments (Hulme and Edwards 1997). Yet NGOs alone will never have the resources to affect large-scale change, thus making cooperation with governments essential.

One must remember, however, that current work by Plan and CARE to engage in context-changing activities are not reflected in the projects I studied in upper Cañar. Also, regional development plans and changes in national policy do not automatically translate into improvements for individual people. Projects are still implemented at the local level. Future field study is needed to see if current local-level implementation will be any more effective than in the 1990s. Unfortunately, Plan and CARE have not done followup studies after the end of projects. There is still a tendency to believe that if the aid is given, then the job is done. They have been content to claim success, move on to the next project, and promote it with the optimism of a new beginning. The results of this study, especially in agriculture, indicate why it is easier to not return. However, follow-up studies are essential in the process of institutional learning, and could certainly lead to more effective projects in the future. In the meantime, NGOs should not stop trying to improve agriculture. The problems and needs are real, and the results might be different in other regions, in different contexts, or with other projects.

2

Making a Statement or Finding a Role

British NGOs in Latin America

Jean Grugel

> Even the best NGO projects are rarely sufficient to enable beneficiaries to escape from poverty. And most NGO projects are not financially sustainable.
>
> —*Development Initiatives 2000*

> The U.K. government believes that globalization creates unprecedented new opportunities for sustainable development and poverty reduction. It offers an opportunity for faster progress in achieving the International Development Targets. . . . The challenge is to connect more people from the world's poorest countries with the benefits of the new global economy. And that means globalization must be managed to benefit everyone.
>
> —*Department for International Development (DFID) 2000*

The aim of this chapter is to examine the contribution made by the U.K. overseas development NGO sector to poverty alleviation in Latin America. This inevitably implies probing the ways in which poverty is conceptualized within the NGO community and its influence over how poverty is understood within U.K. government circles and, more widely, within the European Union (EU). Any contribution that U.K. NGOs make in terms of poverty relief must be assessed on two separate—though ultimately related—fronts. First, what do they do on the ground? How far are they able to address either what they understand to be the immediate symptoms or the root causes of poverty in Latin American communities? How do they contribute to alleviating poverty in particular localities? Second, what are their strategies for transforming the nature and the scale of the responses by Northern governments and global governance bodies to poverty generally, and in Latin America in particular? Can they contribute to bringing about deep structural changes that address the global causes of poverty?

U.K. NGOs make their policy for Latin America within the context of globalization and the Europeanization of aid. As a result, in the search for funding and influence, they address a European audience and are increasingly integrated into European development spaces. Their strategies, then, are no longer directed narrowly toward shaping British policy or delivering aid on the ground. Moreover, the governance agenda and the European shift toward decentralized aid has had considerable consequences for NGOs. In particular, the scope of their activities has broadened. They are no longer simply aid deliverers but now play a role in national and global networks. U.K. NGOs thus attempt to use their leverage, nationally, regionally, and globally, to push for global transformation to bring about real and lasting changes to the poor in the South.

The chapter proceeds in the following way. First, I contextualize the work of the U.K. development NGO community by examining where the sector "fits" in the United Kingdom and in the EU. In particular, I emphasize the deepening relations between the NGO community and the Department for International Development (DFID). I also examine the impact of the growing internationalization and regionalization of U.K. NGO activities. I then discuss the complex ways in which poverty is conceptualized by NGOs. Finally, I identify the role of U.K. NGOs in Latin America, focusing on the kind of connections that have typically developed to link U.K. NGOs with the region. Here, the core of my argument is that there has been a marked, but far from straightforward, shift from project-based activity to advocacy. This transition is clearest within the larger NGOs. For small NGOs, the shift from projects to advocacy is a difficult transition to make. Moreover, for all NGOs, there are pressures in favor of project-based activities that range from funding to the belief systems of some NGO workers. Where NGOs remain focused on project work, there is a growing emphasis on local ownership of projects. I use the Intermediate Technology Development Group (ITDG), the International Institute for the Environment and Development (IIED), and Homeless International to analyze more fully the nature of U.K. NGO project work.

U.K. Development NGOs: Professionalization, Regionalization, and Internationalization

U.K. development NGOs are in a state of transition. First, their funding sources are being transformed. The U.K. NGO community differs from most other European aid communities in that the bulk of its funding still comes from nongovernmental sources. Less than 20 percent of total estimated NGO income in 1998/99 came from DFID. Nevertheless, this independence easily can be exaggerated. Figures for funding are somewhat misleading, in that development NGOs can claim tax breaks, access lottery funds, and draw on other government funds in addition to core or project funding. As a result, government support actually represents around 46 percent of their total income (Development Initiatives 2000). At the same time, the official figures mislead as to the incomes of particular NGOs. They can conceal dependence on U.K. government on the part of some NGOs due to contracts for aid delivery, especially in the provision of technical services such as water and emergency aid, or in core funding. In fact, while the total amount of funding from DFID for NGOs has remained more or less constant since the 1990s, core funding to the larger NGOs has steadily increased.

Second, the community is becoming more diversified as some NGOs become actors on a regional and global scale while others remain small. Oxfam U.K., for example, manages a budget of almost $200 million, while some of the smaller NGOs have very reduced overheads and rely on voluntary contributions or sporadic funding for projects from the Joint Funding Scheme (JFS) run by DFID. Smaller NGOs also find it difficult for the most part to access EU funding, despite encouragement and support from BOND, the national platform of development NGOs. Moreover, the larger NGOs are increasingly moving out of simply delivering aid—for themselves or for government—toward acting as knowledge banks, information brokers, facilitators of relationships, and active participants in global civil society. This is strengthened by the fact that as NGOs professionalize, they become important to DFID or even at times to the Foreign and Commonwealth Office (FCO). NGOs are now consulted over arms transfers, risk management, or lobbying strategies at the World Trade Organization (WTO), for example, as well as over the design and delivery of aid.

The relative financial independence of the U.K. NGO sector allows it considerable autonomy from DFID as to the positions NGOs adopt on international issues. Certainly, most NGOs have resisted joint activity with DFID within the international system. The very public criticisms of the NGO community to the U.S. and U.K. bombings of Afghanistan that were carried out in 2001, for example, are testimony not only to the fact that NGOs still value independence, but also to their confidence in their authority to speak for broad swathes of U.K. public opinion. Professionalization, however, is not without its problems. Inevitably, while some NGOs move closer to government, the sense of marginalization that others perceive increases. Some of the smaller NGOs have expressed the fear that an increasingly professionalized NGO sector, efficiently delivering tasks for government, is becoming distant from its core supporters within society. The extent to which professionalization serves as a barrier to poverty alleviation—as some voices within the NGO community suggest—is thus an important issue. There is the risk that NGOs' profile as a voice independent from government, an image that they have carefully built up over years, will be eroded. There is also the possibility that it will cause deepening fissures within the NGO universe, as the larger NGOs take on a range of functions that embed them within governance networks. For some NGOs, this means that the NGO community as a whole is gradually compromised in terms of its capacity to criticize government action (Grugel 1999).

U.K. NGOs are acutely aware that they now have a dual mandate. They are responsive to government and try to access public policy debates, but they also play an important role within British society and need to retain public goodwill for funding and support. Around 30 percent of U.K. households give regularly to charity. NGOs publicize their work to society at large and aim to speak about development in nontechnical language. Participation in NGOs is encouraged through schools, churches, university groups, and other civil society organizations. As a result, there is a strong sense of ownership within British society over U.K. NGOs and an unwillingness to see them simply as agents of government. Of course, this also shapes the kind of images NGOs present to the public. The NGO community is driven toward the presentation mainly of the most dramatic aspects of their work—in emergency relief or famines—rather than their long-term contribution to either advocacy or small-scale development. There is, as a result, something of a tension between the public presentation of NGO work and the activities that they undertake. It is partly due to the fact that British NGOs rarely emphasize their work in Latin America.

The ambiguity of the NGO–government relationship can be traced through almost all levels of NGO–DFID interaction. A particularly good example can be found in the NGOs' responses to the DFID's "White Paper on Globalisation" in 2000, which lays down the framework for U.K. development policy. The NGOs were consulted during the writing of the paper and made extensive submissions to DFID. Yet the White Paper ultimately reflected the treasury focus that globalization and liberalization, in themselves, constituted the building blocks of development. As a result, NGOs have been critical of the paper's benign interpretations of globalization and the notion, found in parts of the paper, that globalization is a solution to poverty. For the NGOs, the paper understates the scale of the present development problems in the South and the difficulties poor communities have in accessing the benefits of globalized trade. The NGOs also reacted negatively to aspects of the DFID paper outlining how aid should be implemented. These disagreements make clear that, while consultations take place regularly, NGOs are far from being equal partners in U.K. aid design.

Nevertheless, professionalization and deepening ties with government are now unavoidable. The centripetal force of the EU as an actor in development cooperation and the emergence of cross-European networks of aid agencies act to drive professionalization and contribute to a regionalization of NGO strategies and activities. Although it is difficult to obtain precise figures, some studies put overall EU funding to NGOs at as much as US$7.3 billion. It is obviously important to access this funding and to contribute to shaping EU development policy in general. As a result, U.K. NGOs are now active not only in Westminster and within U.K. public opinion and civil society, but also inside European policy and solidarity networks. The EU has encouraged, and indeed funds, a number of NGO networks to make its interactions with the NGO community easier. The larger U.K. NGOs play an important role in APRODEV, a broad-based network of large European NGOs; the network of Catholic NGOs, CIDSE; the Save the Children Alliance; and EURODAD, the debt and development European umbrella group.

European NGO lobby groups have scored a few notable successes in their relationships with the EU. Consultation with NGOs is now an obligatory part of the aid process. NGOs have established a reputation (perhaps an exaggerated one) as efficient organizations able to deliver value added for relatively small outlays of cash. Their role in scrutinizing EU activities is also regarded as vital. Perhaps their greatest success, however, within the United Kingdom and Europe, has been in the role they have played in insisting that solving poverty requires political, not merely technical, responses. In particular, NGOs have attached importance to the role of civil society, human rights, and democratization in poverty alleviation. In this, they have genuinely contributed to a sea change in how aid is conceived and administered. While NGOs have not been solely responsible for the emphasis on civil society in EU aid, they certainly played a role. According to an APRODEV report, the EU recognizes that the advantages of NGO-delivered aid lie principally in that NGOs are organizations committed to civil society development in the South:

> Strengthening civil society is important for several reasons. For the same reasons as in Europe, it is good to have a policy dialogue between civil

society and its government. In addition, the strengthening of civil society can contribute to the empowerment of marginalized parts of the society which can lead to poverty reduction and the development of a more just society. (APRODEV 2000, 5)

NGO influence over the discourse of aid and even how parts of the aid budget are delivered is not matched by influence over the size of the aid budget as a whole or the aid allocations contained within the different budgetary lines. Development NGOs have been especially critical of the fact that aid funding in the 2002 European Community budget is effectively smaller than in the previous year. Moreover, the most basic of poverty-related aid lines, such as food aid and humanitarian aid, have been cut by 8 percent for 2002 in comparison with the previous year (Liaison Committee 2001a, 3). In fact, not even levels of EU funding to NGOs are completely secure. In 2001, the EU reviewed its cofinancing scheme, which effectively functions as an exclusive source of funds for NGOs. The Liaison Committee of European development NGOs has been unable to prevent funding cuts and has been critical of both the decision to cut funds and of the fact that they were barely consulted over the report (Liaison Committee 2001b). The NGOs accuse the EU of ignoring the fact that they are one of the few stakeholder groups for lobbying and advocacy in Europe that work in partnership with the Southern NGOs and other civil society actors in developing countries—something that discursively, at least, the EU claims to be engaging in promoting (Liaison Committee 2001b, 4). In sum, while the NGOs have been able to enter the development policy networks in the EU, they remain relatively weak actors within them.

How Do NGOs Conceptualize Poverty?

Poverty has recently returned as the central *problematique* in global development. The U.K. government and the EU argue that the goal of aid is to reduce poverty. But they tend to conceptualize poverty in quite a straightforward way as a lack of economic, social, cultural, and political capital. Poor people are seen as disadvantaged in terms of influencing political outcomes; poverty is self-perpetuating and hard to escape. The role of development cooperation, consequently, is to build and develop forms of social capital that, over time, provide communities and individuals with the resources they lack to function as citizens and consumers within society. At the same time, U.K. government and EU institutions also view the political structures and economic circuits typical of developing countries as poverty-intensifying. In short, EU official development cooperation takes an approach to aid that assumes that poverty is essentially the result of internal structures within developing countries. It is seen as separate from, not related to, the workings of the global economy. As a result, antipoverty EU strategies go hand in hand with a view that poverty can be eradicated and development assisted by deeper integration into a liberalized world economy and political reform within developing countries. Finally, poverty is seen mainly in behavioral terms: its causes and manifestations are visible, and poverty can be measured. It is absolute, not relative. Because of this methodology, EU-funded antipoverty programs tend to adopt a results-oriented focus.

European NGOs, by contrast, take a more complex view of poverty. In the first instance, poverty is regarded as multidimensional. U.K. NGOs capture this by describing poverty as the sum of sets of "crosscutting issues." These include gender, education, health, the environment, citizenship, and human rights. To be poor is to experience multiple deprivation. IIED, for example, which has specialized in studies of urban poverty, argues that poverty cannot be captured by income analysis:

> [Our] research has long pointed to the limitations of measuring urban poverty by income only. Other aspects of deprivation include the contravention of the urban poor's civil and political rights (including the right to make demands within political systems) and poor quality, insecure housing and lack of basic services (with the large health burden and other costs that these impose). IIED's work stresses the importance of understanding and addressing the housing and infrastructure needs of the poor and the necessity for urban groups to have more influence on public programmes and resource allocations. (IIED 2001, n.p.)

Perhaps even more significant, however, is the fact that many NGOs tend to view poverty as an outcome of global, as well as national, structures. Poverty is the result of the ways in which the global political economy has expanded over time and space. Its root cause thus lies within international structures, rather than simply nationally rooted forms of political and social stratification or a simple analysis of state bias or inefficiency. So, for example, Oxfam U.K.'s analysis of poverty in Ecuador suggests that even its immediate causes are a complex mix of international and national factors, made worse by natural disaster. These include:

- An economic model that promotes exports and cuts social services in order to repay the country's huge external debt;
- The reduction of the international price for oil (over 50 percent of Ecuador's exports);

- The collapse of almost a third of the banks (nine banks) working in the country;
- The failure to reform fiscal policy, including the recent elimination of property and income taxes, further increasing the gap between rich and poor;
- And over $2 billion of losses or damage to infrastructure caused by El Niño. (Oxfam 2001)

The logic of this approach is that poverty elimination requires advocacy and pressure to bring about global change. A range of international issue-areas within the global political economy requires reform. These include trade policy; environmental policy; the introduction of a regulatory code for financial services and investment; the monitoring and control of transnational practices; changes in how commodities are produced, priced, and traded; and a reduction in, or even elimination of, the external debt. More fundamentally, a power shift is necessary within international and governance structures with the aim that they reflect more closely the makeup of the global population, rather than that of the western states or the interests of large capitalist conglomerates. At the same time, these global economic and political reforms should be allied and underpinned by a transformation in the values embedded within international society; NGOs work to promote a more ethical universe and an international order predicated on respect, dignity, the value of the person, and the centrality of rights.

This maximalist and long-term agenda is complemented by strategies to empower communities in the South to also demand global and national change. According to IIED, one principal function of Northern NGOs is "to provide assistance and research resources to local groups and help to get their concerns heard and understood at the political level" (IIED 2001). This is also the primary aim of the North-South cooperation group within BOND, the U.K.'s national platform of development NGOs. Strengthening local social movements and empowering civil society thus becomes a way to combat vested interests and to provide the poor with the organizational capabilities and political ability to struggle for pro-poor reforms inside their own countries.

In sum the U.K. NGOs' focus on poverty broadly combines attention to:

- the multiple way that poverty is lived in developing countries;
- the salience of the global political economy as a barrier to equality; and
- the importance of participation and civil society in combating poverty.

Their arguments are in line with mainstream debates about poverty within the U.K. development studies community that emphasize the ways in which institutions and power reproduce poverty and inequality globally and nation- ally (Moore and Putzel 2000).

Nevertheless, there is something of a tension between how NGOs de- scribe and utilize notions of poverty within the NGO community and within their own programs and the language they use to address their funders. Along with other European NGOs, the U.K. NGO community speaks to DFID and the EU in the language of cost-effectiveness ("NGOs are cheap") and adopts a results-based methodology. Their aim appears to be to push official funders to live up to their own goals and rhetoric on antipoverty, rather than to press them to adopt a more radical approach. They have focused attention, for example, on the contradiction between the official poverty focus with U.K. and EU aid, and the fact that aid allocation actually reflects political criteria. This means in practice that the middle income Eastern European countries receive a far larger aid allocation than the poorest countries. NGOs have also been particularly critical of the EU's endorsement of cooperation with in- dustrialized countries that effectively functions as subsidized funding for European private enterprises to develop overseas markets (B7–665 line in the community budget), particularly since this comes at the expense of real cuts in the poverty-eradication and the human rights budget lines (Liaison Committee 2001a, 9). The NGOs also are keen to point out "the lack of coherence between poverty alleviation and the European Union's other poli- cies" such as its trade policy (APRODEV 2000).

U.K. NGOs in Latin America

Latin America is not a major recipient of U.K. aid, or indeed European aid generally. Only around 10 percent of all EU aid is channeled into Latin America. Most of that, however, flows through European NGOs. Since 1992, more than 40 percent of the aid projects cofinanced between the EU and NGOs have been in Latin America. British bilateral aid to Latin America represents less than 8 percent of the U.K. total. Again, however, NGOs are prominent in its delivery and design.

The impact that British NGOs can make in the region is inevitably small, if it is measured in terms of the number of projects that can be financed or the scale of U.K. responses to disasters or emergencies. Nev- ertheless, Latin America has an important place within the U.K. NGO community in two senses. First, Latin America has proven to be fertile terrain for developing strategies of decentralization cooperation and part- nership relationships with Southern NGOs and grassroots movements. In some cases, Latin America has furnished NGOs with an opportunity to develop civil society aid projects and cooperation policies that have served as a model for their work elsewhere (Grugel 1999). British NGOs were among the earliest to embrace the notion that antipoverty strategies require an integral approach that encompasses developing civil society and encourages participation. The richness of Latin American civil society movements has made it possible to posit relationships of equality and co-ownership with U.K. NGOs. In interviews, U.K. NGO workers return time and again to the notion that working with Latin American social movements means two-way traffic; cooperation is a learning experience for U.K. NGOs. This is in line with recent findings by Friedman, Hochstetler, and Clark (2001), that Latin American social movements participate within global civil society on terms of equality. Second, Latin America is a constant point of reference within U.K. NGO advocacy strategies. So, although in terms of spending, Latin America appears relatively unimportant, its influence over U.K. activity is considerable.

Elsewhere, I have argued that U.K. NGOs operating in Latin America stress the importance of political entitlements and citizenship as vehicles for poverty elimination, rather than focusing straightforwardly on economic entitlements (Grugel 2000). I explained this eminently political focus as the result of the convergence of factors such as the growing use of the term "civil society" throughout Europe to express commitment to political and social change based on the resurrection of the values of communities. Changes in the mode of delivery of aid across Europe have made NGOs sensitive to the demands of international donors that embraced the language of civil society; the term echoes the demands for civil society empowerment as a project for democratic deepening in Latin America, and it reflects the growing participation of NGOs within the sphere of "global civil society." This political orientation flows from the fact that the Latin American poor experience relative deprivation rather than absolute poverty, in comparison to Asia and Africa. Moreover, it rests on an assumption that empowering civil society and participation in networks within global civil society is itself an antipoverty strategy. It is certainly in line with the NGO view that poverty is an outcome of crosscutting areas of deprivation and the consequence of structures, national and global, that prevent poor people from realizing their potential.

U.K. NGOs engage in two distinct kinds of work in Latin America: project-based initiatives and advocacy. Projects are traditional forms of NGO activity. They involve financing, in part or in total, the costs of small-scale development with the aim of making meaningful changes to people's lives. The problems with projects as a development strategy is that they can make a difference to only a few people and perhaps only then for the life of the project. As a result, advocacy has become more and more important to the

NGOs. Advocacy means that they can focus on the root causes of poverty. Edwards and Hulme (1992, 20) describe advocacy as "lobbying government and other structures from outside." They go on:

> The rationale for this approach is simple: many of the causes of under-development lie in the political and economic structures of an unequal world—in trade, commodity prices, debt and macro-economic policy; in the distribution of land and other productive assets among different social groups and in the misguided policies of governments and the multilateral institutions. . . . It is difficult, if not impossible, to address these issues in the context of the traditional NGO project. (Edwards and Hulme 1992, 20–21)

Edwards and Hulme argued that NGOs' advocacy successes are inevitably limited because NGOs are peripheral to the international system. Moreover, Doolan (1992) has suggested that U.K. NGOs find advocacy difficult in practice because they are increasingly forced to respond to emergencies rather than concentrating on long-term work. He also suggests that the U.K. public view charity, not advocacy, as the main anti-poverty vehicle, raising the possibility that a new political focus on the part of NGOs would not necessarily be well-received (Doolan 1992, 209). Nevertheless, ten years on, we can see that the advocacy focus has become more important than ever. Advocacy is, in fact, an almost inevitable outcome of Europeanization and professionalization. It is the emergence of large coordinated networks that has made the research and lobbying that advocacy requires feasible. CISDE's *Strategic Plan for 2001–2004*, for example, presumes that, while support for the project work of the NGO members will of course continue, most attention will be paid to advocacy within the umbrella organization.

Europeanization means that it is not always possible to examine U.K. NGOs' advocacy in ways that separate it from the work undertaken within the European networks. In order to get a flavor of NGO lobbying at the EU and at the national level, I have chosen to focus on the activities of two very different groups: EURODAD, the European-wide network of NGOs concerned with the external debt, in which U.K. NGOs play an important part, and the exclusively U.K.–based World Development Movement (WDM). EURODAD lobbies on behalf of all indebted countries; as an illustration of its work in Latin America, I have focused on its recent campaign around debt renegotiations in Honduras. In the case of the WDM, I examine the strategies adopted with respect to Latin America and development issues in general.

EURODAD, Poverty, and Debt in Honduras

European NGOs were vocal throughout the 1980s and 1990s in identifying the development impact of the external debt in developing countries. They were broadly successful in bringing this issue to the public's attention in the developed countries and in forcing the countries of the North and the international financial institutions (IFIs) to consider questions of poverty in their negotiations with developing countries over debt. This led to the heavily indebted poor countries (HIPC) initiative, which allows for staggered debt reduction for the very poorest countries. It is supported by the British treasury and DFID, as well as other leading states in the developed world. The HIPC initiative is conducted through negotiations between the governments of the debtor countries and the IFIs. The G-8 is more informally influential in the proceedings. Debtor countries are required to submit a poverty reduction strategy paper (PRSP) to the IFIs, which if approved, is designed to cut the external debt while releasing funds for antipoverty measures and for development. Debtor governments are encouraged to consult civil society organizations within their country over the design of the PRSP.

EURODAD brings together the European groups concerned with the impact of the external debt on countries and about the ways in which World Bank and IMF poverty reduction strategies, encouraged in their rescheduling discussion with developing countries, impact poverty. EURODAD closely monitors the negotiation process, lobbies the IFIs and the G-8 to maintain the commitment to poverty reduction in the negotiations, and aims to support civil society organizations in developing countries in their quest for influence in drawing up the PRSPs.

Honduras became eligible for debt reduction under HIPC in 1999. Indebtedness, a failing state, regional conflict, and natural disaster together had contributed to a dramatic increase in poverty since the 1980s. According to the World Health Organization, by the 1990s Honduras had the worst quality of medical attention in the Americas. By 1999, it was estimated that 57 percent of all urban and 75 percent of all rural Honduran households were living in poverty. In 2000, a structural adjustment loan contracted by the Honduran government was due to expire. Because Honduras had now been admitted to the HIPC initiative, this was replaced by a poverty reduction growth facility loan (PRGF). Meanwhile, over US$9 billion was pledged by the international community for reconstruction through grants and loans following Hurricane Mitch in 1998, which killed over 6,000 people and devastated large swathes of the country.

EURODAD sees its role in Honduras as that of

- pushing for the disbursement of all the funds now available to the government in Honduras into programs that are genuinely aimed at decreasing poverty;
- encouraging the IFIs to keep in mind their commitment to civil society consultation and "ownership" of the debt reduction program, rather than necessarily pushing for privatization of government assets and services as the strategy for growth;
- lending support to the umbrella group, Interforos, made up of around 800 Honduran community and civil society organizations, in its struggle for consultation and influence over the PRSP; and
- keeping the issue on the agendas of governments in the developed world.

In support of these aims, EURODAD has made clear through the submission of letters both to governments in the developed world and to the IFIs that the Honduran government is failing in its task to consult civil society over debt and poverty reduction. The Honduran government drew up its PRSP without consultations with civil society organizations. Nevertheless, it was accepted by the IFIs in June 2000. As a result, Interforos (2000a) prepared its own PRSP. Pressure was then brought to bear on the IFIs, via sympathetic governments in the G-8, and the Honduran government was told, in July 2000, that the government's plan should be implemented only after consultation with civil society. This was a small success. However, once the government and the IFIs have agreed upon the overall strategy it is hard to see what role Interforos could effectively play beyond reacting to government decisions. Meanwhile, EURODAD insists that the reasons for Interforos' exclusion does not solely lay with the Honduran government. The IFIs should also take some responsibility because they impose a timetable that allows little time for community responses and inputs:

> From a glance at the HIPC/PRGF timelines and its links with the PRSP process, it emerges that inflexible timetables and conditions set by external stakeholders might have influenced the initiative, rather than local, national stakeholders. Nationally owned cannot be equated with governmentally owned. (EURODAD 2001, 6)

Consultations with social organizations, in effect, are tagged onto an agenda developed to suit the IFIs and national governments. They are a concession without meaning.

It should be noted that there is considerable difference in how EURODAD/

Interforos on one hand and the IFIs/Honduran government on the other view poverty. The Honduran government's PRSP argues that poverty is "the historical outcome of high population growth combined with low economic growth" (Government of Honduras 2000, 3). It is a result of an overall insufficiency of income, rather than unequal distribution of wealth. This seems to have been accepted by the IFIs. The logic of this approach is to stimulate economic growth and raise productivity. As a result, policies to support market opening, reduction of public spending, reform of the financial sector, and privatization can legitimately be presented as antipoverty strategies. In other words, the Honduran government, supported by the IFIs, is using the HIPC initiative as a source of funding for opening the economy, coupled with mild programs of targeted social spending. Oxfam has articulated clearly the NGO rejection of this approach:

> The traditional disconnected view of poverty reduction continues [within the PRSP], with growth on the one hand and increasing financing of the social sectors on the other. Although we strongly believe that growth is absolutely essential to poverty reduction, without a stronger focus on the distributive impact of growth and access to productive assets, we do not believe that such an approach will succeed. Our partners in Honduras describe the poverty reduction approach of the existing programmes as social welfare in orientation, without a sufficiently nuanced understanding of gender and regional disparities. (Oxfam International 2000)

Interforos has, in fact, gone further in its criticisms and suggests that the very economic model is at the root of poverty in Honduras. Nevertheless, the PRSP provides funds to keep liberalization on the agenda, rather than offering a kick-start for an alternative project of growth with equity. Interforos argues that a new basis for development itself is urgently required in Honduras, if social inclusion and poverty reduction targets are to be met (Interforos 2000a).

Finally, EURODAD is pushing the IFIs and the G-8 to take steps to control how the PRSP is conducted in Honduras. There are problems, EURODAD suggests, in the very structures through which aid disbursements are made. In this, EURODAD is drawing on the experience of reconstruction after Hurricane Mitch in 1998. Of the US$9 billion made available to the Honduran government for reconstruction, only 30 percent of the funds have actually been spent on identifiable reconstruction projects (Interforos 2000b). This is, in fact, a coded way of suggesting that corruption within the government has led to a siphoning off or a misallocation of funds.

In sum, EURODAD's approach is to suggest that poverty will not be reduced significantly in Honduras unless there is internal reform, greater attention to civil society and ownership of poverty reduction strategies, a broader understanding of what poverty actually is, and change within the ways in which global governance institutions operate. That EURODAD's lobbying has had some success in Honduras is clear simply by the terms of the debate; however, it has yet to scale up from acting as a knowledge bank and advocate to local civil society organizations on the ground, and lobbyist to the G-8 and the IFIs, to having a full voice in the process. On the debt issue, then, NGOs remain somewhat on the periphery of the policy-making process.

The World Development Movement

The World Development Movement (WDM) has operated a twin strategy, combining global lobbying with fund-raising and awareness programs within the United Kingdom for over thirty years. WDM encourages citizenship involvement and consumer power deployed for equitable development, through, for example, support for fairly traded products such as coffee and bananas. It has also organized boycotts of goods and companies and exposed companies that infringe labor rights, such as Del Monte in Costa Rica in 1997. It has been consistently active around the debt issue and campaigned actively against the Multilateral Agreement on Investment (MAI), which was successfully stalled in 1998.

WDM's most recent campaign is against the General Agreement on Trade in Services (GATS), which has been agreed upon by the WTO and means that all governments must open their public services contracts to foreign as well as domestic competition. WDM allege that GATS serves as a bridgehead for the penetration of transnational corporations into the developing world. Developing governments, which need to belong to the WTO for trading purposes, will have no choice but to open their service sectors to foreign companies. Moreover, service providers that are non-profit or that provide a social good, such as water, drainage, waste disposal, and so forth, will be treated under the same rules as nonessential commercial services or those offered by companies that aim to maximize profits. Opening service provision in this way has mainly been the result of lobbying by transnational corporations at the WTO.

In the WDM campaign, the example of Bolivia figures prominently. Popular protest scored an unusual success in 2000 in that it appears to have reversed the privatization of water in Bolivia. As part of a general privatization of services, the Bolivian government sold the public water system to a European consortium of companies, in which the U.K. group International Water was a prominent member. Sharp rises in the cost of water were immediate.

For many low-income families water became a more expensive weekly commodity than food. As a result of sustained popular protest in Cochabamba and other Bolivian cities, the government rescinded the privatization process. Nevertheless, as the WDM points out:

> If current negotiations at the WTO continue, it would be difficult, if not impossible, for the Bolivian government to go back on its privatization decision. The protests would be futile, as the government's hands would be tied. Negotiations of the GATS are putting the privatization of services, including public services, on an entirely new footing. As a result of these negotiations, governments around the world will be under immense pressure to privatize services, resulting in commitments which are effectively irreversible. (WDM 2001)

In taking on the GATS, the WDM is directly attacking the assumption that greater liberalization can lead to even development. The WDM is criticizing the very structures that underpin the global political economy. It is thus a far harder issue to influence even than the debt reduction process. WDM is currently pressing the U.K. government on GATS, although it recognizes that this is a particularly difficult issue to put on the government's agenda, since service delivery is a major overseas industry in the United Kingdom. The U.K. Department of Trade and Industry has consistently been favorable toward GATS and has been actively courting U.K. business, rather than the NGOs, in order to coordinate a common approach (Mandelson 1998). Nevertheless, the WDM has chosen an opportune moment to highlight the impact of global practices such as these on poverty and development, as mass pressures have been shown to be effective in cases such as the Multilateral Agreement on Investment (MAI). By feeding information into the public arena, the WDM hopes to shape the debate in the long term and to promote popular mobilization around the GATS issue in a way similar to the MAI.

Projects

WDM is unusual in that its sole mission is advocacy. This pushes it toward research and lobbying around poverty and the global political economy—where, it argues, the root causes of poverty can be found. For most U.K. NGOs, however, the task is to straddle both project-based work and advocacy, even when they take the view that advocacy will ultimately be more effective. As a result, there is a move, at least within the larger NGOs, to try to link advocacy and project work together. This is a response to a view that advocacy may take NGOs into policy-making arenas, without necessarily scoring notable successes, and may close them off from contact with Southern NGOs. So, for example, NGOs grouped together in CIDSE now argue that advocacy work should be strongly linked to projects and should be based on grassroots experience. A 2002 meeting of the advocacy and lobbying group of CIDSE argued that advocacy work should reflect the common concerns of Southern partners. Similarly APRODEV rejects any simple categorization of NGO activities into operational and advocacy work (APRODEV 2000, 5). Oxfam U.K., meanwhile, supports local campaigns for labor rights in the textile and agro-export industries in Chile, funds training and advocacy workshops in Brazil, and supports human rights groups in El Salvador and Guatemala. They also fund more traditional projects such as microcredit, housing and water programs, and emergency programs in Honduras and Guatemala.

Smaller NGOs have been less affected by the growth of advocacy. Their focus has tended to be more exclusively on projects. Perhaps partly because of their size, some small U.K. NGOs adopted quite early a view that projects should be controlled in the South and should respond to demands generated locally. At the same time, some U.K. NGOs have specialized in running projects in particular issue-areas and, over time, have built partnership relationships with groups in the South engaged in similar activities. This kind of specialization undoubtedly improves the quality of projects. Thus the Intermediate Technology Development Group (ITDG) opened a Latin America office in Peru in 1985 to coordinate regional activities; this office now functions autonomously. Its aim is the promotion of viable technology alternatives that build on local knowledge and skills. In providing genuine technological alternatives in agroprocessing, energy, and credit, ITDG attempts to articulate a needs-based development approach that is respectful of the environment and generates alternative employment for poor people, for whom the "choices" are either marginalization or insertion into the global political economy at the bottom of the processing chain. ITDG's approach is multifocused in that it aims to provide technical services, for example in hydroelectricity, water provision, and agroproduction, combined with a sustained research program that links technology with poverty alleviation.

Another example of a specialized NGO is the International Institute for the Environment and Development (IIED), which specializes in urban poverty, urban environmental policy, and urban governance. In Latin America, it has worked in Buenos Aires in particular. Like ITDG, IIED maintains a joint focus on poverty-related project activity and research. IIED specifically draws on the knowledge and expertise of workers in the South. It also works for larger agencies, coordinating their activities and projects and advising them on urban development. Its antipoverty programs include microfinance for housing and neighborhood development, and research into the impact of urban poverty on children:

> Children have particular requirements and vulnerabilities, with regard to both their physical and social environments. Overcrowded, precarious housing, hostile neighbourhoods and inadequate infrastructure and services can threaten both their immediate well-being and their long-term development and prospects. In many cases, an awareness of their particular needs could, with little additional investment, make a substantial difference to the quality of their lives. Not enough is known, however, about practical and effective ways of addressing children's interests within urban development. Their concerns are rarely taken into account in most planning decisions, community development projects or housing or upgrading schemes. (IIED 2001)

A less technical, but similarly specialized, focus is taken by Homeless International, which is dedicated to fostering local initiatives in communities experiencing poverty. All its partnerships with Southern community groups and NGOs are long term. In this way, Homeless International tries to avoid the pitfalls typical of project-based development—that projects fall apart as soon as the Northern funders withdraw. Homeless International works in Argentina, Bolivia, and Brazil, and its projects encompass microcredit, social housing schemes, and health and sanitation initiatives. Its partner in Argentina is the *Fundación Vivienda y Comunidad*, in Buenos Aires, which concentrates on funding housing improvements, including the provision of sanitation and water, to low-income families and to communities that have been negatively affected by cuts in state and federal social services since the 1990s under the structural adjustment process. In Bolivia, Homeless International works with *Fundación Pro-Habitat*. Whereas Fundacion Vivienda y Comunidad mainly offers technical services, Pro-Habitat tackles issues of participation, management, and education among low-income communities in La Paz. Its aim is to provide basic knowledge, through architects, community educators, medical assistants, and artists:

> The main thrust of their work has been in a Chagas control programme, working on a housing improvement and preventative health programme to combat disease which is spread through carrier bugs living in the cracks in mud-brick walls and the thatched roofs of poorly constructed houses. (Homeless International 2000, n.p.)

Both ITDG and IIED offer eminently technical projects that contribute to small-scale development. Homeless International is equally specialized. All three do quite different jobs from the kind of advocacy work that the more politicized NGOs have generally embraced. Their contributions are specific and confined geographically to particular communities. They aim at changing the life chances and quality of life of small groups of people caught up in poverty. Their understanding of poverty is thus as an immediate, lived experience. On a small scale, they can be—and indeed they are—effective. Nevertheless, their impact is necessarily reduced by the fact that they do not address—and indeed do not aim to—the underlying causes of poverty within Latin American communities.

Conclusion: Evaluating the Role of the U.K. NGO Sector in Poverty Alleviation

Deepening poverty globally, and the growing marginalization of more and more of the world's population, has become almost an embarrassment to global governance organizations such as the World Bank and the IMF, and to supranational and national bodies of the developed world, such as the EU and the U.K. government. The result has been a tendency to argue that globalization can—and should—be made to favor the poor. This is the essence of the message contained within the U.K. Department for International Development (DFID)'s White Paper on Globalization in 2000. While NGOs in the United Kingdom and across Europe generally have responded positively on the whole to this renewed focus on poverty alleviation, they have also challenged the simplistic view that globalization can serve in some automatic or direct way to alleviate poverty.

U.K. NGOs aim to contribute in a range of ways to undermining this somewhat facile account of both globalization and poverty. Some take a long-term view that only through a radical overhaul of the global structures in which Latin America's poor ultimately operate can any meaningful improvement be achieved. These NGOs aim to contribute to nothing less than a reordering of the global political economy through advocacy. Clearly a long-term strategy, any efficacy NGOs may have depends upon strategic target setting. Recently, U.K. NGOs have been particularly active in advocacy campaigns around debt and the operation of the WTO. Other NGOs see advocacy as a way both to challenge the global political economy and to undercut the legitimacy of Latin American governments that do not take the needs of the poor into account or listen to poor communities in terms of policy making. A third group of NGOs remains focused on projects that aim to improve the life experiences of the poor, frequently from a conviction that it is not enough to wait—or even work for—global change.

It is difficult to say what works and what does not. Apart from the normative bias inevitably embodied in the notion of "success," there are methodological pitfalls: How can we know the real impacts of the work? What is our time frame? Are we measuring relative or absolute results? Whose "poverty," exactly, are we are measuring? But, more fundamentally, it could be argued that any successes NGOs have had are small and barely touch the scale of the problem. In one sense, this is of course true. But the evidence presented here suggests that U.K. NGOs, like almost all Northern organizations committed to creating a fairer world, are central to change because they indicate a society-based will for transformation. In a range of inevitably imperfect ways, they engage in social and political struggles for a better world and an ethical global order. In a very real sense, therefore, their core significance lies simply in the fact that they exist and that they signal a commitment to change.

3

Perceptions

NGOs in a Context of Socioeconomic Change, Argentina at the End of the 1990s

Patricia Feliu

This chapter begins by describing the characteristics of present-day Argentinean nongovernmental organizations (NGOs) and their transformation and growing numbers associated with the changes the country has experienced in the past decades. This new context has brought about a reformulation in the relationship between the Argentinean state and Argentinean society.

From there, the chapter will go on to illustrate different perceptions about the role of NGOs in the context of these social, economic, and political changes. It will present four key perspectives, using specific examples: the perspectives of NGOs themselves, of international organizations, of the impoverished population benefiting from projects, and of the government.

These perceptions about NGOs will then be synthesized into images which, looking beyond their diversity, polarity, and even sharp contradictions, house elements with considerable potential. These elements may eventually be key to influencing decision making and constructing new and different situations.

Characteristics of NGOs in a Globalized Country

"NGO" is a concept with many definitions. Here, it is used in its widest sense to refer to civil-society organizations: nonprofit, collective forms of organization which depend upon neither the State nor private enterprise. This definition does not consider particulars of their internal organization, such as whether the NGO relies on paid or volunteer labor.[1]

Approximately until the 1970s, Argentinean civil-society organizations were structured around the then-current model of the state: a welfare state, agro-exporter with an incipient national industry. The basic forms of organization were: unions (*sindicatos*), guilds, business federations, cooperatives, professional associations, and mutual societies (these suffered the greatest changes); as well as neighborhood associations and local development groups, church groups, and foreign cultural groups. Political participation through party politics was greater, and political life and culture were more dynamic and formed an integral part of people's everyday lives.

Since the mid-1970s, Argentina has suffered profound social, economic, and political transformations. For the region as a whole, these emerge in concepts such as state reform, economic adjustment, crisis of representation, and social fragmentation. In this period, civil-society organizations went through significant transformation and their numbers grew exponentially. According to the United Nations Development Programs (UNDP)'s NGO directory (2000) there are 265 organizations working specifically in the area of social development in Argentina.[2] We will take this information as a basis for the following discussion, as it is the most recent and centered upon this type of organization.[3]

In recent years, more organizations and a greater number of different organizational models have emerged. These include, for example, social development organizations whose objectives are associated with the satisfaction of basic needs, survival, and human rights. These organizations are categorized as either techno-professional, direct-assistance, or grassroots organizations. Their interests center upon the development of human and social capital and the strengthening of civil society. They are also identified as organizations that emphasize the viewpoint of the people.

The changes that have affected Argentina since the mid-1970s have been accompanied by new conditions of existence that have negatively affected the most vulnerable sectors of society, producing a growth in their demands and changes in their forms of expressing these. Work flexibilization, the underground economy, an unemployment rate of 16.4 percent with 32.7 percent of people living below the poverty line and 10.3 percent in extreme poverty: together, they describe a social model that implements exclusion.[4] Applying these measures to the whole of the country, with an estimated population of just over 36 million, would give us nearly 12 million people living below the poverty line, and over 3.5 million people living in extreme poverty.

The population's demands are no longer expressed as large or massive mobilizations of workers' groups; rather, it is fundamentally the unemployed, or those who suffer deterioration in their working conditions, who act (for

Table 3.1

Distribution of NGOs by Year of Creation

Year of creation	Number of organizations	Percent
1940–1979	45	17.0
1980–1999	215	81.1
No information	5	1.9
	265	100.0

Source: By author, based on data from *Con fines Sociales. Organizaciones de la Sociedad Civil de Promoción y Desarrollo de Argentina*, PNUD-GADIS, Buenos Aires, 2000.

instance, public employees whose salaries were recently cut by 13 percent as part of the "zero deficit" plan). These actions address specific themes, in specific places, and in a confused relationship with the political sphere (corruption, clientism, manipulation). In this period, territorial grassroots organizations have also grown. These include long-standing types of organizations such as neighborhood associations, local development groups, neighborhood clubs, public libraries, and school cooperatives, as well as newer organizations such as community kitchens and day care centers.

The current distribution of NGOs in the national territory is not even, but rather concentrated in the principal cities in order of importance: Buenos Aires (46.6 percent), followed by the provinces of Buenos Aires and Santa Fe; finally Río Negro, Córdoba, Jujuy, Formosa, and Chaco.

Based on the UNDP study, it is possible to group the themes addressed by these NGOs into three levels of importance, with the first level indicating the most common themes:

1. education, health, childhood, women, youth, neighborhood organizations, and environment;
2. rural development, communication, human rights, nutrition/food, the handicapped, indigenous peoples, and appropriate technology;
3. economy, employment, international relations, violence, politics, microenterprise, housing, the elderly, culture, discrimination, ethics, civil-society organizations, crafts, climatic change, citizenship, social development, drug addiction, state reform, and AIDS.

It is important, however, to realize that each organization addresses more than one theme.

In their great majority, the NGOs include law as a thematic area. This is expressed in different ways, such as legal, judicial, justice, and legal frame-

Map 3.1 **Social Organizations by Geographic Location**

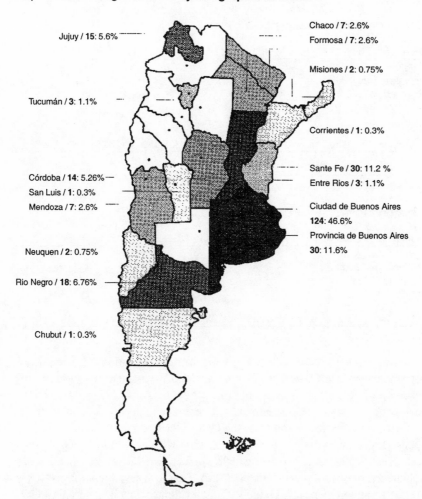

Jujuy / **15**: 5.6%

Chaco / **7**: 2.6%

Formosa / **7**: 2.6%

Misiones / **2**: 0.75%

Tucumán / **3**: 1.1%

Corrientes / **1**: 0.3%

Córdoba / **14**: 5.26%

San Luis / **1**: 0.3%

Mendoza / **7**: 2.6%

Sante Fe / **30**: 11.2 %

Entre Rios / **3**: 1.1%

Ciudad de Buenos Aires
124: 46.6%

Provincia de Buenos Aires
30: 11.6%

Neuquen / **2**: 0.75%

Rio Negro / **18**: 6.76%

Chubut / **1**: 0.3%

Source: Elba Luna, "Mapa institucional," in *Con fines Sociales. Organizaciones de la Sociedad Civil de Promoción y Desarrollo de Argentina,* PNUD-GADIS, Buenos Aires, 2000.

work, ultimately, questions of rights that aim at the exercise of respect for the individual/inhabitant/citizen. Possibly, this is because the new conditions of existence fail to take them into account.

In regard to the area of activity or mode of intervention of these organizations, it is important to emphasize that they encompass a wide range. One basic classification of activities is: (a) technical assistance to the beneficiary population, (b) technical assistance or consulting to other organizations, and

Table 3.2a

Human Resources Used by NGOs

Type	Number of NGOs	Percent
Paid (only)	20	7.5
Volunteer (only)	70	26.5
Paid and volunteer	133	50.1
No information	42	15.8
Total	265	100.0

Source: By author, based on data from *Con fines Sociales*, PNUD-GADIS, 2000.

Table 3.2b

Category "Paid and Volunteer" by Main Type of Labor

Main type of labor	Number of NGOs	Percent
Majority are paid	39	29.3
Majority are volunteer	87	65.4
Equal numbers	7	5.3
Total	133	100.0

Source: By author, based on data from *Con fines Sociales*, PNUD-GADIS, 2000.

(c) research and study. Another commonly used classification is (a) grassroots organizations, where members are beneficiaries, (b) assistance organizations, made up of volunteers who are not direct beneficiaries, and (c) nongovernmental development organizations, with technical and professional staff.

Based on the information from the UNDP NGO directory's individual response sheets, we obtained the following data with respect to NGOs' human resources: Of a total of 16,702 people working in NGOs, 86.2 percent are volunteers; only 13.8 percent are paid staff. That is to say, Argentinean NGOs appear to support themselves largely through volunteer labor. Observing NGOs by types of human resources (paid labor only, volunteer labor only, or paid and volunteer), we obtained the distribution shown in Table 3.2a.

If we look at the paid and volunteer category with its total of 133 organizations, it is clear that the tendency toward volunteer labor remains (Table 3.2b).

NGOs' many sources of economic resources can be grouped into three levels, with the first level indicating the most common sources of NGO funding:

1. Individual donations (51 percent), educational activities, membership fees, national government, and fund-raising events;
2. Foreign NGOs, consulting services, bilateral cooperation, businesses,

sale of publications and products, multilateral agencies, and agencies of foreign governments;

3. Provincial government, subsidies, fee-for-service, other donations, municipalities, members' resources, scholarships, funding drives, national cooperation, microenterprises, national NGOs, private organizations, own patrimony, and library services.[5]

NGOs tap into a wide range of funding sources, and in general a given NGO will obtain funds from a variety of sources. Of the 265 registered organizations, however, more than a third (34.7 percent) do not give information about their estimated annual budget; organizations are normally reluctant to offer this sort of data.

What becomes clear from this information is that NGOs in general, and those focusing on social advancement and development in particular, do not have a clearly defined profile. It is not possible to classify them by a single set of criteria as each organization defines itself by distinct combinations in a range of ways.

Different Perceptions about the Role of NGOs

Nongovernmental Organizations' Perceptions of Themselves

Key difficulties identified by NGOs in their activities are access to information, regional differences, and above all the differing capabilities of the organizations themselves, which put them in situations of advantage or disadvantage relative to others. Another preoccupation for NGOs is the amount of time invested in fund-raising, which affects the sustainability of their activities through time. NGOs also warn of the functioning of "clientist" mechanisms among NGOs, that is, a tendency for some NGOs to work with unclear guidelines and little transparency.

NGOs' perceptions of their relationships with different actors can be characterized in the following ways. From the state, they demand more funding and complain of (a) lack of planning (due especially to the high level of turnover of public servants) and policies toward NGOs that decrease their impact (including frequent changes in policies and programs); (b) lack of transparency in state actions; and (c) excess of formal requirements, to which some NGOs do not have the human or economic resources to comply. It becomes clear that NGOs' relationships with the state pass exclusively through the executive branch in its different levels: national, provincial, or local (municipal). It is with the latter that they achieve better possibilities for collaboration, fundamentally because of the scarcity of technical personnel locally—personnel that NGOs can offer. The legislative branch in its three levels is, on the other hand, disarticulated from NGOs' activities. Relationships with businesses or business foundations are also very rare.

Some NGOs express difficulty in establishing links with international organizations because of the influence these exercise on state policy. Many are concerned about the lack of freedom to carry out projects based upon local needs, feeling themselves pressured by emerging trends from abroad.[6] Looking beyond the great differences among organizations, in general the level of autonomy and participation NGOs feel they can exercise is questioned, whether in relation to international organizations, powerful interest groups, or governments.

In this sense, many NGOs identify themselves as watchdogs of public action and reservoirs of critical consciousness. Others, however, maintain that their function is located in the tension between their critical consciousness and the place that powerful groups assign to them. Some cannot forget that it was largely international organizations that installed the theme of NGOs' representing civil society, including the necessity of NGOs' presence due to their supposed transparency of action. These new rules that inform international organizations' social policies implicitly support their economic policies, which are intimately related with the refinancing of the external debt —contracted with those same international organizations.[7]

In one of the World Bank's Voices of the Poor workshops,[8] held with a grassroots organization in a poor urban neighborhood, one conversation turned to the role of the World Bank in the life of the people:

> If our interests are not in agreement, why give to the World Bank, why give them information about the needs, the realities of this area? To what point is it useful for us to do all this work for the World Bank if they don't have the same interests as we do?
>
> The World Bank says it is interested in the poor, but I believe that the World Bank is far from resolving this problem.

NGOs are worried about other aspects of the quality of their own activities. The accelerated growth of social needs has created ample opportunities for "non-serious" NGOs, and the lack of fiscal control over NGOs has motivated hidden commercial activities, generating a lack of credibility in some sectors. In this sense, there is a demand that the state control the functioning of NGOs and stimulate the growth of a greater number of "serious" organizations; the NGOs themselves should also exercise control over each other to avoid fraudulent activities.

NGOs question themselves on many themes, and so form spaces to connect with one another. The establishment of organizational networks allows NGOs to share objectives and has improved their functioning. NGO networks may organize by theme, or as general social policy networks. In 1991, the national forum of NGOs was launched,[9] and in 1998 a network was formed for NGOs to dialogue with the World Bank: GTONG-BM.[10]

International Organizations

International organizations such as the World Bank, United Nations, and the Inter-American Development Bank give important encouragement and legitimacy to the participation of NGOs. The diversity of international organizations' programs is expressed in the different summits and fora they have organized, as well as in their lines of credit, subsidies, and donations. These influence not only the content of the public agenda, but also the areas of action that NGOs define for their projects.

The United Nations Development Program (UNDP) bases its actions on the idea of "human development," valuing people's capabilities, organizations, and participation in the construction of the social order. Thus the UNDP supports the strengthening of civil society and its organizations. Its interest in this theme is manifested in a book published in 2000: *Con fines Sociales: Organizaciones de la Sociedad Civil de Promoción y Desarrollo de Argentina* (With Social Aims: Civil Society Development Organizations in Argentina).

The World Bank, for its part, has the objective of reducing poverty. It centers a great part of its actions around the concept of social capital, with society's organizations being part of the manifestation of this. The World Bank considers that NGOs' participation improves projects' abilities to reach the most disadvantaged groups and gives greater flexibility and transparency to project implementation. As a mechanism for citizen participation, the World Bank incorporates the perspective of alliances, promoting interrelationships among the three sectors: public, private, and civil society.

> From the viewpoint of the World Bank, supporting this type of initiative is central, insofar as it demonstrates the potential of collaboration between government and civil society, a proven road in international experience and a very effective way to generate policies and projects that improve people's quality of life. . . . From the viewpoint of civil society, what is hoped for is commitment to this fight against poverty; adequate knowledge, especially at management level; and a capacity to direct this social energy toward transformation. (Cesilini 1999, 13–14, 16)

Concrete examples of the World Bank's interest in the participation of NGOs include the program "Alliances for Poverty Reduction," the NGO Working Group on the World Bank (GTONG-BM), and the publication of a directory of NGOs in the city of Buenos Aires.

An Example: World Bank Consultation with NGOs

The World Bank's country assistance strategy (CAS) consultation for Argentina, organized by the GTONG-BM, was a monumental experience. With the huge number of attendees and themes addressed at the consultation, many considered it the largest experience of multisectoral social dialogue carried out in the country to date. This experience allows us to consider the dynamics (construction and tension) established by the various actors as they related with one another.

The consultations were organized through five regional fora and one national forum which took place during February and March of 2000. The consultation was by its nature dispersed, and the World Bank was not obliged to synthesize the results. The bank committed itself to respond to the proposals, signaling which had been incorporated into the CAS and which had not, and giving reasons.

The consultations had barely been proposed when questions began to arise about the appearance of participation, provoking a contradictory, reflective process. This situation became clearly apparent during the organization of the Buenos Aires pre-forum, in the disputes raised by various NGOs. Following confrontations, the announcement of the pre-forum was worded in the following way: "Rich Country, Poor People? Equity: Social Debt,"[11] critically paraphrasing a World Bank document.[12]

In response to the consultations, various organizations maintained that the objective of the Bank was to hold a public event that would situate that organization as a reformed institution, capable of incorporating social demands. Nevertheless, other aspects emerged:

> It is possible to state that the intense debate and cross-cutting organizational structures produced a qualitative leap with respect to the traditional one-to-one interaction among grassroots organizations, funding organizations, and/or the state. (Banco Mundial 2000, 14, 16)

The conclusions generated by the consultations revolved around a strong criticism of the model of structural adjustment supported by the World Bank. There was demand for a greater participation of NGOs in public life; greater fiscal oversight of social programs financed by the World Bank; incorporation of themes that did not figure in the World Bank's agenda, such as land, habitat, and housing; and the complete public diffusion of the contents of the CAS. The need also emerged to analyze regionalization, including the development of specific indicators to suit each region, focusing on a participative, regionalized construction of social indicators.

The thematic axes of the consultations were: justice, anticorruption, and security policy; gender; health; education; work and employment; productivity development; financial and tax systems; environment; infrastructure and transport; and poverty and social policy. With reference to the theme of poverty and social policy, the central points of the proposals developed in the consultation by the NGOs were:

- Fight poverty through an improvement in the distribution of income, and combat inequity and exclusion;
- Monitor social programs and seek transparency; ensure the participation of beneficiaries in the design and control of programs;
- Invest in social capital for the strengthening and training of organizations and networks; and
- Promote indigenous peoples (including issues of identity, leadership, and bilingualism).

The final document was presented in the national congressional building in a ceremony presided over by the then-president of the Commission on Population and Human Resources. As he hosted this final meeting, he lamented that he had not participated in the consultative process and signified commitment to be involved in the future.

The World Bank's response[13] to this document took into account all areas touched upon in the consultations, and synthesized some points, including:

1. Observations on the consultative process:

   Dispersed—not synthesized: "The intention was to learn more about priorities and perspectives. . . ."

2. The role of the World Bank and its work:

   The goal of the World Bank is self-generated and sustainable development, it also has a role to assist in emergencies, and in countries with average incomes it should take the role of mediator among various actors.

   Its goal is to assist the country in the planning and design of policy, not just to finance.

3. Each thematic area had its response. In regard to the themes of poverty, equity, and social protection, some responses were:

Economic reactivation should be led by the private sector and not driven by public spending.

International experience teaches that the best way to distribute is through social expenditure; it reduces poverty and income inequality considerably. . . . In Argentina social pressure is progressive.

The reality is that poverty is increasing, this preoccupation points to the need to direct the social protection system in Argentina, including health services and other social services, to manage these risks and reduce the vulnerability of the economy.

The Impoverished Population, or Project Beneficiaries

Taking as a source of information the Voices of the Poor project, it can be observed that the impoverished population in general does not identify techno-professional NGOs as part of community life. While NGOs of this type did not participate in focus groups, neither did the population which was consulted identify them as part of the organizations that carry out activities in the community.

Community members named in their diagnostics, whether or not they valued their activities, the organizations in which they participated, the so-called grassroots organizations made up of beneficiaries; direct-assistance organizations such as the church, generally made up of volunteers; and also the services and plans of the government. Less frequently, political parties and businesses were mentioned.

Grassroots organizations appeared frequently in all of the consultation sites, with diverse characterizations. Emphasis was on the community center and clubs (both are typical men's spaces) and the day care center, neighborhood kitchen, and the "Cup of Milk" centers (primarily women's spaces).

It is the meeting center for the neighbors to resolve problems about land or neighboring communities. (rural area)

Because it serves to organize people. (rural area)

The day care center gives a good service, they are trustworthy, serve meals and it is free, a shame that there is only one. (urban area)

There are many children and sometimes they even eat standing up, they receive a cup of milk in the afternoon. There is no community kitchen for elderly people, there's one which is 40 blocks from here. (urban area)

The church is one of the most frequently named organizations, though in a number of cases more in relation to religious than social services.

> Father Robert comes and he gets (us) a lot of things. (rural area)

> The church gives milk on Sundays, they do baptisms and sometimes there is a party for the children. For others there's the evangelical (church), according to one's preference. (urban area)

Government services and plans are perceived as very important organizations because they give opportunities, educate, train, and provide work; in some cases they become axes of community life:

> The school gives work. Before, we hunted and fished, now in the school we do carpentry and construction work. (rural area)

> The women also work in the school, and the children study. (rural area)

> The truth is that if it weren't for the doctors, who would look after us? (rural area)

> The school has a computer, it is progressing, they have night classes, and also a cafeteria. (urban area)

> The First Aid station needs more resources, it needs equipment and medicines. (urban area)

> Plan Vida is a disaster, they only give milk and on top of that it changes location every day, it's very disorganized, there is no communication. (urban area)

> Plan Vida aside from the things they have given, made us begin to work together. (urban area)

An exceptional case was a cooperative in the town of Los Juríes in the province of Santiago del Estero. This was a *campesino,* or farmers' cooperative, that was identified as a social development organization.

> The cooperative centralizes different government programs. Through it, the programs arrive here, loans from abroad are distributed to people that need them, to the members. Also, through the cooperative we receive information about other organizations, and solutions for people's problems. (rural area)

People's opinions of political parties are restricted to the assistance these can give to solve problems.

> The Basic Unit No. 26 (of the Justicialista Party) gives you metal sheets for roofing, but they take a long time; they also help you giving what they can: wood, planks. (urban area)

> They always help with the paperwork in the municipality. Yes, and they also take charge of everything when someone has to be buried. If not, who would pay for the burial? (urban area)

Instances of direct participation by the consulted population in the organizations that carry out activities in their community are few. Many organizations are associated with corrupt conduct and clientism, but there are also some cases that demonstrate participation and strong institutional life, for instance in the case of the campesino cooperative.

With respect to containing networks for crises, two kinds stand out. On one hand, there are the networks structured around government plans at their different levels, for instance Plan Vida. On the other hand, informal organizations are created through the initiative of neighbors, for instance the community kitchens that begin by offering a plate of food and later consolidate themselves offering alternative solutions to other necessities such as clothing, housing materials, schoolwork assistance, training courses and so forth. Normally, this consolidation is accompanied by at least one level of support from a more structured institution; in this study the majority of these were church or government bodies, with the latter having a tendency toward clientist conduct. The exception was the campesino cooperative, an autonomous, sustainable, and representative organization.

The Government

Governments understand NGO's function based on their need to reconfigure their relationship with the people in a way that permits a more legitimate understanding of their interests, and as organizations that can contribute a distinct viewpoint toward improving public policy. Governments see in NGOs the potential for a new linkage through which the state can comply with its obligations while the NGOs maintain their autonomy.

Governments maintain that the strength of a democracy is based upon the quality of its social institutions. A solid social fabric is fundamental to building a democracy on principles of solidarity and equity. Despite changes over time, the following public bodies, created in the 1990s, indicate the inclusion of civil-society organizations in Argentinean public policy:

- National Center for Civil Society Organizations (Centro Nacional de Organizaciones de la Sociedad Civil [CENOC]), Ministry of Social Development and Natural Resources. CENOC was created by the then-subsecretary of social development. Unfortunately, in the process of moving to the level of the secretariat and then to the ministry, CENOC gradually lost ground and is now largely inactive.
- Center for Information on Organizations Working in the City of Buenos Aires (Centro de Información sobre Organizaciones que Operan en la Ciudad de Buenos Aires [CIOBA])

Recall that it is only the executive branch of the government that establishes contact with NGOs. Local governments, particularly, have improved their ties with social organizations, particularly grassroots social organizations: approaching and including them. The legislative branch, on the other hand, is very disconnected from NGOs and does not have a direct relationship with them. It would be interesting to analyze the normative processes of the state. For instance, Argentina's new Constitution, written in 1995, is taken as an example of citizens' rights; yet at the same time laws are passed promoting work flexibilization, privatization of state enterprises, zero deficit, and so forth.

Images of NGOs

It is commonly maintained that during the development of the welfare state, the emergence of civil-society organizations is not stimulated (or permitted), as clientistic mechanisms come into play allowing little or no citizen participation. It appears to be forgotten that in the short democratic life that Argentina has experienced, grassroots organizations such as mutual societies, unions, guilds, improvement societies, and public libraries were perfectly common— and the cooperative movement was very strong. It is important to remember the role that was played by political parties in this past civil-society framework, as representatives of civil-society's interests. It also bears pointing out that clientelism is not a particular characteristic of the welfare state, but rather, of authoritarian concepts of domination, most obviously manifested in the defacto military governments but also deployed within the centralized government model of the current free-market state.

The transformations in the last quarter-century have been very significant. State reform has involved decentralization within a framework of a crisis of representation, and in the face of weak local governments. The economy has undertaken an adjustment that has involved balancing the national budget, paying external debts, and reassessing financial activities, including the privatization of state enterprises such as oil and communications within a deindustrialization policy. This was accompanied by a regressive distribution of income (Beccaría 1992, 93–116), changes in relative wages, and a deterioration in social services (education, health).

These were huge transformations with an often contradictory character; on one hand, the GDP grew and price indices were favorable; on the other hand, unemployment and regional crises grew also, worsening like never before people's living conditions. This situation has been described in the World Bank document "Poor People in a Rich Country: Report on Poverty in Argentina" (Banco Mundial 2000). Economic growth has shown itself only through the concentration of wealth, because this growth is not built upon a model of social equity. Growth has thus led to the progressive implementation of mechanisms of exclusion.

From these macrolevel changes, tendencies have unfolded toward fragmentation and breakage in the social sphere. State intervention has shifted priorities, discarding the concept of universal social protection and instead implementing focused, assistentialist policies. Decentralized social policies open up participation to NGOs. The state abandons its representation of the poorest sectors of society, as these are covered by new kinds of social organizations. These sectors not only grow, but also develop new ways of interaction between public and private spheres, between state and market. There emerge private associations for public benefit, their actions oriented toward meeting social needs in a context where living conditions have deteriorated greatly.

In the face of this new social situation of weakened democracy, concepts about civil-society organizations vary. They range from the very optimistic, in which civil-society organizations are understood as dynamic alternatives in democratic life that aim at cooperative mechanisms of social responsibility. Other optimistic views see NGOs as taking a confrontational role against the state and the new interventions and impositions of globalization. Pessimistic views, on the other hand, see NGOs as agents reproducing inequality: accomplices of existing power structures, in the words of James Petras (1997, 10), "the community face of neoliberalism"; or as agents that replace the state as it slides toward market rationalism (providing survival strategies for professionals); or as appendages of a state in social decline.

NGOs can conceive of themselves as simple networks that challenge poverty and capture resources, or they can also see themselves as effective mechanisms to counteract the processes of exclusion and social segmentation: not only strengthening, but deepening the processes of democratization. These organizations can be understood as links in the engineering of new social policies; as consequences of new forms of poverty and marginalization; or as a critical expression of the current situation.

Optimistic images, whether presenting NGOs as dynamic or confrontational alternatives, maintain that these organizations have considerable potential for the reconstruction of the social framework. The principle ideas that underlie this position are:

- The participation of NGOs permits more efficient and effective policy implementation; above all, their involvement achieves mechanisms for transparency and citizen control. NGOs maintain a more direct relationship with communities and thus more adequately identify their needs. They are organizations that are based upon the social enterprise model and are essentially citizen's initiatives.
- The production of social capital is necessary for development. Social organizations embody part of the social capital generated in a society. This is not limited to the formation of citizens convinced of their civic duties and dedicated to their communities (active citizenship), but is also based on the formation of participative processes and entering into a concept of solidarity, referred to as alliances or networks. These organizations can be thought of as schools for democratic participation.

The pessimistic images, on the other hand, argue the impossibility of starting from a neoliberal model and achieving a framework that reconciles the concentration and centralization of capital with the microdistribution of symbolic power or strengthening of civil society. They posit:

- The incongruence of trying to relate the idea that people's well-being is a shared responsibility of the social whole, if the government's model of political economy is based on structural adjustment directed toward the most disadvantaged sectors and producing huge gaps between rich and poor, and subject to international power structures.
- The absurdity of funding organizations that identify the causes of the new poverty in inefficiencies and distortions of the political system, rather than in the adjustment policies that they themselves impose, producing the corruption (complicity) of the political system.
- NGOs are identified as the "most appropriate" actors to implement the imposed social policies because they are posited to be uncontaminated by political corruption. But in reality, NGOs are actors dominated by others, they are expressions of social fragmentation and growing poverty. (Basualdo 2001)

NGOs are a social phenomenon; regardless of our opinions or convictions, they are a form of organization that people have chosen in these years—

this is what they have done, their practice. A great deal of community activity is channeled through this kind of organization as a demonstration of determination: to keep fighting, to not give up, the so-called "*aguante*" (Asociación Civil Madre Tierra 2000). And different discourses now incorporate NGOs, placing them among society's spokespeople.

The level of heterogeneity of NGOs is great. Their versatility is such that we can only define them from different angles, as social organizations that represent collective aspirations and projects that are enormously diverse, each defined by its mission, objectives, actions, target population, and relative location in the process of the construction of social relationships in each time and place.

But the fundamental limitation of NGOs' work is that their actions are not sustainable: they disappear when the subsidy disappears, and their radius of action is limited to a group of beneficiaries. From this emerges one of the challenges facing them, which revolves around the articulation between the social and the political.

It is not easy to find a path to a functioning democracy; this involves many meetings and partings of dynamics, groups, and ideas. Yet what is certain is that from the perspective of social policy, *NGOs*, the *local*, and the *participative* do not revert to an independent process. Their relationships with the macro, with the political economy, the political system, the national model, is necessary, as is the identification and localization of all the social actors, including those with economic power—for it is not possible to think about transformation without including intervention in the process of accumulation.[14]

Every social situation, however small or precarious it may be, designs a rationality that is articulated with larger processes. Social policies that are invasive rather than empowering, obviously have local-level effects. But the interchange and consumption of material and symbolic goods can strengthen social sectors. All practice aims for the construction of spaces of social relations among actors, spaces where ideas and actions are interwoven. Social relationships thus function like connecting bridges that allow for the creation of new and different situations. Seeing this process, we would be able to envision the possible construction of a critical mass that would influence decision making, once it achieves sufficient force.

4

Visions of Development

Catholic NGOs and Indigenous Communities in Northwestern Argentina

Laurie Occhipinti

Nearly every NGO defines the group that it works with, or serves, in particular ways. Various organizations may work with poor women, with inner city youth, or with silver miners, and so forth. The ways in which an organization defines its target group are indicative not only of whom it serves, but of the kinds of projects in which it is interested. The ways problems are defined and understood form the basis of the work of the NGO and its role in the community (see for example Escobar 1995; Pigg 1992). Here, I am interested in NGOs working with indigenous peoples.

I suggest that projects aimed specifically at indigenous groups base their work on the premise that poor indigenous peoples are not simply a subset of the poor, but that their cultural differences form a fundamental element of their poverty. This is not to say that the NGOs are necessarily interested in changing that culture; often, their goal is the very opposite, to preserve what is seen as the uniqueness of indigenous culture. Yet in doing so they face a very peculiar conundrum: what sets indigenous cultures apart is often their economic organization, based on noncapitalist, nonmarket production—the antithesis in many ways of development itself. How does one create development without changing the economic base of the culture, and by extension, the culture itself?

In this chapter, I consider two NGOs in northwestern Argentina and how their ideas about the indigenous cultures with which they work shape their projects and their programs. The work of each organization is shaped by its own understandings of the local culture and its visions of the past and future. In each case, some of these ideas are explicit and well developed. Others are unstated, simply assumed, but have an enormous impact on the work of the NGO. I argue that these ideas are fundamental to understanding the NGO's role in the community and the impact of NGOs' positions as cultural brokers.

The Organizations and the Communities

The indigenous cultures of northwestern Argentina are numerous and varied. Indigenous peoples make up only a small fraction of the nation's total population and are concentrated in the northern extreme of the country. The indigenous cultures of Argentina are confronted by a nation-state that is still in the process of defining the role of its native peoples, a global economic system that is foreign to traditional ways of subsistence and exchange, white settlement and development that encroaches on traditional lands, and a natural environment that has been and continues to be subject to pressures of degradation. In this context, NGOs have emerged as one of the most significant actors in the establishment of a more equitable status for indigenous peoples in Argentine society. NGOs have taken a leading role not only in economic development, but in promoting and defending indigenous rights in every sphere from land reform to organization, education, and lobbying for legislative change.

Fundapaz

Founded in 1973, Fundapaz works in northern Argentina, with a variety of programs ranging from reforestation projects to a cheese factory. The NGO has several regional programs with a central administrative office in the city of Buenos Aires. Its programs espouse two goals: to increase the productive capacity of the small producers, farmers, and artisans in the communities in which it works and to work to improve social organization in the communities. The organization portrays its work as that of a bridge between poor rural populations and the dominant society—a bridge upon which ideas are allowed to travel in both directions (Fundapaz 1988). Most of its funding comes from nonprofit European development agencies, many of which are religious in nature. Other funding comes from government sources and large international agencies such as the World Bank. As a private nonprofit organization, Fundapaz is not officially affiliated with the Catholic Church, but sees itself as having "Christian inspiration" and maintains close ties with the church.

In the province of Salta, Fundapaz works with the Wichí, an indigenous people whose economy was based primarily on hunting and gathering until the middle part of the twentieth century. From its base in the small town of Los Blancos, Fundapaz makes regular forays into the surrounding villages, focusing on community organization and sustainable agriculture.[1] A team of six professional staff members includes individuals with both technical and organizational skills who divide their time fairly evenly between the Wichí and *criollo* (white) communities. At any given time, Fundapaz projects may include such things as promoting the construction of family gardens through the provision of tools and seeds, introducing new breeds of goats more suited to the harsh ecological conditions, helping to dig wells and ponds to cache fresh water, and building community centers. Fundapaz promotes different kinds of projects in the Wichí and criollo communities, according to local needs, preferences, and practical project considerations. The NGO has also had a long-term commitment to help local communities gain legal rights to the land that they occupy, a struggle that took over fifteen years (see Occhipinti 2000). In this process, which resulted in the distribution of titles in the Los Blancos region in 1997, Fundapaz acted as mediator between Wichí and criollo communities, as lobby group in pressuring the government, and as technical adviser.

In its promotion of development projects in the Wichí communities, Fundapaz faces formidable challenges. The material standard of living of the Wichí is much lower than elsewhere in the province or in the nation. In the region near the town of Los Blancos, none of the Wichí communities has electricity.[2] A lack of potable water is a problem endemic to the area, as much of the ground water is too salty to drink. Public services such as health care and education are inadequate throughout the region. Many adults are illiterate, and women and children, in particular, often have limited fluency in Spanish. Household cash incomes range from virtually nothing to about $150 per month.[3] The economy of these Wichí communities is based on a precarious combination of wage labor, subsistence agriculture, and foraging. Wage labor takes the form of irregular day work for white farmers in the area. This work is highly unreliable and pays only a few dollars a day.[4]

One question that Fundapaz staff frequently raise is: What do the Wichí want? The answer is far from simple. From one perspective, the many voices within the Wichí communities create a complex and often contradictory landscape of wants and opinions. There is no single "Wichí vision" of economic development. Nevertheless, there are certain shared assumptions, a degree of consensus, and expressions by local Wichí leaders that suggest an idea of development that is broad in scope, including not just economic well-being but cultural preservation and a degree of local autonomy. At a meeting of many Wichí community leaders in July 1997,[5] one middle-aged man expressed his goals for the Wichí and some of the challenges that they face as a people:

> We need to teach our children, so that they also learn. We are entering
> secondary school, college, but they do not teach the things of our culture.
> We are looking for this path, which is the land, legal status for our commu-
> nities, health, education. Our organization, to be Wichí, must be organized
> according to our own culture. The national constitution talks about the
> different cultures. They are asking now what we want, what [form of] or-
> ganization, what customs, so that these are not lost. For these reasons we
> must talk to our young people, so that they learn from our path.

As this speaker expressed, in many ways the immediate goals of development proposals—health, education, production—are secondary to deeper
concerns. The underlying issue goes beyond the number of goats that a family receives as part of a husbandry project, but is about maintaining a sense
of cultural identity. Many Wichí leaders and community elders feel that while
young people need formal education to help themselves and their communities, they also need roots in those communities and a sense of their own
heritage. There is a sense of urgency that underlies the discussions of leaders
at meetings such as this one, a sense that their cultural identity and the cohesion of their communities is threatened. Generations of broken promises and
unfulfilled expectations have left a significant part of the Wichí community
with a sense of fatalism, cynicism, and even despair, as another leader expressed in the same meeting:

> There are programs, there is help, but they do not reach here. Justice does
> not reach indigenous people. . . . The indigenous people will always be
> poor until they die.

In the Wichí communities, Fundapaz, like other organizations, has become a significant resource in its own right, beyond any secondary benefits,
such as increased production, that the projects it introduces may bring. What
many of the Wichí involved in projects welcomed most were the short-term
benefits associated with the projects themselves—food and wages that were
available to project participants, as well as tools and materials that were often also included. Within the community, the usefulness of the projects was
transformed in such a way that it did not appear to matter if the end result
was a shed, a fence, or a well, as long as it employed a significant number of
community members, who were paid in cash or in kind for the days that they
worked on the project.

In the work of economic development, it is sometimes easy to forget that
the Wichí communities have their own agenda for change, one that does not
always coincide with the goals of specific programs. As projects are put into
place, they are transformed from their original intent by the actions and ideas

of the people in the community. Such transformations adapt projects to meet the needs perceived by the community, without necessarily producing the transformation envisioned by the projects. The Wichí accept the strategies and often the discourse of projects but for their own motivations: a reformulation of development that represents a creative response to local needs (see Crush 1995, 8; Comaroff and Comaroff 1992, 5). In the economic landscape of the Wichí, development projects were a desirable form of employment, one that was fairly reliable and eagerly accepted. Fundapaz acted to bring such projects, and the communities cultivated this relationship to ensure access to the resources that it brought. Fundapaz has become one resource among many in the subsistence strategy of Wichí households that utilize every available resource.

Yet the role of Fundapaz goes beyond simply acting as a conduit for resources. Fundapaz is in a unique relationship with these communities, one that is not matched, under the current situation, by government projects or other outside initiatives. It has a long-term presence in the region, and a commitment that goes beyond the scope of any single project. In addition, the Wichí clearly recognize the importance of Fundapaz as a bringer of knowledge and as an advocate. As one community leader said, "We take advantage of you [aprovechar de ustedes]. Besides [Fundapaz], we do not have anyone. We don't know much about the outside world—but you do. . . . There are many things we need." There is a clear recognition that Fundapaz is an ally, an advocate in an environment where such are scarce, as well as a crucial conduit of material resources.

Recently, Fundapaz has made a conscious shift in methodology, trying to move from a situation in which projects were often presented as givens, to a more proactive relationship between the communities and the organization. One of the Los Blancos team members described this shift: "We talk to the clan, to see all of their needs. Then we go looking for projects. We have to knock on different doors, to find the projects that can meet these needs." This shift in methodology represents a change in the relationship of the organization with the community. As another staff member commented, "Before, Fundapaz did everything—we had the idea, we made the projects, we came in with the resources, and everyone signed up. People recognize that this has changed."

This shift is in response to a sense that the old method of simply presenting a project to the community as a package deal was imposing outside decisions, at best; at worst, it was paternalistic. Yet locally, the primary concern in the communities was often less with the result than it was with the process, the resources that were immediately available, and the ongoing relationship with the NGO. From this point of view, a community center (which may never be used after its construction) was more desirable than a fence around a permanent water supply if the former meant a steady source of employment for two months in the dry season, while the latter entailed only a few days' labor. Thus, the suggestion that the community itself should propose the project that it wanted was often met with indecision—what was most wanted was the work of the project, rather than the finished product. While the NGO's goal was increased community self-sufficiency through a completed development project, the community saw the project as a medium for bringing more employment; their goal was to ensure a continuing influx of projects to create a series of employment opportunities.

OCLADE

OCLADE (Obra Claretiano de Desarrollo [Claretian Development Project]) is a non-profit NGO established and run by the Catholic Church of the prelature of Humahuaca. It runs programs throughout the prelature, which encompasses most of the puna (*altiplano*) of northwest Argentina and the sub-Andean valleys directly to the east (including the departments of Santa Victoria Oeste and Iruya). This area may well represent one of the poorest geographical regions in Argentina, with high indices of illiteracy, infant and child malnutrition, and unemployment.[6] Because of the size of the area and the difficulties of transportation and communication, particularly in the rainy season (December to March), the resources of OCLADE are sometimes spread thin.

Its major programs focus on community organizing, economic development projects (mostly in the realm of subsistence agriculture), and various projects aimed at improving health and education for women and children. Funding comes from various religious intermediary organizations, both Catholic and Protestant, from nonreligious development organizations, and from several government programs. About 25 percent of total funding comes from some level of the government; the rest is from NGO sources and direct support from the Catholic Church. In 1997, OCLADE had about twenty-five full-time employees, including administrative staff, local development workers, and support staff. There are also numerous people working at the local level, all of whom receive no salary or very small stipends, who do the bulk of the work associated with projects. While NGO administrators refer to them as "volunteers," the women themselves see their involvement with the NGO as paid work, and the positions available in the preschool and as literacy educators represent an important source of employment for local women.[7]

The *departamento* of Iruya was one of the first communities in which OCLADE began to work in 1983.[8] Iruya is a scenic town in the high Andean valleys, a land of dramatic cliffs and swift rivers. The people of Iruya are known as *Kolla*. Their local economy is based primarily on subsistence agriculture, supplemented by meager sales of produce on the regional market and migrant labor to plantations in the lowlands. The average household has a cash income of perhaps $600 a year, and holds less than a half of a hectare of land.

At the present time, OCLADE has one professional staff member in the community who works principally with child and infant feeding programs as well as preschool programs in several communities in the interior. In Iruya, OCLADE has been most active in the areas of health and education, in part due to the personal skills and interests of some of the people who were key to founding the organization. OCLADE has also acted as an important conduit of material resources into the community; projects have provided materials to construct systems for drinking water and for irrigation and to build health posts. There have also been several attempts to create productive associations and cooperatives for both agriculture and crafts. While these had some success in the short term, they met with long-term failure, and none of them are currently active in the community, an issue that I discuss at length below.

OCLADE's health and education programs respond to clear needs in the community. Nonetheless, to an extent these projects treat only the symptoms of poverty, rather than aiming at changing the productive conditions that provide an inadequate income. Short-term solutions create a dependency on outside interventions and do not resolve the underlying issues: child malnutrition is the result of poverty, and only improving the productivity and income of households will address such a problem in a meaningful way. Members of the community, when asked, say that they welcome the programs and the assistance that they represent; however, it is also true that few members of the community see OCLADE as a truly important resource for their community, in sharp contrast to the relationship between the Wichí and Fundapaz. People's concerns about "development" focus on their farms, on migrant labor, and on maintaining a lifestyle that they see as both their inheritance and their legacy to their children. OCLADE's projects may seem peripheral to many of these concerns, its concerns outdated or secondary. Nicolas, a very active leader in one of the villages near Iruya, said:

> To me, OCLADE was formed to work with the problem of malnutrition and infant mortality. But afterwards, they kept going on to do the same things. They think that things don't change, that people here need the same things as when they started, ten or fifteen years ago. They gave things, before, to improve the life of the people. The community center, the health post, the school, the pre-school. Then last year, there was a big meeting [the assembly of the prelature] and we saw that we need irrigation canals and the commercialization of our production. A lot of these things now, they see that the government has to do them.

Leaders like Nicolas have begun to look elsewhere for projects to improve agricultural productivity, sensing that OCLADE has little interest in investing resources there. As there are no other major NGOs active in the highlands, local leaders have chiefly turned to the federal and provincial governments for funding to improve agricultural conditions. There are significant difficulties that they face in this, as project funding is scarce and difficult to obtain.[9]

Negotiations of Status

In the last several years, both Fundapaz and OCLADE have shifted to a more "participatory" methodology, one that encourages local program participants to become more active in identifying the needs of the community and more involved in project planning at early stages. This shift is not coincidental, but is reflective of trends in the world of NGOs more broadly. In Iruya as in the Wichí communities of Los Blancos, this shift has created challenges in the relationship between the NGOs and the communities they serve. While it may seem from an outside perspective to be a wholly desirable and empowering shift, it has met with resistance locally in both cases and presented considerable challenges for the organizations.

Both NGOs stress the importance of empowerment, but on the level of their praxis it must be considered how much room each gives for the empowerment of both individuals and communities. Each NGO faces distinct challenges to implementing a more participatory methodology; these challenges are based both in the NGOs' own strategies and "cultures" and in the cultures with which they work.[10] Of the two NGOs, OCLADE has a more deeply internalized system of hierarchy, which interacts with a status-oriented culture to prevent empowerment on an individual level. While both NGOs' philosophies are about self-sufficiency and maintaining cultural values, the underlying differences around status and authority differ, and contribute to different stances and strategies in achieving these goals.

OCLADE

The administration of OCLADE is based in Humahuaca, the center of the prelature, located about three hours by vehicle from Iruya. Locally, one promoter lives in Iruya and makes periodic visits to program sites in the surrounding villages. She is a cheerful woman in her thirties, from the provincial capital, and trained as an elementary teacher. Until 1997, all of the decisions about programming were made centrally by a few key administrators. Since that time, the NGO has begun to decentralize planning through a number of smaller administrative groups that now make many programming decisions on a regional level. The group for Iruya includes the promoter, one or two other people who work closely with OCLADE in Iruya, and several other people who work with the organization in other capacities in Humahuaca.

This group meets periodically to manage much of the administration for local projects. For example, it evaluates project proposals presented by communities and decides which should be funded, and it deals with problems that arise within ongoing projects. At the present time, none of these team members comes from Iruya, and their regular meetings are not open to the participation of individuals from the community or other interested parties.[11] Although certain individuals within the organization and the church more broadly resist the hierarchical nature of the organization (which is often accompanied by a paternalistic view of the local culture), the overwhelming tendency in OCLADE is toward a notable degree of hierarchy, with ultimate authority vested in the bishop and his office.

It is not only the NGO's perceptions of the community, but the community's perception of the NGO that shapes the relationship. The people of Iruya, part of a peasant society stretching back through generations, have a strong sense of hierarchy and rigid social classes. OCLADE is seen as part of a hierarchy of external powers, benevolent or otherwise, that imposes its will on the community. The average Kolla sees herself as part of the lower echelons of a natural social order comprised of clearly defined status relationships, that is, landlord–peasant, priest–parishioner, mayor–citizen, husband–wife. With OCLADE, this relationship takes the form of uneducated farmer–NGO professional, separated by barriers of education, race, and class. The strong, internalized sense of social hierarchy in the culture, reinforced by OCLADE's own tendencies toward a hierarchical administration, makes a shift to a more participatory model doubly complicated. Just as a parishioner would not want to offend or challenge the authority of a priest by making too many suggestions, neither would a Kolla farmer want to input too many ideas to the OCLADE staff.

Fundapaz

The relationship between the Wichí and Fundapaz is quite different, based on both the NGO's organization and the indigenous culture. Wichí political organization is highly egalitarian, and there is little sense of hierarchy or class within the villages. Instead, respect is accorded to individuals based on their age and on the knowledge that they are seen to possess. The face-to-face relationships of the villages are often extended to the outside world, and there is little understanding of the ways in which external politics function.[12] As an example, even those Wichí who have a long involvement with development projects have only a vague idea of what the process of obtaining funding for any given project entails. A common view, frequently expressed, is that Fundapaz has a large warehouse somewhere, and chooses to parcel out materials according to its own whims.[13] This kind of idea demonstrates that many people in the communities do not understand the process, and feel that it is beyond their control or influence. As Fundapaz tries to change the nature of the relationship between NGO and community, there is a degree to which the Wichí view this shift as the retraction of resources, as a diminution of the relationship itself, within the context of reciprocity that frames the Wichí worldview.

Fundapaz's own organizational structure is much less hierarchical than OCLADE's. The administrative office in Buenos Aires shapes the overall mission of the organization and coordinates grants and funding, but has little involvement in the day-to-day operations of the Los Blancos team. The team itself is comprised of five members and the local director, who divides his time between the administrative office in the provincial capital and the Los Blancos office. The other team members—two couples in their early thirties and one woman in her fifties—live in Los Blancos and make frequent, regular visits to the communities. Their training is varied, with one agronomist, two specialized in natural resource management, and one having a broader background in social sciences. Only one team member, a woman from the criollo community, does not have a professional degree.

On a daily basis, the team members interact as equals. Pablo, the director, is an energetic, tireless man who greatly respects the opinions of the team members and backs up their opinions on program decisions. In their meetings in the Wichí communities, the Fundapaz team is careful to allow time for extended discussions, often in Wichí,[14] and to solicit opinions both at meetings and in informal conversations. The Wichí, for their part, are much more forthcoming with their opinions than their Kolla counterparts.

The Wichí value the knowledge of the professional staff of the NGO, but in keeping with Wichí notions of knowledge and experience, the status of the team members is tempered by their youth. In a heated discussion on land titles one afternoon, a Wichí elder summed up his frustration with the Fundapaz position in the following way: "You, Marcelo, are young. I was fighting this fight when you were still a baby at your mother's breast. You don't understand what we have been through."

Seeing Indigenous Peoples

In their engagement with local cultures, the NGOs emphasize not only issues of economic development, but issues of indigenous rights and cultural autonomy. In a certain sense, the indigenous cultures themselves are seen as being not just outside of the dominant culture, but as existing as an alternative social model. Each NGO has created an image of the local community that stresses its indigenous nature, as an alternative to the "materialistic capitalist ethos" of Argentine society. In doing so, the NGOs focus on aspects of indigenous culture that are particularly attractive to their own philosophies and beliefs, at times finding themselves at odds with local opinions and even the indigenous cultures themselves.

Both Fundapaz and OCLADE have an enormous degree of respect for the indigenous culture where they work. There is a high degree of awareness of the degree to which the native peoples of Argentina have historically been dispossessed of their lands and relegated to a low position on the socioeconomic ladder. Both NGOs put the integrity of the indigenous culture as one of their highest priorities when planning and implementing projects, and both have invested an enormous amount of time and energy into issues of land rights as well as promoting indigenous rights. There can be no question that these NGOs have served as effective advocates for the indigenous communities.

At the same time, however, it must be understood that the ways in which the NGOs perceive the cultures that they work in has a tremendous impact on their work. This perception shapes how the organization understands the causes of poverty as well as its visions of the future. Perceptions of local cultures influence not only the personal relationships between NGO staff and community members, but the kinds of programs that the NGO implements. It is in their preceptions of the indigenous cultures that the two NGOs are most divergent. OCLADE tends to romanticize an idealized "traditional" Kolla culture, an image which at times stands in the way of programs. Fundapaz, while very culturally sensitive, grapples with the question of what kind of economy is compatible with Wichí culture (even as the Wichí grapple with the same issue), while putting a great deal of emphasis on ecological sustainability.

OCLADE

The Catholic Church in Iruya and the surrounding region, and by extension OCLADE itself, is motivated by the tenets and discourse of liberation theology, a transformative movement within the Catholic Church beginning in the 1960s. This perspective shapes the work that the NGO does and the role that it sees itself playing in the community. One element of the teachings of prominent progressive theologians was that the ultimate Christian mission was to end the suffering and oppression linked with poverty, through the transformation of economic conditions for the poor. In this spirit, OCLADE was founded.

In order to transcend traditional church efforts at charity, development projects were needed that linked social organizing and community development with programs that created economic development and improved local conditions. In this particular vision of economic development, improving economic conditions is a means to an end, rather than an end in itself. The goal is human dignity—the ability of individuals to live meaningful lives, of communities to thrive, and, in the long term, through incremental local change, the transformation of society itself. In this way, the work of OCLADE is seen as a mission, with a higher moral purpose—a goal that differentiates it in important ways from, for example, government development agencies (see, for example, Scott 1998).[15] The NGO itself exists as part of the larger mission of the church, and its goals are intimately linked to a broader agenda of increasing the presence of the Catholic Church as well as in meeting the immediate development needs of the communities it serves.

OCLADE is part of the church itself, administratively and financially completely dependent on the prelature, while Fundapaz identifies itself as having roots in a progressive Christian vision but exists as an independent organization with no formal ties to the church. In its literature, OCLADE draws heavily on Biblical references and on religious metaphors, and its staff includes many members of the clergy as well as lay volunteers who are committed to the church first and to the NGO as a part of that church. Notwithstanding the important role of local volunteers, it is significant to note that OCLADE's professional staff, its entire administration, and the majority of persons on its advisory boards are not native to the highlands, but come from urban areas of Argentina and from Europe.[16] The organization and staff are thus highly cognizant of the cultural differences between themselves and the local parishioners they serve, and the Kolla culture is forefronted in much of the work that they do. The church actively promotes visible symbols and displays of Kolla culture, ranging from *Pachamama* ceremonies to the use of traditional instruments as part of church services. Other regional NGOs have been created within the church specifically to promote indigenous rights.[17]

As the church has worked to increase local acceptance of indigenous identity and promote indigenous rights issues, certain themes have been highlighted and particular features of local culture have been stressed and drawn out. In Iruya, these have focused first on the poverty and oppression suffered by local people and second on the nobility and goodness, in an absolute sense, of the "traditional" way of life, that is, subsistence agriculture and herding (see Olmedo 1990). These themes are not unrelated in the local imagination: highland farmers frequently describe their life as one of "suffering" and "sacrifice." Farming is seen as a choice that one makes—rather than migrating to the city or leaving the area, the peasant family chooses to stay on the land, to live a life of hardship, in order to have something of the land and of a way of life to hand down to future generations. The church's frequent references to the sacrifices made by local people, to the obstacles faced by local residents in continuing their way of life, and to the suffering and oppression suffered by the Kolla are resonant with themes and ideas in the culture itself, and thus find a receptive audience.

The development work of the NGO takes place in this context, and is not without unconscious and untheorized paradoxes. The NGO itself is essentially founded on the premise that the local economy is inadequate, that there are high levels of poverty and its associated ills. Yet the life and traditions of the Kolla farmer are part of the very object that the church would like to respect, preserve, and give higher value to. In the church's discourse, and in local constructions of identity, subsistence agriculture is part of the very essence of Kolla identity. The life of the peasant farmer is an implicit model of virtue, to which is contrasted the crass materialism (in both a literal and philosophic sense) of Argentine culture. The paradox is nearly inevitable— to create "development," to raise incomes that all agree are inadequate, depends largely on finding viable alternatives to subsistence agriculture, alternatives that include more participation in the market economy.

OCLADE continues to emphasize health programs and literacy, treating the symptoms of poverty, rather than fostering programs to improve cash incomes through better marketing of produce. Subsistence production is regarded as an essential part of "traditional" Kolla culture, and any movement away from subsistence production seems to threaten that image. The agency focuses on improving traditional agriculture, even as the standard of living that it provides seems to be inadequate. Subsistence agriculture, the traditional way of life of the Kolla, is seen to be the key to maintaining autonomy and independence, by the NGO and indeed by many villagers.

OCLADE has thus focused on projects to promote subsistence agriculture, avoiding commercialization of agricultural produce, despite indications that Kolla farmers would have welcomed increased marketing opportunities. One exception, a sellers' cooperative, was a short-lived attempt to improve marketing options in a couple of villages. The project was instituted by OCLADE and managed by local residents. Its rapid collapse was explained to me by NGO staff as the result of local fighting and factionalism. From another perspective, however, the leadership of the cooperative had only a rudimentary understanding of regional marketing and basic bookkeeping. Further tensions were caused by the reluctance of many local farmers to deal with the cooperative rather than with a buyer who had been coming to the community for many years and had established a position as a local *patrón*.

Two factors prevented more careful oversight and a greater commitment from the NGO to the sellers' cooperative. First, there is an institutional ambivalence about engaging in commercialization. Local subsistence agriculture is idealized, even though it is seen as providing an inadequate standard of living by residents and NGO staff alike. Second, OCLADE has a very strong ideology of community, of cooperation, and of collectivism that shapes its programming decisions and its daily operations. The idea that people should work together to improve things for the collective, a very strong idea of Christian communism in the primitive sense, derived from OCLADE's religious background, and makes issues of conflict and conflict resolution particularly problematic. When there is seen to be "too much fighting," the organization tends to pull the project out, to suspend the program, or to stop working in a community. This is often justified by saying that there are other communities that "really want" a project, and if the first community cannot work together, there are others who could benefit. When people do not get along, it is seen as a moral failure, one that people themselves should overcome for their own good, rather than as a structural problem that needs to be figured on and planned for.

Fundapaz

For Fundapaz, projects among the Wichí have focused on the introduction of subsistence agriculture, which seems to be ecologically sustainable and economically possible, but may be fundamentally at odds with the Wichí concepts of both time and labor. The Wichí have not adopted the patterns and seasonal rhythms necessary for agriculture. A project to encourage families to construct garden plots, for example, met with only a lukewarm response. As one of the staff members of Fundapaz noted, "We have to look at what they will use, or what they can sell. Otherwise, unless they see a specific reason like use or sale, they will not bother doing it. . . . If the Wichí don't do something, it is because they are not interested in it."

The gardens promoted the use of vegetables such as radishes and carrots which grow well in the region, but which the Wichí do not consume as part of their regular diet. Because they are easily grown, white farmers in the area tended to grow their own and were not interested in purchasing the surplus. Something as apparently straightforward as building gardens is working at the level of wholesale cultural change, despite the number of years that the Wichí have been living in relatively settled communities. It has to do with habits of work, most obviously, but also habits of consumption, patterns of land use, and the frequent movement of individuals between households and communities.

Despite the difficulties involved, Fundapaz focuses on subsistence agriculture. The "traditional" economy of the Wichí, hunting and gathering, is seen to be important to maintaining the culture but inadequate to support the community given the extent of ecological degradation in the region and the limited land available for foraging, as ranches owned by whites have permeated traditional territories. There is a high degree of respect by Fundapaz for traditional hunting and gathering practices, and to the extent that it is possible, projects are planned during times when game and wild fruits are scarce. Nevertheless, Fundapaz emphasizes alternative economic strategies, which it sees as necessary to development. Despite the cultural barriers to smallholding, it is seen as an option that will allow the Wichí to maintain a degree of economic autonomy, lessening their dependence on highly exploitative wage labor.

Fundapaz has focused a great deal of energy over the past decade on promoting land titles as a means to security; without security of land tenure, the entire Wichí economy and culture was seen as being at risk. Any development options for the Wichí are seen as being land based—whether it is agriculture or the limited extraction of resources such as timber. Land titles will allow the Wichí to erect fences to exclude cattle, allow capital investment in water sources and community buildings, and ensure access for foraging.

Here, as with OCLADE, there is a paradox involved in promoting subsistence agriculture. The local staff are well aware of the cultural obstacles to smallholding, and in fact these obstacles are a frequent topic at planning meetings and in informal discussions. The discussions frequently center on a few traits that are seen (rightly or wrongly) by the staff as being part of Wichí culture; most frequently named are a tendency to rapidly consume goods and produce, rather than stockpiling; the rapid diffusion of goods through the community beyond their intended recipients; and the mobility of individuals, when many projects call for a core group of participants. At times, creative solutions to these issues are built into plans, while at other times the consequences are simply accepted as part of doing business with the Wichí. But the real obstacles to smallholding may be deeper.

The area encompassing Los Blancos, called the Chaco Salteño, is a harsh landscape of scrubby trees, cacti, and thorny brush. Finding development strategies that are ecologically appropriate is at the top of Fundapaz's agenda. There is a sense of impending ecological crisis in some of the agency's work, an idea that the region is rapidly degrading, and that without intervention the area will become increasingly inhospitable. The destruction is blamed on the introduction of cattle in the 1940s, and on deforestation caused by the extraction of the best lumber. Fundapaz's projects thus seek to avoid these economic alternatives with the Wichí. Although many Wichí would like to own cattle, the agency refuses to entertain projects that would introduce them.

However, from another perspective, cattle may be the element that allows the impoverished white farms to sustain their level of subsistence; the capital represented by cattle make those marginal farms viable.

Fundapaz does not fall into thinking that the Wichí are "noble savages" who, if left to their own devices, would prove to be excellent stewards of the land and its resources. The mystique that is part of an international indigenous rights discourse, that indigenous peoples are necessarily at one with the earth, is not part of the agency's discourse. Instead, there is a recognition that within a local area, the Wichí tend to use up resources rapidly, and consume them thoroughly. This belief makes Fundapaz even more resistant than it might otherwise be to promoting either cattle or the extraction of timber. Yet Fundapaz sees the Wichí as having a deep knowledge of the environment and a long-term commitment to preserving it. Fundapaz thus seems to take on the role of mediator in the nature-culture relationship, in order to protect the Wichí from their own worst inclinations and short-term needs and desires, and to foster the long-term interests hidden beneath.

Conclusion

Both NGOs discussed here attribute the causes of poverty to the cultural divide between the indigenous cultures and the dominant society. Often this is described as the isolation of the indigenous group, the failure of the wealth of the dominant society to reach into these remote areas, or the lack of resources. Occasionally it is blamed on historical patterns of domination, as in land claims, but this theme is treated cautiously. Both NGOs see local economic change as a result of external forces impinging on local resources, especially land and labor. The "outside" world is rarely seen as offering anything beneficial in terms of change, but rather as a threat to local cultural integrity. Social change is seen to be driven primarily by the relationship of local villages with the external world, and is also viewed as a threat to the local culture.

Implicitly, creating economic autonomy is one of the underlying goals of development programs. Both NGOs view participation in the larger capitalist economy—through commercial agriculture, herding, or wage labor—as culturally alienating for the indigenous groups. The indigenous societies are almost invariably understood as being *outside* of capitalism (not as integrated at lowest level). The focus tends to be on subsistence practices—which are almost always going to be inadequate at dealing with poverty in these contexts—rather than on "enterprise." The focus of projects is not on more integration with the capitalist economy, but on less.

It is significant that both NGOs are completely administered and managed by nonindigenous staff.[18] The perspective they bring to this work tends to accentuate the emphasis on the indigenousness, as it were, of the local culture. Their work, in planning, in formal project administration, and in the informal relations between staff and members of the local community, is thoroughly shaped by their status as cultural outsider. In a sense, the NGO itself is a cultural outsider, one that local people may manipulate and use to suit separate purposes, as with the Wichí, or dismiss to a certain extent as irrelevant, as has happened in some of the Kolla villages with OCLADE.

The NGOs' emphasis on subsistence production accords with the theme that the indigenous societies are culturally vulnerable. Foremost in the literature and thinking of each organization is the idea that the indigenous culture is unique, and that it is threatened or endangered. The threat comes primarily in the form of poverty, as local economies seem to provide an increasingly inadequate level of subsistence. In Iruya, malnutrition and child mortality is taken as evidence that families live on the edge of hunger. In Los Blancos, the alternatives to subsistence agriculture—irregular wage labor and hunting and gathering—are both seen as inadequate to support families. In their programs, both NGOs stress local autonomy—subsistence production—as a way to ensure cultural survival. Projects thus focus on reducing risk, and on ensuring a greater reliability of subsistence. Land ownership and local production that is not dependent on the market are seen as ways for local people to maintain control of their own economic well-being.

Without economic change, in the forecast of each NGO, the indigenous culture cannot survive, beset by an array of difficulties: young people will leave their native communities in search of work; family ties and kinship networks will break down; norms of sharing and cooperativism will be lost as each household struggles to survive. Eventually, in the worst-case scenarios, under the flood of media images, the scant attention paid to indigenous cultures by the educational systems or the dominant society and the increasing ease of transportation and communication, the cultures will disappear, subsumed into the underclass of Argentina. The survival of the indigenous culture is linked with the ability of its communities to be self-sufficient. Neither organization proposes that a whole-hearted adoption of capitalism and the market will do—in part because of the economic and social marginality of both groups, and in part because of cultural issues. The market economy is seen at its base to be incompatible with the cultural values of the indigenous population and intrinsically threatening to their way of life.

Success, however defined, rests on the level of congruity between the needs and desires of the community and the NGO's strategy for development. The degree to which the NGO finds acceptance in the community and the willingness of people to participate and take on a proactive role in the organization depends largely upon its finding ways to address the real needs and desires of local people. In indigenous communities, the cultural distance between NGO staff and community members makes it difficult to gauge the extent to which ideas are shared, and seems to require a high degree of introspection and self-awareness on the part of the NGO in examining its actions and strategies. Both Fundapaz and OCLADE begin with the premise that development has to be negotiated with the community, albeit at different levels. The issue then becomes, how is it possible to negotiate these ideas?

These NGOs come to the table with their own ideas about what constitutes "development" for the Wichí or the Kolla. An essential and fundamental element of their vision is that the future of these unique cultural groups not be complete assimilation, that development allows them to remain (or to become) self-sufficient, if not isolated. This idea of indigenousness is so ingrained that it may come to hinder negotiation, if it does not coincide with the visions that local people have of their own future. For both of these NGOs, the emphasis on preserving or maintaining the indigenous culture itself takes priority over strictly economic concerns. There is, of course, nothing wrong with this, as long as the NGO and the community share a similar vision. The key to success rests in the organization's ability to engage in a dialogue with community members about how they see their own future, without becoming trapped in a static notion of saving a "traditional" culture.

5

Market Articulation and Poverty Eradication?

Critical Reflection on Tourist-Oriented Craft Production in Amazonian Ecuador

Patrick C. Wilson

It seems to us that since with nature you can domesticate the animals, you
can domesticate the plants, what we aspire to do is domesticate beauty:
the beauty that is normally preserved in the folkloric communities.

—*Rebeca Santos, president of Sinchi Sacha*

In January of 1999, the *Fondo Ecuatoriano Canadiense de Desarrollo* (the
Canadian Fund for Ecuadorian Development, FECD) sent an auditor to the
Amazonian community of Santa Rita to assess the social and economic impacts of a ceramics project on their community. The project, funded by FECD,
was designed and installed by a Quito-based NGO, Sinchi Sacha. Sinchi
Sacha designed the project to improve the economic situation of the community through the sale of ceramics to tourists. The project also had the goal of
improving the social standing of women in the community, as women would
produce the ceramics and be the primary economic beneficiaries.

Since the inception of the project in 1997, however, the ceramics plant
had largely failed to provide the economic and social benefits it promised.
The plant, staffed entirely by women, created greater market dependency for
those working there, but the women ceramists were not able to generate the

profit necessary to effectively maneuver in the market. The plant also introduced new social tensions to the community, as community members avidly disagreed on the appropriateness of women working outside of their homes independently of their husbands. Plant director Nancy Grefa suffered malicious rumors and spousal abuse as a result of her work at the ceramics plant, and also lamented the deteriorating economic condition of her family. Her low earnings did not allow her family to buy what they needed in the market, and the time she spent at the plant took away from the time she would have otherwise spent farming. Yet the ceramics plant is an example of craft-oriented development projects being copied throughout Amazonian and Andean indigenous communities. Such projects are rooted in the belief that market-oriented craft production will empower communities economically while also helping to preserve local cultural traditions. The ceramics plant provides a clear example that these projects do not always aid communities in poverty alleviation, nor in cultural valorization.

Many of the problems experienced at the plant (and which spilled over into the community more generally) resulted from the only partial knowledge and understanding that Sinchi Sacha personnel had of local sociocultural conditions in Santa Rita, both while designing and implementing the project. The NGO's well-meaning intentions, rooted in promoting gender equality and environmental sustainability, ultimately threatened to undermine gender relations among and between families, because the project design violated local beliefs regarding gendered division of labor and appropriate and acceptable gendered roles within the family. Furthermore, the imposition of a cash economy on the women working at the plant put at risk the agricultural subsistence economy of their families, as women abandoned their agricultural labor in favor of the ceramics plant. When the plant failed to generate the expected profits, some families were left with neither sufficient food in their fields nor money to go buy more food in the market.

This chapter begins with a review of women in development (WID) and gender and development (GAD) theory. Sinchi Sacha referred to different tenets of both WID and GAD theory in the design of the ceramics plant, so it is important to place the design within its theoretical context. Likewise, the ceramics plant was designed to promote the sustainable use of resources in the area by providing a viable economic alternative to forest cutting. It thus reflects current trends among development projects promoting sustainability, as it sought to forge a dignified relationship between local cultural practices and the market to aid in the economic empowerment of local peoples. The middle sections discuss "culturally appropriate sustainable development" in the context of ceramic production in the Amazon. The final sections highlight the social and economic problems that resulted both at the level of the individual women working at the plant and at the level of the community as a whole from Sinchi Sacha's ceramics project.

Gender and Development

Since the 1970s, women have been an important, and sometimes even central, consideration for development practitioners. The exact nature of the relationship between development and gender considerations has changed over time, from a tendency to exclude women from development projects, to making women the primary beneficiaries. Prior to the emergence of the WID approach in the early 1970s, women were generally thought of in terms of their reproductive roles: reproduction, childcare, and education (Braidotti et al. 1994). Third World women were treated as tradition-bound, and therefore as a hindrance to development and modernization (Scott 1995; Chowdhry 1995). Yet through a process of critical reflection, development theorists and practitioners began to realize that it was necessary to account for the economic roles that women play in a variety of contexts.

An extremely influential book by Ester Boserup (1970), *Women's Role in Economic Development*, was crucial for instigating a process of reflection regarding the impact of development projects rooted in modernization theory on women's well-being, as a well as dialogue regarding what women's role in the development process should be. Boserup argued that the male-biased nature of development projects, which tended to assume a strict dichotomy of men as economic earners and women as domestic caretakers, removed women from the important productive practices they engaged in (such as certain agricultural activities), while also devaluing women's work by dismissing it as unimportant. Therefore, the net result of these development projects was a decrease in the social status of women, and a devaluation of women's economic roles.

The WID approach sought to include women in the development process as central and crucial economic actors. Suggesting that in many nonindustrial societies women and men contribute more or less equally to the household economy (Boserup 1970), a critique of women's subordination became economic in nature. Looking past social causes of inequality, the emphasis on women's productive roles meant that their subordination (and by implication, overcoming that subordination) was seen within an economic framework (Razavi and Miller 1995, 4). Therefore, proponents of WID suggested that women's subordination in a wide array of contexts could be overcome by including women in economic development projects.

The WID approach has since come under scrutiny for its tendency to oversimplify women's social situations, and in many cases to ignore the social context altogether. While WID emerged in the context of attempting to shatter domestic-bound representations of women globally, it in many ways reproduced and reinforced those roles through the types of development projects instituted in the 1970s. Furthermore, many critique the WID approach for viewing women as a tool for enhancing development, while failing to examine male bias in the design of development projects. The WID approach, therefore, has been criticized for not reflecting seriously on how *development* needs to be restructured to benefit women (Razavi and Miller 1995).

In some cases, by not understanding local gender relations, development projects that sought to improve women's situations ultimately placed an additional burden on women's shoulders:

> Women's projects in development programmes address women's problems only partially, by, for example, introducing income generation activities. Such programmes imply that women have time to do more work. . . . The feminist concern for changes in the sexual division of labor is evaded; rarely do development programmes lead to increasing men's work burdens. (Braidotti et al. 1994, 83)

Many women, particularly in the Third World, are responsible for a disproportionate amount of domestic work and subsistence activities. Some WID approaches tended to pile on additional labor through project implementation targeting women, not recognizing that the women's domestic labor load would remain unchanged. The inability of many WID advocates to recognize and valorize women's labor in domestic and subsistence contexts has been argued as one of WID's principal failures (Hirshman 1995).

The WID approach also was criticized for its tendency to treat women as a homogenous category (Porter 1999). Third World feminists have critiqued First World feminists for imposing a First World feminist agenda on Third World women without seeking to understand the unique cultural context of women's lives in different locales (Mohanty 1991; Hirshman 1995). The WID approach often obscured important differences between women from different cultural contexts and how they perceived and interpreted their own situation, both socially and economically.

These critiques led to gender and development (GAD) approaches, and a focus on social relations, especially gender relationships, in local contexts. GAD approaches have encouraged an understanding of how social relations of power between men and women in different cultural contexts can influence the types of projects likely to benefit both women and the larger society (Porter 1999). While GAD is certainly an improvement over the WID approach, it also has its critics. Some suggest that GAD has the tendency to reduce "gender" to "women"—thereby excluding men, this time, from the development equation (Razavi and Miller 1995). GAD has also been criticized for ignoring relations of power between men and women in both domestic and public contexts, even while ostensibly analyzing gender relations (Smyth 1999).

A final concern with some GAD approaches has been their inability or unwillingness to provide critical reflection on development as an industry. Not unlike WID in the 1970s, the GAD approaches of the 1980s and 1990s have often uncritically embraced greater market incorporation as the catch-all solution to economic "underdevelopment," without considering the possible impacts of market incorporation on local economies and on social relations. These neoclassical approaches have been championed by the large development banks, and most important, have defined the approaches of numerous NGOs working in the Third World.

Since the 1980s the number of NGOs working in Latin America and elsewhere has dramatically increased. The rise in popularity of NGOs over the past twenty years reflects the promise they hold in the eyes of many to aid in poverty alleviation, stem human rights abuses, extend democracy, and promote environmental sustainability (Fisher 1997). The presumed advantages of these organizations over state institutions is thought to lie in their lack of burdensome bureaucracies and political agendas. Furthermore, as many Latin American states adopt neoliberal agendas that include scaling back and eliminating some social services for economically marginal populations, NGOs have increasingly been called upon to fill these gaps (Bebbington et al. 1993).

NGOs, Culturally Appropriate Sustainable Development, and Craft Production

In the past twenty years, discourses of development have shifted to promote ecological sustainability as an emphasis of development projects. A strong discourse of environmentalism has suggested that the key to conservation of natural areas may lie in the involvement of indigenous peoples in conservation or sustainable development projects (Orlove and Brush 1996). Representations of indigenous peoples as "native environmentalists" or "ecologically noble savages" have contributed to this process by creating stereotyped images of indigenous peoples living in harmony with their natural surroundings. While these stereotypes have recently come under criticism for their inaccuracies and paternalistic overtones (see Ramos 1998; Conklin and Graham 1995; Stearman 1994), they remain popular images in development discourse. As such, countless development projects promoting environmental sustainability have been implemented in indigenous communities during the past twenty years.

Sustainable development projects in indigenous communities have frequently sought environmental conservation with cultural sensitivity. Their premise is that valorizing local cultural practices can help both to preserve local cultures and promote conservation efforts. For example, a forestry management project in Amazonian Ecuador encouraged indigenous Quichua people to abandon cattle ranching, a recent introduction to the region, for a much older and more ecologically sensitive local tradition of agroforestry (Shiguango et al. 1993). The valorization of craft production has also been a strategy used by many NGOs to forge links between indigenous populations and external markets, particularly tourist markets, hoping to provide indigenous artisans with economic outlets while promoting sustainability. One famous example of indigenous communities empowering themselves economically, politically, and socially through craft production and sales is that of the Otavalo Indians of Ecuador, who have achieved wide recognition and economic success through the sales of their sweaters, tapestries, backpacks, and other woven goods (see Colloredo-Mansfeld 1999).

Many NGOs working in indigenous communities have tried to replicate the successes of groups such as the Otavalo weavers or the Zapotec weavers in Mexico (see Stephen 1993), through implementing craft production projects in indigenous communities. Women artisans have often been the protagonists. This is partly due to the rising popularity of GAD models, but it is also the result of lingering assumptions about the relationship between women and cultural continuity. Women have frequently been thought to be more tradition-bound than their male counterparts, and therefore more "authentic" bearers of culture. As Carol Smith (1991) has pointed out for Mayan women in Guatemala, women are thought to preserve culture by maintaining "traditional" dress styles and indigenous languages, while men tend to assimilate dress styles and more often speak the dominant national language.[1]

Proponents of indigenous women's crafts projects cite the potential of such projects to aid in poverty alleviation while also strengthening local cultural pride and ethnic identification. They also offer the potential to valorize women's work, thereby increasing women's social and economic standing within these communities. With these promises in mind, the Quito-based NGO, Sinchi Sacha, designed and implemented a ceramics plant in the indigenous Quichua community of Santa Rita in Ecuador's Amazon basin.

Sinchi Sacha, Sustainable Development, and the Huacamayos

The Huacamayos mountain range runs along the western edge of Ecuador's Amazon basin and is a highly biodiverse region. Looking to the west from the small city of Tena, capital of Napo province, the mountains form a dark green and purple barrier to the Andes mountains rising behind them. Often enshrouded in clouds or fog, the Huacamayos provide a striking visual. Nestled among the foothills of these mountains are numerous Quichua communities that engage in small-scale agriculture, cash cropping of coffee, *naranjilla* (a citrus fruit frequently used for juices and preserves), cacao, and other products, as well as cattle ranching. In recent years population growth has exacerbated existing land shortages, forcing members of these communities to expand their agricultural and ranching frontiers westward, further into the foothills of the Huacamayos.

In the early to mid-1990s, Sinchi Sacha and PROBONA (another Quito-based NGO that works for the conservation of Andean forests) began organizing a series of activities to provide the communities of the Huacamayos with alternatives to forest cutting and further expansion into the foothills. They first worked on community organizing and urged these communities to form a regional organization of the Huacamayos that would specifically be responsible for community economic development and ecological conservation. These efforts resulted in the creation of the *Comité Intercomunitario de los Huacamayos* (the Intercommunity Committee of the Huacamayos), of which the community of Santa Rita was a founding member, and which consisted of seven communities in 1995.

In the beginning, Sinchi Sacha and PROBONA appointed local coordinators of the committee; they focused on small-scale projects in member communities, such as building walking paths to sites of potential tourist interest, creating ethnobotanical gardens, and establishing nurseries of native plants. The following year the organization grew to include eleven communities in the area; that same year it was renamed and officially recognized by the Ecuadorian government as the Union for the Administration, Use, Utilization, and Community Management of the Area of the Huacamayos, or the Unión Huacamayos for short.

The Unión Huacamayos is a representative organization that is primarily responsible for coordinating development projects in its member communities. The communities elect leaders who act as intermediaries between Sinchi Sacha (as well as other groups and individuals) and the union's base communities. The union and its member communities are also affiliated with a regional indigenous federation, the *Federación de Organizaciones Indígenas de Napo* (FOIN), which represents more than 100 indigenous Quichua communities in Napo province.

Since the founding of the Unión Huacamayos in 1996, it has remained highly dependent on Sinchi Sacha and PROBONA for both operational and project funds. Jesús González, executive director of Sinchi Sacha, takes credit for devising the union as an organization, as he hoped to create an indigenous organization primarily concerned with issues of sustainable community development. Sinchi Sacha then wrote proposals for projects to be implemented in the Unión Huacamayos's communities. This was a good relationship for Sinchi Sacha, as it provided them with communities with which to collaborate on development projects. Yet, the arrangement left the Unión Huacamayos highly dependent on Sinchi Sacha. The Unión's leaders did not obtain the skills and knowledge necessary to write their own proposals, market their own products, or otherwise promote their organization.

Over time, Sinchi Sacha shifted its focus from small projects to more ambitious sustainable development initiatives for the Unión's member communities. The NGO drafted a three-pronged sustainable development proposal for the communities of the Unión Huacamayos, of which the ceramics plant in Santa Rita was one part. The proposal also included an ecotourism project in another community, and an ethnographic museum to be managed collectively by all the communities in the Unión. The Canadian Fund for Ecuadorian Development (FECD) provided more than $200,000 to fund the project, over $100,000 of which was earmarked for the ceramics plant. The project began in earnest in 1997.

The ceramics plant was designed with the idea of the complementarity of craft production and environmental sustainability. Sinchi Sacha views economic development as a necessary reality for indigenous communities in the Amazon, but it also feels that development does not need to come at the expense of environmental sustainability. Its projects attempt to forge linkages between indigenous communities and the market that are based in the valorization of local artistic production, viewing artistic practices to be at the core of indigenous cultural identity. As Jesús González says:

> The base of understanding for the Amazon is in its art. If a community . . . does not have a structured artisan tradition, the process of (cultural) decay is greatly accelerated. Therefore, we have viewed craft (*artesanía*) as the base of our participation. Art and craft. (personal communication 1998)

According to González, cultural vibrancy is related to the health of local artistic traditions. Therefore, Sinchi Sacha's projects typically involve the introduction or recuperation of local art forms, transforming them for market production.

Sinchi Sacha argues that local motivations for engaging in artistic craft production are limited by the lack of market outlets. The NGO suggests that the basis for artistic preservation is not cultural, in and of itself, but rather economic, and that if local crafts do not have a viable market local peoples will dedicate themselves to other activities. In its proposal for funding for their project "Huyacamayo Urcu I," of which the ceramics plant was one component, the need for market articulation was defended in the following way:

> Artistic activity alone does not represent a great incentive, neither economic nor cultural, because of the lack of access to markets and the excessive exploitation suffered at the hands of intermediaries. (Sinchi Sacha 1996, 54)

Therefore, Sinchi Sacha set out to implement the ceramics plant in Santa Rita hoping to find market outlets for pottery produced at the plant through the growing Amazonian tourism industry.

Santa Rita and the Ceramics Project

The community of Santa Rita is organized around a large grass-and-dirt square. About forty-five houses, an elementary school, and a partially completed basketball court are clustered around the perimeter. To the right of the town square is a dirt path wide enough and occasionally dry enough for a 4 x 4 truck to pass. This path runs along a small, fast-moving river, the Chicama. Two hundred meters along the path and across the river is the ceramics plant. Situated atop a clearing, the plant consists of six thatched-roofed cabins, each with a unique function. A wooden bridge crosses the river, and a sign carved in wood identifies the cluster of cabins as *Rupaj*, which means "hot" or "burned" in Quichua.

A footpath leads to the first cabin, an oval structure equipped with tables and shelves. This structure is utilized by the women ceramists for making hand-thrown pots. During my ten-month stay in Santa Rita there were seven women who dedicated themselves full-time to working at the plant. They spent the majority of their time in this room. Walking through, one enters a circular structure with a thatched roof and cement floor, but no walls. This shelter contains the majority of the machinery for the plant, featuring a hydroelectric turbine that (although never fully functioning) was intended to power pottery wheels, as well as to provide electricity for the entire plant. There are six pottery wheels, a drum for mixing raw clay with sand and water (also powered by the turbine), and the turbine itself. Behind this structure sits a third cabin, oval in shape, which was to serve as a meeting place, an instructional facility, and a small library. This building was almost never used, a library was not constructed and the educational functions of the plant were never realized.

Behind these initial three buildings is a shelter containing the kilns, the bathrooms, and another shelter for preparing clay. The shelter with the kilns was designed to contain three kilns, two large ones, and a smaller one; but by early 1999, only a one large kiln and one smaller kiln were installed. Both kilns are fired using gas canisters, commonly used as cooking gas in Ecuador, which could be bought for about eight dollars a canister in 1998. The bathrooms were also never installed, and some of the toilets and sinks arrived broken.

In its proposal for funding, Sinchi Sacha argued that a ceramics project would be the perfect fit for the communities of the Huacamayos, because it would help to invigorate a disappearing ceramics tradition and tap into a growing tourism industry in the Amazon. Sinchi Sacha planned to market ceramics in several ways. First, it would help organize trips for foreign tourists to the Amazon. The Huacamayos region, being located in the westernmost edge of the forest, provides relatively quick, easy, and inexpensive access to the Amazon, and Sinchi Sacha hoped this would lead to an influx of tourists to this region rather than to the more expensive tourist destinations deeper in the forest. The three components of the Unión Huacamayos sustainable development proposal were combined to be complementary, so that tourists could stay in the tourist cabañas in one community, visit the ethnographic museum where they could purchase ceramics and other local crafts in the gift shop, and also visit the ceramics plant in Santa Rita.

Another strategy for marketing the plant was to advertise it as a locale to come and learn traditional ceramic techniques from indigenous women. In this sense, the plant was designed to not only be a workshop, but also a school where one could come and learn to make pots. Sinchi Sacha also planned to sell ceramics produced in Santa Rita at a handicraft shop it operates in the heart of the tourist district in the old section of Quito, and to market the ceramics internationally.

The project's focus on local cultural practice was seen as key to its success. Local support for and involvement in development projects has been shown to be much greater when the project seeks to strengthen existing local cultural practices rather than trying to introduce new ones (Kleymeyer 1992; Healy 1992). Production of "traditional" crafts for the market can help to strengthen social traditions, stem out-migration of young men looking for work, and reinforce the household unit as the basis of production (Nash 1993).

In Santa Rita, as in other communities of Napo province, ceramic production had long since ceased and was almost forgotten. Yet ceramics have a long history in the Amazon and remain a vibrant craft among some

Amazonian groups, such as Quichua communities in Pastaza province located just to the south of Napo. Members of Pastaza communities, commonly referred to as Canelos Quichua (as opposed to the Quijos Quichua of Napo province), have a highly refined ceramic tradition, in which women produce ornate, delicate hand-thrown pots, with thin rims and elaborate geometric designs drawn in red, brown, black, and white. Women make the pottery within their homes, and much of the pottery produced is destined for domestic consumption.

Sinchi Sacha refers to the ceramic tradition in Pastaza as both motivation and justification for their project, as it provides evidence that ceramics remain an important cultural attribute of many Quichua communities. According to Norman and Dorthea Whitten, who have done extensive research and writing on the Canelos ceramic tradition, there are important connections between ceramic styles and cosmological belief systems and shamanic practices, which highlights the important place of pottery in Canelos cultural practices (Whitten and Whitten 1987, 1993). Not only have some Canelos Quichua successfully marketed their wares to tourists, but ceramic production also serves as an important locus of cultural continuity for them (Whitten and Whitten 1993).

Nevertheless, while ceramic production thrives in Pastaza, there is no such tradition still in practice among the Quijos Quichua of Napo province. During their earliest trip to Pastaza and Napo, in 1968, Whitten and Whitten note the lack of a ceramic tradition in Napo:

> Traveling north, we crossed the Napo River (into Napo Province) on a small ferry, drove on to Tena and Archidona. . . . Throughout this area we asked about *mucahuas* (bowls for serving chicha[2]) and *tinajas* (large jars for storing chicha), and we received the same response, "No, we don't have them." (Whitten and Whitten, 1985, 4)

In fact, in Santa Rita the women were learning ceramic production anew. Only the oldest women in the community could remember their mothers making pottery in their homes for domestic use.

For several reasons, Sinchi Sacha viewed this as an advantage. First, ceramic production is a cultural activity with a long history, and while it has been out of practice for at least forty years in Santa Rita and the neighboring region, the eldest do have memories of these practices. At the same time, this tradition risks extinction, as no one currently makes pottery. Finally, since the ceramics tradition is not vibrant in Napo, Sinchi Sacha felt it was able to alter both the methods of production and the styles produced, tailoring them to large-scale production for tourist consumption. Therefore, instead of hand-coiled pottery, they trained the women in wheel-thrown pottery, which greatly expedites production.

Sinchi Sacha also trained women in the production of coffee and tea cups, bowls, plates, shot glasses, and later even ashtrays, rather than in forms, such as serving bowls for chicha, chicha storage containers, or funeral urns, which are more typically produced in Pastaza and are found in the archaeological record in Napo. Sinchi Sacha argued that these wheel-thrown products were more durable than the thin-rimmed hand-coiled ceramics, and the styles were more suitable for Western consumers, who could find uses for coffee mugs much more readily than large chicha storage containers. With wheel-thrown pottery production, Sinchi Sacha estimated in its proposal to the CFED, ceramists in Santa Rita could produce between 1,300 and 2,000 pieces per month.

Sinchi Sacha transformed ceramics production from being primarily domestic, as among the Pastaza Quichua, to being centralized and highly mechanized in Santa Rita. As Jesús González explained:

> Where we [Sinchi Sacha] are working, the people are beginning to make ceramics anew. I believe that much of the ceramics plant, as you have seen, is using high technology, high temperature kilns so that this ceramic practice can recreate itself in modern society. . . . If you can't sell it, it is going to end. Sadly, that's the way it is. If the artistic practice doesn't have a market outlet, the work stays in museums only, and nothing more. Therefore, we have attempted to forge a relationship between the cultural practice, ceramics, and its ties to the market. (personal communication 1998)

Significantly, and in contrast to what is primarily observed in Pastaza province, ceramic production in Santa Rita is removed from its domestic context and is situated within the ceramics plant. This provides centralized access to high technology, including hydraulic-powered wheels and gas-fired kilns. Sinchi Sacha argues, however, that a balance can be struck between technological introductions and traditional practices, which will allow for the effective sale of ceramics in the market. Arturo Crespo, the first ceramist contracted by Sinchi Sacha to help install the plant and train the women of Santa Rita to work at it describes it thus:

> One establishes a dignified relation between the market, Western technology and traditional practices in order to provide for necessities and basic services, establishing small-scale community and familial economies. (Sinchi Sacha 1997, n.p.)

The utilization of technology for the recuperation of traditional practices is not, according to Sinchi Sacha, necessarily contradictory, because of the need to "modernize" these practices to make them suitable for the realities of the market economy and the tourist trade.

Ceramics, Gender, and Development

Due to the potential fundamental role that gender serves for inheritance of tradition, the women ceramicists are the transmitters of the principal documents of cultural identity.

—*Arturo Crespo, pottery instructor for Sinchi Sacha*

While the ceramics plant was built for the community of Santa Rita, women were the sole ceramists at the plant. Initially twenty-four women came to the training workshops at the plant, but the men were not invited to participate. Sinchi Sacha made a calculated decision to work only with the women of the community for several reasons. First, Sinchi Sacha was pursuing an agenda compatible with some GAD advocates, in which they hoped to improve the social standing of the women in the community by providing them with income and a degree of independence from their spouses. Second, ceramic production in the Amazon had historically been a female activity and one in which men were forbidden to participate. Finally, Sinchi Sacha argued that providing women with income would bring a greater benefit to their families and the community as a whole, as women would dedicate earned-income to improving the condition of their families.

Sinchi Sacha's ceramics project in Santa Rita is partly a product of the different paradigms relating to women's roles in development. Sinchi Sacha wanted women to be producers of the ceramics and the income earners at the plant. Sinchi Sacha also wanted to promote Quichua cultural survival through reintroducing traditional artistic practices to women, whom they saw as the carriers of culture. Rebeca Santos, president of Sinchi Sacha, suggested that Napo Quichua women's predominantly domestic role makes them critical agents of cultural maintenance and transmission:

The woman reproduces the culture and reproduces life. Not only because she gives birth, but also because she worries much about nutrition. Therefore, from the outside, it seems that there is a patriarchal vision, and included is the horrible saying "the man of the house." But in reality it is the mother of the children that really raises the children, worries about education, clothing. (personal communication 1998)

Sinchi Sacha also has the goal of promoting more equitable relations between the sexes in indigenous communities. Rebeca Santos views relations between the sexes to be very poor in Santa Rita and in Napo Quichua communities generally, with domestic violence and mistreatment of women occurring at alarming rates. She says, "Each time I speak with peasants or indigenous people, without exception, the men beat the women, they yell at them, they treat them poorly, they don't respect them, they abuse them. Including sexually, they abuse them. This is an illness of Ecuador, almost comparable to hunger" (personal communication 1998). Arguing from a GAD perspective, Santos suggested that increasing women's access to earned income could improve their status in society, and thereby possibly lead to better treatment. The successful elaboration and sale of pottery, Santos felt, had the potential to spark a transformation in gender roles, as women would gain more economic power and external validation of their work through the sale of their pottery.

The gender component of the ceramics plant in Santa Rita has as one very important element the almost complete exclusion of men from the project. The design of the project targets women, and women only, as the beneficiaries, with the assumption being that the family as a whole will benefit. While the project was ultimately forced to include men, the original plan was to utilize male labor only for the construction of the ceramics plant. In Rebeca Santos's words:

> Originally, I only wanted to work with women. In reality, I resented the men so much that it seemed that they did not deserve . . . not even help, because it seemed to me that they were people who did not respect their women. And if they have such a bad attitude . . . (personal communication 1998)

Sinchi Sacha justified their exclusion of men from the project by suggesting that potting was a strictly female activity in Quichua culture:

> The ceramics in Amazonian Ecuador always have been in the hands of women. Therefore, in all of the Quichua communities—and I believe also in the Shuar ones—they have an internal law among themselves that the men should not touch the clay. This is a feminine labor, it is one that females perform. And they have the idea that if the men touch the clay from childhood, it effeminates them. (Rebeca Santos, personal communication 1998)

There was also an economic and social motivation to include only women in the ceramics project. As Rebeca Santos suggests, providing women with avenues for generating income has the capacity to improve their social status within the family and community, and the condition of the family as a whole:

> There have been many studies done where one sees that if you pay a salary to a man and to a woman, only half or less of the salary paid to a man is used for the family. And 120% of the money paid to the woman is used [for the family]. Because all of her money plus her work goes to the family. Therefore, in this difficult situation, we have prioritised working with women, because we feel it is going to help to better the quality of life of the family. (personal communication 1998)

Santos argued that as the women learned the potting trade, and as their earning power increased, the entire family would benefit as a result. This strategy ultimately backfired, as the project introduced new sources of conflict between women and men in Santa Rita, as well as between Santa Rita and Sinchi Sacha.

Empowering or Endangering Women?

> I have come to recognize that we have worsened the condition of women [in the community]. What we have achieved is an increase in violence towards the women. This has been extremely sad, because it can't be that such a great effort to give something progressive to the women of the community has resulted in worsening conditions. In the house they beat them [the women] to death for nothing. Worse than before. The project has provoked a terrible violence against them. . . .

> —*Rebeca Santos, president of Sinchi Sacha*

In August of 1998, following a community celebration, the female director of the ceramics plant, Nancy Grefa (appointed by Sinchi Sacha), was brutally beaten by her husband. He accused her of having an affair with another man while working at the ceramics plant, while also withholding the money she earned at the plant from him. As director of the plant, Nancy Grefa worked long hours. The design of the ceramics plant obliged her to work outside of the home. She would typically arrive at the plant by 7:00 or 7:30 A.M. and work there until three or four in the afternoon. This led to rumors about her and the other women ceramists, as both men and women suggested that it was inappropriate for women to work outside the home unaccompanied by their husbands. Envy and jealousy grew, as some community members spread rumors that some of the ceramists were engaging in extramarital affairs while not under the supervision of their husbands.

For almost four weeks, as Nancy Grefa recovered, the women completely abandoned the ceramics plant. They feared similar consequences. They talked about how the men in the community were spreading rumors about them because of their work at the plant, and they questioned whether they would continue working there. The number of women working at the plant had already dwindled from twenty-four original participants to seven during the first months of operation, and now even more were considering leaving.

Playing off development theory dating back to the early 1970s, Sinchi Sacha argued that integrating gender into development projects was necessary if the project was to be effective. Yet, Sinchi Sacha poorly understood gender relations in Santa Rita, and as a result introduced new sources of conflict between men and women in the community. Since working in the ceramics plant compelled women to work outside their homes, it went contrary to commonly held beliefs about appropriate gendered activities, and ultimately undermined Sinchi Sacha's attempts to improve the social and economic condition of the women in the community. The taboo against women working outside of the domestic context strongly deterred some from involving themselves in the project, leading to a low rate of participation, which hampered the project's potential for success. Many women left because they felt it to be an inappropriate atmosphere for women to work.

Others left because the ceramics plant added an unwanted burden to their workloads. For the women who continued working there, this became another source of tension between them and their husbands, as many traditionally female tasks were left unattended while women worked full time at the plant. Quichua women are typically responsible for the cooking and the childcare, and they do a substantial amount of the gardening as well. Much of this work was going unfinished while the women worked at the plant, and they were concerned. As Nancy Grefa explains:

> We have to leave our children in the house with nothing, no food. And since we don't have anything in the house, sometimes we'll go in the afternoons [after working during the day at the ceramics plant] to the finca to plant and harvest a little food. Sometimes we'll have nothing. (personal communication 1998)

This is one common result of development projects targeting women, as the gendered division of labor often discourages men from helping their wives to absorb the increase in labor demands placed upon them (Braidotti et al. 1994). Men became frustrated with their wives when household tasks were left unfinished, food was not prepared, and children were left unattended. This also served to discourage many women from working at the plant, as their domestic chores and agricultural activities limited their ability to spend large amounts of time working there. In fact, other than Nancy Grefa who, as president of the women's organization in Santa Rita, felt a strong responsibility to work there, and her sister, who continued to work there out of solidarity with Nancy, the only other workers were three young, single women and two elderly women (one of whom was Nancy's mother) whose domestic burdens were much lighter.

Entrenching Poverty and Market Dependence

In August of 1998, after women had been training at the ceramics plant almost one year, the seven principal ceramists in Santa Rita proudly set up a thatched-roof stand at a small cultural fair being held in the city of Archidona, five kilometers from Santa Rita. This was the first time the women had ventured from their community in hopes of selling their product, and they meticulously organized and reorganized the bowls, cups, and plates on the display table. The pots were roughly made, some hand-coiled and some wheel-thrown, but possessed a kind of elegance in their asymmetry. Made from a brown clay, many of their inner faces were glazed blue and white. The women had drawn petroglyph symbols, copied from the numerous boulders found in the region, into the pieces.

Three young women, students in my English class, asked me to help them write a sign that read *Ceramics from the Community of Santa Rita*, which they hung behind tables holding about forty pots. This was an exciting moment for the women ceramists, who had dedicated countless hours during the previous eighteen months to learning the ceramic trade. Now, they were prepared to turn their hard work into profit through the sale of their product. The cultural fair marked the unofficial inauguration of ceramics production in Santa Rita, as the women were making the shift from training to production for sale.

The excitement of the cultural fair quickly turned to disappointment. The women sold only two pieces during the week-long fair, both to me on the morning of the first day. They earned approximately two dollars from their sales, a disappointing result. The fair was located alongside and behind Archidona's municipal building, and had less than ten stalls altogether. Its disadvantageous location coupled with its small size and lack of flair meant that it did not generate much attention. During the week, some local townspeople would lazily stroll past the stands, but there was little interest in buying, and the women from Santa Rita made little effort to sell to them. This was only the latest in a series of economic disappointments and community problems directly or indirectly related to the construction and operation of the ceramics plant in their community.

The ceramics plant was not generating profit for the women working there. The lack of profits exacerbated conflicts between women and men in the community, as well as between people with family members working at the plant and those without. It led to accusations of women withholding money from their spouses and from the community as a whole. From the beginning of production in late 1997 to the end of my fieldwork season in early 1999, the women estimated they had made the equivalent of fifty dollars each over the entire eighteen-month period. Husbands and other community members, who saw the women working long hours daily in the plant, assumed that the plant was producing substantial profit, and therefore accused the women of keeping the money for themselves. If the plant was not profitable, they argued, why would the women spend so much time there?

At Santa Rita's Community Assembly in December of 1998, Nancy Grefa spent over two hours justifying the financial situation of the ceramics plant to the rest of the community. She detailed all earnings and all expenditures, attempting to illustrate why the ceramics plant only had approximately twenty-five dollars in savings, because of lack of sales. Community members accused Grefa and the other women working at the plant of withholding money from their husbands and the community as a whole. After the assembly, Nancy spoke with me about the difficulties of managing the money for the ceramics plant:

> Rebeca Santos gave me 500,000 sucres once [approximately $63] for transportation and to buy gas for the kilns. I spent the 500,000 sucres on gas and transportation, but some people in the community say that I took the money for myself.

In an attempt to settle the concerns of community members, the assembly decided to designate a man to serve as treasurer of the ceramics plant, possibly because it was assumed a man would manage money better than the women—thereby sabotaging Sinchi Sacha's initial commitment to empower women.

The failure of the plant to produce profit illustrates the dangers of haphazardly forging market ties with populations that have only tenuous market relations. The ceramics project employed a neoclassical development approach; it attempted to transform women's labor, which had historically been strictly domestic in nature, for market production and consumption. Sinchi Sacha was not cautious or critical of the market; on the contrary, the incorporation of indigenous peoples into the marketplace through the production and sale of "folkloric crafts" was viewed as the best way to preserve indigenous cultures. As Jesús González says, "if you can't sell it, it is going to cease to exist." Yet the case of the ceramics plant in Santa Rita is illustrative of those situations where crafts do not find a significant market. While the aim of this project and many like it was to aid in the alleviation of poverty in the community, it is apparent that it has done little to achieve that goal.

The case of Santa Rita's ceramics plant raises important concerns about the impacts of failed development projects on recipient communities. For NGOs sponsoring projects, the impact that project failure has on the NGO itself is limited and frequently mediated through an analysis of the extraneous circumstances that led the project to failure. For example, NGOs and other development organizations frequently place the blame on shortcomings of the local environment rather than inadequacies within the project design or implementation (Fisher 1997).[3] Furthermore, NGOs and other development organizations have a large degree of authority to assess their own project's performance, which often leads to creative myth making (Reyna 1997). The cultural coordinator for Sinchi Sacha suggested to me one afternoon in their Quito offices that the ceramics project was likely to fail. He was less downhearted, however, about what the ultimate outcome of the plant would mean. He said that even if the ceramics plant failed, the project had made a positive impact. According to him, Santa Rita will always have the ceramics plant to be proud of, which community members built with their own hands.

Yet for the community members, who invested their time and labor in the project, the stakes were much higher. Villagers in Santa Rita invested a tremendous amount of time, energy, and personal resources in the construction of the ceramics plant. The women who work there have done so at the expense of caring for their children, their gardens, and their households. The time invested at the ceramics plant, therefore, has been at the expense of activities that are central to maintaining their household economies. Since the ceramics plant required a huge investment of time with little or no economic return, the families active in the plant were becoming poorer. As Nancy Grefa explains:

> Before I started working at the ceramics plant, we didn't need to buy anything from the town. We had everything we needed on the finca. We even had chickens and a pond for tilapia. But since I've been working at the plant, we haven't been able to keep the finca producing, and we now have to buy food from town.

One impact of the ceramics project, then, has been to forge closer linkages between the women working at the ceramic plant and the market. For some, this has come at the expense of agricultural subsistence activities. The women at the ceramics plant are not only producing for the market, but they have also been forced into greater market consumption. Moreover, the ceramics plant has been less-than-profitable, and the "dignified relationship" that Sinchi Sacha hoped to foster between community members and the market has not materialized.

Efforts to market the ceramics to foreign tourists or to sell the products in Quito or internationally were ineffective. Jesús González had promised Santa Rita that the plant would be profitable, and that there was a large tourist base from which to draw for sales. Early on, Sinchi Sacha would occasionally organize small groups of tourists to take a day trip to Santa Rita. Most of the pottery that the community sold was on these trips. Yet, community members were not trained to accommodate or entertain tourists, and the tourists usually appeared with no prior warning from Sinchi Sacha, leaving Santa Rita unprepared for their visit. On at least one occasion, the women had no pottery ready to sell on the day of a visit.

Furthermore, outside of the occasionally planned trip by Sinchi Sacha, the community did not have the resources or know-how to attract tourists on their own. The community also lacked the means and training to market their product themselves, so they relied fully on Sinchi Sacha to generate a demand for the ceramics. As a result, Santa Rita's dependence on Sinchi Sacha was complete. Over time it became apparent that a significant market for the ceramics did not exist, and that one would not soon emerge.

One day, Nancy Grefa and I sat in one of the thatched-roofed cabins looking over a table of recently fired pots. As we were going through them, I asked her to point out some of the ones that she made and explain what they meant to her. She picked one up and began talking about the pot, its historical importance, and what it meant to her and the community now:

> We used this pot to eat and to put . . . well, really it was only mostly used to eat. These are the kinds of pots our grandmothers used to make. Our ancestors and our grandmothers used to make them like this—even larger. Before, our grandmothers used to draw petroglyphs on these pots. The ancestors used to know how to draw figures that represented people, so that the shamans could send the tourists. Therefore, we also make these drawings on our pots, so that the tourists are called to us and visit us. They [the drawings] have the spirit power of the rock. . . . So this petroglyph symbol is because [the tourists] aren't listening. So it will send the tourists. Because sometimes they don't come to visit. So this petroglyph calls them from wherever they may be walking and uses the power of the spirit to bring them here to the community. That's what this petroglyph means.

NGOs, Culturally Appropriate Development, and
Poverty Alleviation

The example of the ceramics plant in Santa Rita raises important issues related to culturally appropriate sustainable development projects. Domestic NGOs have often been praised for their presumed social closeness to the communities in which they work (Fisher 1997). Yet, many of these NGOs come from a middle-class, urban background, and vary substantially in their degree of contact with, and understanding of, rural communities.

Sinchi Sacha's staff are all urban intellectuals, who, while possessing impressive scholarly knowledge of Amazonian Ecuador, lack sustained interaction with the communities where they work. They typically travel to Napo province for a few days each month, but their presence is intermittent at best. A more constant presence on their part might have led to a deeper understanding of gender relations in Santa Rita, for example, thereby circumventing sources of potential conflict. As it happened, Sinchi Sacha's best intentions for the ceramics plant and the community of Santa Rita were undermined by its superficial comprehension of local gendered relations of production, and of the cultural history of ceramics production in the region. The project also suffered from the NGO's lack of ability to transfer key project components (particularly marketing) into local hands.

NGOs working for poverty alleviation frequently propose greater market articulation as an important component of their projects. Projects such as the ceramics plant in Santa Rita are designed with the premise that greater access to capital will improve the economic situation of impoverished groups. These definitions of poverty, however, are rooted in modernist, developmentalist notions of capital accumulation. They often devalue subsistence activities that, while not market oriented, have proven very effective in sustaining community well-being. The presumed strength of projects like the ceramics plant which promote "culturally appropriate" development is that they should aid in the achievement of more equitable relationships between local peoples and the market. This, however, has not necessarily been the case. Producing traditional crafts alone does not forge advantageous relationships with the market.

Forging advantageous relationships with the market requires an intimate understanding of market forces, so that local peoples can locate potential markets, promote their goods, and sell them to generate profit. The cases of the Otavalan and Zapotec weavers illustrate that producing beautiful crafts is not enough. In both of these cases, local peoples had developed a detailed understanding of their markets, and were able to control all phases of the textile economy, from production, to marketing, to sale (Colloredo-

Mansfeld 1999; Stephen 1993). In Santa Rita, however, this was not the case. The women at the ceramics plant were being trained in the production of pottery alone, while they remained fully dependent on Sinchi Sacha to organize the sale of their product. This made it unlikely that Santa Rita would be able to independently market their ceramics, and made it less likely still that the plant would ever generate favorable profits for the ceramists and their community.

6

Women, Microenterprise Development, and Poverty in Bolivia

Ana Mayta

ACRE—*Acción Creadora*, or Creative Action—is a Bolivian NGO that works in four outlying neighborhoods of the city of El Alto, three neighborhoods in the city of La Paz, and two rural communities in the Bolivian altiplano.

The four El Alto neighborhoods where ACRE works are receiving points for immigrants from different rural communities. They border one another: Villa La Merced with 578 inhabitants, Porvenir (meaning "the future") with a population of 498, Bolivar Municipal with 670, and Villazón with 450. These are all recently settled areas and still lack basic services such as sewage and electricity. Residents are mainly small-scale merchants and artisans, of Aymara ethnic background.

The three La Paz neighborhoods where ACRE works are also receiving points for immigrants, but these are primarily people who have already been living for several years in urban areas. The neighborhood of Pantisirka has a population of 670, San Luis has 580, and Alto Ciudadela has 460. Residents are mainly small-scale merchants and artisans, of Aymara, Quechua, and Guaraní ethnic backgrounds.

The two rural communities where ACRE works are Achica Abajo, located at Viacha in Ingavi province, and Achacachi in Omasuyos province. Achica Abajo has 798 inhabitants, and is located 38 kilometers to the west of the city of La Paz, near the small town of Viacha. The climate there is cold, with an average temperature of 8 degrees centigrade. Achica Abajo's population is of Aymara background, and the main economic activity is herding, including cattle, sheep, and camelids. Residents of Achica Abajo also grow crops for their own consumption, primarily quinoa and potatoes. Their market center is the city of La Paz, and they also buy and sell in local weekly markets or *ferias* in and around Viacha.

Achacachi is located farther afield, nearly a hundred kilometers west of the city of La Paz. The town of Achacachi has a population of 5,400 and the entire municipal area has a total population of over 60,000 people.[1] The population of Achacachi is of Aymara origin, known for maintaining their ancestral forms of social organization (in many cases now converted into *sindicatos agrarios* or agricultural syndicates), and for their warrior tradition. Achacachi is a farming town, producing potatoes, broad beans, and the typical Andean tubers *oca* and *papalisa*. Herding of cattle, sheep, and llamas is also an important economic activity in the area. Locals sell their products in the weekly ferias; Achacachi is a meeting point for farmers from different neighboring communities and buyers from the city of La Paz.

The NGO–Community Relationship

In each community, both rural and urban, ACRE began its work with a diagnostic. This diagnostic provided data about local economic activities, the number of inhabitants, and their priority needs. This process also gave us, the NGO's founders, the opportunity to get to know local people. After completing the diagnostic and observing the needs of women textile producers, we started with a project known as "Strengthening the Quality of Textile Production." The project's principal objective was to work with women who were producing handmade textiles, to improve the quality of their finished products. To this end, ACRE organized courses in improving hand-dying, using natural dyes, and preparing the raw material. We focused on improving wool treatment to obtain a higher quality finished product. ACRE also organized courses in business administration, where we provided the women with tools for good microenterprise management.

Nevertheless, this entire process turned out to be inadequate because key resources were still lacking. There was no capital for textile enterprises to purchase raw materials. Nor was there assistance in the area of marketing. Starting in 1998, however, ACRE identified an international NGO willing to seed-fund microenterprises for extremely poor families. This international NGO's funds are targeted toward people that have the motivation and initiative to start a microenterprise, but who lack capital and are not able to access loans.[2] Through this international NGO, ACRE was able to access financial resources for these businesses. At the same time, ACRE began to assist the women in the marketing of their products, by seeking out new markets, making contacts, and guaranteeing to the buyer that the merchandise would be delivered on time.

Table 6.1

Microenterprise Activities and Markets

Activity	Local market	External market
Producers of textiles (sweaters, shawls, scarves, caps, gloves, etc.)	La Paz (minimal sales)	United States Germany
Producers of hand-crafted wall ornaments	La Paz, Santa Cruz	United States
Producers of hand-embroidered table cloths	La Paz	
Producers of other clothing (parkas, jackets, etc.)	La Paz	
Small-scale merchants (neighborhood stores and sales posts selling a range of products)	La Paz	

Source: Compiled, by author, from ACRE women's groups.

By the year 2000, women artisans who received this sort of integrated support had managed to double their income, with the export of their products into international markets. At the time of the initial diagnostic, women textile producers were earning an average of US twenty dollars per month from the items they produced; by 2000, under the revamped Project to Strengthen Microenterprise Development they were earning use US forty dollars per month—still small, but a tangible improvement.

Currently, with the Project to Strengthen Microenterprise Development, ACRE works with groups of women who produce a range of different products, according to the skills and ability of each individual. These activities all fall in the broad area of "microenterprise" and are listed in Table 6.1. As can be seen in the table, women who produce alpaca wool textiles and wall ornaments sell very little in the local market, but their products are in demand in markets outside Bolivia. Yet these producers themselves cannot seek out these markets due to their low education levels, lack of information, and inability to communicate in the language of external buyers. ACRE therefore seeks out markets on behalf of these groups of women, makes contacts, guarantees delivery of orders to the client, guarantees payment to the producers, and guarantees the quality of the product to the buyer.

Based on our work in ACRE, we can state that the residents of the neighborhoods and communities where we work have understood the role that the NGO is playing there, and that the NGO has also learned about the culture and the customs of these communities. It is very important to know one another, in order to be able to understand one another and work together in a coordinated way to pursue a common objective. In this way, we can achieve satisfactory results both for the NGO and for the groups of women micro-entrepreneurs in the communities.

According to our experience, training, financial capital, and marketing are all fundamental for microenterprise development. Each factor complements the other, and none should be overlooked to achieve a favorable result. In addition, the initiative of the women microentrepreneurs themselves and their own desire to improve their situations are a key ingredients in the microenterprise development process. It is here, with the microentrepreneurs' own goals and initiative, that microenterprise development programs must start, if they are to be efficient and have a positive impact.

Local Perceptions of NGOs: Solutions in Their Hands

Generally, in Bolivia, in communities where NGOs are present, there is a wide variation in the perceptions of the different groups involved in the change process about the role played by NGOs. This depends upon the way in which NGOs enter and begin their work in a given community. Some NGOs are paternalistic and think they have the solution to reducing poverty in their hands, without taking local people into account. Some NGOs bring donations of food for families, thinking that in this way they are going to resolve the problem of poverty. The people become accustomed to receiving, and begin to perceive NGOs as organizations that bring gifts.

At the beginning, when ACRE arrived at one community to work with grassroots groups, it became a bit difficult to make the locals understand the reason for the NGO's presence in the community. The majority of the local population believed that an NGO has the obligation to give gifts, so they asked what we were going to give them, and what donations we were going to make. The community was accustomed to this kind of relationship with NGOs. Other NGOs had previously appeared in these communities bringing gifts of food or other products for immediate consumption, as their response to the extreme poverty of these people. This kind of paternalistic assistance did not have the desired effect, and their work made no impact. No change was achieved; everything continued as before, even after the NGOs had worked there for several years.

Analyzing the work of earlier NGOs, the population's opinion of them, and the results and impacts achieved, we can state that there needs to be a change both in the mentality of community groups and of the NGOs who wish to work with them. NGOs must cease to be paternalistic and not think that they hold solutions to poverty in their hands. They must allow the protagonists to participate in laying the groundwork for the process of change, according to their own necessities and requirements. Change must begin with the initiative of the protagonist herself. Any change that is planned must accord with her own requirements for her development and improved way of life. Change must not be imposed; it must be a voluntary choice made by local actors in the process.

Poverty: Symptoms and Causes

In the past decade, Bolivia has lived through enormous changes in its social, economic, and political spheres. Even so, in the world context Bolivia still projects the image of a poor and dependent country. It is a nation burdened by an external debt that hampers its capacity to carry out its various functions and to satisfy the subsistence needs of its population.

Bolivia is one of the poorest countries in Latin America. Economic indicators show slow growth in GDP, high informal sector growth, a large external debt, a low coefficient of savings and investment, decline in exports, and increasing deterioration of terms of trade. There is corruption, excessive bureaucracy, mistrust in the justice system, and a deficient transport infrastructure.

Social indicators also underline Bolivia's poverty. The country has one of the highest birth rates (average 4.2 children per family), infant mortality rates (67 per thousand), and death in childbirth rates (390 per hundred thousand) in Latin America. One in two rural women is illiterate. Of Bolivia's total of 2.4 million youth, more than a quarter (26 percent) do not have access to education. Notable are the country's low level of expenditures on education, the low life expectancy of the population (61.8 years in 1998), scarce human resources in the area of technology, high levels of unemployment and underemployment, and increasing levels of unskilled labor. In Bolivia, poverty places severe limitations on well-being and economic and social development, and it is compromising the country's social, economic, and political stability.

As a structural phenomenon, poverty apparently affects women and men equally; yet because of the nature of systemic relationships between women and men defined by gender, women suffer greater poverty than men— particularly in rural areas. One of the most complex variables in the analysis of the phenomenon of poverty is the way in which it relates to women, that is, the poverty resulting from asymmetries and gender differences that reproduce and accent a woman's situation. Among the factors that intensify the process of the "feminization of poverty" are inequality, marginalization, and social and political exclusion of women. It thus becomes necessary to identify and evaluate the variables that reproduce women's poverty, in order to be able to generate interventions that provide the most effective benefits to women.

We speak of a "situation of inequality" because it is evident that Bolivian women still find themselves in conditions of palpable disadvantage. Deficiencies in their educational levels are expressed in a lower school attendance rate for girls relative to boys, as well as higher rates of illiteracy (22 percent for women as opposed to 9 percent per men).[3] Women in rural areas have less opportunity to inherit land from their parents; sons obtain approximately 80 percent of parents' lands, according to indigenous customs in the communities where ACRE works. The 2000 Human Development Report cites GDP per capita for men in Bolivia to be nearly three times that of women.[4] We also speak of "social and political exclusion" because, although women in the communities where we work are present at monthly community meetings, we have observed that women seldom speak or participate in meetings, and their opinions do not appear to be considered when decisions are made. Only men's opinions are considered and taken into account.

Poverty is found in a world characterized by inequality and inequity, a world where some fully exercise their rights and liberties as citizens, while others do not have access to the fundamental liberties of action and decision. The structural character of poverty relates to the slow process of development and growth of the nation, which cannot be modified in the short term. Nevertheless, it is imperative that the government adopt policies and programs to fight poverty. Bolivia is still far from being able to guarantee a dignified standard of living for its population. The current population growth rate (2.11 percent annually) supposes an increase of 150,000 inhabitants per year, which will worsen the deterioration of living conditions—considering that, according to UN statistics, around 94 percent of the Bolivian population already lives at or below the threshold of poverty.

Different international summits have discussed the problem of poverty and approved recommendations and lines of action for poverty reduction. Countries, for their part, have committed themselves to formulating strategies, and identifying timelines and financial resources to overcome poverty, but still the population has not received any benefit. In Bolivia poverty worsens every day.

The NGO ACRE focuses its work in rural areas and in the urban periphery where many migrants from rural areas arrive. There is a strong incentive for families to emigrate from rural areas to the cities, because rural land has been divided into smaller and smaller parcels over time, and the production from these parcels is often not enough to supply families' subsistence. Thus, many families migrate from the countryside to the city to improve their situation, without realizing the educational and other requirements (e.g., possession of an identity card and/or birth certificate) that are necessary to find employment in the urban context.

Failing to find paid work, many families turn to traditional artisan activities as a way to earn a living. According to their own experience and knowledge passed down through their families, they may carry out activities such as hand-spinning, natural dying of wool, and weaving or knitting a variety of textiles from llama and alpaca wool; they may make wall ornaments, embroidered tablecloths, and embroidered pictures with local motifs, as well as belts, handbags, and sewn items such as jackets and parkas. These producers face a key difficulty, however, in that their products do not have the quality that clients demand. Also, producers, lacking knowledge of markets, often sell to unscrupulous intermediaries who buy merchandise at very low prices. Sometimes producers are able to recoup only their investment; other times they earn a bit for their labor. In the end, the situation of these migrants to the city has not improved over their previous conditions in the countryside. Their situation may have even worsened.

Education is a factor influencing poverty; currently the level of school attendance in these rural communities and peripheral neighborhoods is very low. When girls have the opportunity to study, most only attend through fifth grade; boys may attend middle school or even high school but seldom graduate. Those who do manage to complete high school do not have the opportunity to pursue a career through university study, which would help them to improve their situation. The family economy is one of subsistence and both parents and older children must work to help provide for the family. Another limitation to accessing university study is that the quality and level of education in rural high schools is low compared with urban high schools, placing rural students at a distinct disadvantage for university entrance.

The people of the rural altiplano and the peripheral neighborhoods of El Alto and La Paz are accustomed to arduous work; they are of *campesino*[5] background, used to working their land, building their own houses, and constructing their own roads. Campesinos work and produce all their lives, but have been left to their own devices by every government; no one has protected or educated campesinos as human beings. Ignorance brings poverty; campesinos work to escape poverty but do not have the necessary resources to achieve this; rather, they are faced with obstacles, such as illiteracy and lack of legal documents, which continue to place them in a situation of social and political exclusion.

Microenterprise and Poverty

Microenterprise development is one strategy to fight poverty. Eighty-eight percent of the Bolivian population is employed in the microenterprise sector, representing key actors in the nation's economic growth. This sector has the potential to create growth with equity. To achieve this, however, it is necessary to empower people and give them the conditions and opportunities to grow their businesses. For example, technical training for the workforce, including women, is important, because to increase a country's productivity it is necessary to develop its human capital. What is needed is a framework to develop microenterprises in a way that accommodates microenterprises' peculiar characteristics, rather than focusing the bulk of resources on large and medium enterprises.

ACRE's Project to Strengthen Microenterprise Development creates an accessible, viable alternative for families with few resources, particularly for women microentrepreneurs who produce textiles and other craft items. These women have the need and will to work and improve their livelihoods, but they do not have access to loans, markets, and other factors necessary for microenterprise development. Yet microenterprise development offers them the potential to increase their subsistence incomes and to give their children more access to resources such as education. ACRE also feels that the Project to Strengthen Microenterprise Development contributes to increasing women's self-esteem and their participation in communities.

The Project to Strengthen Microenterprise Development has three component programs:

1. *Technical training for production*, to improve the quality of finished products, so that these products will meet clients' requirements. This training intends to be effective and practical, geared toward the eventual independence of microenterprises—not "training for its own sake."
2. *Financial capital support*, oriented toward families with extremely limited financial resources that do not have access to loans, and who plan to begin a production or merchant activity.
3. *Marketing support*, intended to strengthen the sales capacity of groups of women artisans through:
   • seeking out markets,
   • making contact with buyers,
   • guaranteeing timely delivery of merchandise,
   • guaranteeing product quality,
   • guaranteeing payment to women producers,
   • market research into fashion and design preferences, and
   • assistance with merchandise export procedures.

The NGO ACRE acts as an intermediary between women artisans and the purchasers of their finished products. ACRE works to ensure the satisfaction of the client, so as to avoid the situation of distrust which often discourages buyers from working with groups of artisans. By providing the client with guaranteed quality and timeliness, ACRE enables these women to compete on more equal footing with the established enterprises generally favored by international buyers.

ACRE considers that microenterprise development for women must take as its starting point each person herself: her knowledge, needs, and priorities—as well as the culture and customs of the community. The NGO should contribute by giving community members the tools to identify their own priority needs, in order to improve their income and living conditions. ACRE encourages women to form groups based on their interests, such as credit, marketing, assessment, and training, for example. Our function is to support existing and new productive units so that they can improve their production and participate in the market competitively, on equal footing with other enterprises.

Socioeconomic Change: View from the NGO

ACRE believes that change happens first through a change of perspective of the women and of community members in general. A woman and her community must be conscious of the change process, as it relates to the needs and priorities both of individuals and of the community. Change must be gradual, that is, a gradual change of attitude of the population accompanied by worthwhile work that gives hope of a better future for their family and their community. This better future includes respect for their cultural identity, their right to make demands and exercise rights in public arenas, and to achieve spaces for political representation.

The social and economic axes—in terms of the right to access education, health, housing, basic services, recreation, and regular income; to possess assets and capital goods; to receive a fair wage; to live free of violence; and so forth—consolidate full citizenship. They presuppose a reduction in gender differences in regard to discrimination, inequality, and exclusion. This is a long process that takes as its starting point the needs of community members. Equity constitutes a decisive goal for the transformation of relationships that exclude people, into equality of opportunity for both women and men.

The foundation of such change is rooted in the construction of new relationships between women and men that are democratic, equitable, and founded upon solidarity, toward the goal of achieving sustainable development and improvement of the quality of life in Bolivia. We must stimulate the necessary conditions for the exercise of the rights and liberties of citizenship, emphasizing the proactive participation of women, without excluding men, but rather, seeking integration and compromise.

What about Impact?

ACRE considers that the Project to Strengthen Microenterprise Development has had the desired effect, citing the following project impacts:

- 188 women now have stable monthly incomes
- 188 women have, on average, doubled their monthly earnings from the sale of products
- women's self-esteem has increased (admittedly, a qualitative judgment on the part of the NGO)

The NGO has worked primarily with women textile producers, although we also have been able to work with other craft producers and a small number of service and merchant microenterprises. In the neighborhoods and communities where ACRE works, textile production and other artisan activities are the main activities for women. Therefore ACRE focuses on these activities, believing that as an NGO is more specialized it will work more effectively and have better results and impact.

During the preliminary diagnostics in the neighborhoods and communities where ACRE works, we made contact with members of the community and got to know them. We also introduced the NGO to them, outlined the work that we do, and explained our objective. At that time, the community members' attention was particularly called to the fact that we could assist them to market their products, once the quality was improved. So people were interested in the NGO, and our courses have enjoyed strong demand. For the relationship with local groups to function well, the important thing is to carry through on promises.

ACRE does not try to reach all families in the areas where it works; rather, people self-select into ACRE's programs based primarily on their desire to work in these activities (such as textile production) and to improve. We believe that we must start from people's desire to improve their circumstances and personal development. If we do not start from here, our work will be useless and our investment of time and money will not have the desired impact. Nothing that is forced upon people can turn out well.

The NGO's work is always carried out jointly; the microentrepreneur and the NGO identify a common objective and work together to achieve results for both parties: specifically, improved income that permits an improved lifestyle. To strengthen a microenterprise, the microentrepreneur must desire the growth of her business—that is key. Without this desire, the NGO can do nothing to assist.

External Influences

One important factor influencing microenterprise development is the market—the demand for the products that the women make. We consider this factor to be key because if there is no market, there is no microenterprise development.

To achieve our objectives and contribute to the development of women's microenterprises, ACRE depends on external factors such as the market. Alpaca textiles and other craft products are oriented toward an export market, and for this reason it is necessary to have access to information and market contacts abroad. We need to be aware of the demand for these products in the countries where we want to establish and maintain markets. ACRE works to develop these market contacts; however, it would be invaluable to receive support from an external organization that would supply information and establish market contacts for us. This would be a great help for these microenterprises, and for us, to achieve our objective more rapidly and effectively.

Another external factor that influences microenterprise development is access to credit. For people with low education levels, limited access to markets, low levels of technology, and low productivity, it is not easy to access a loan through traditional banking institutions. Microenterprises have access to microcredit, of course. Yet we see microcredit as a strategy for administering poverty, not reducing it. Microcredit in Bolivia is expensive, and, according to the Bolivian Viceministry of Microenterprise, 90 percent of people who take out such loans remain in a vicious circle of poverty. They subsist, they feed themselves, but they don't generate surplus, they pay their loans, and sometimes they must borrow from elsewhere to meet their obligations. In this way, they end up poorer than before they accessed microcredit.

Microcredit does not address the root of poverty, it merely alleviates some symptoms without strategizing deeper solutions. Yet if reasonably priced loans were accessible to everyone, with policies favoring the productive sector, most microenterprises could improve and become more competitive. Microenterprises need credit to improve their infrastructure and allow the revamping of production—but they do not need high-interest loans that leave microentrepreneurs poorer than before. Recent protesters and marchers in La Paz have requested that interest rates be lowered and that borrowers not end up paying more than 100 percent of the value of their capital in interest. These high interest rates have also provoked a high level of loan default.

Another important external factor affecting microenterprise development in Bolivia is the degree of openness of markets in other countries to Bolivian products, and the duties that must be paid on Bolivian products entering various countries. Bolivia's exports have declined considerably in recent years.

Trade restrictions are under the control of foreign governments, and these restrictions impact Bolivian microentrepreneurs' ability to access larger markets.

ACRE, as a local Bolivian NGO, can suggest that the Bolivian government work to open markets, with low or zero duty, in countries where there is demand for Bolivian products. We can suggest that the Bolivian government implement policies favoring the productive sector and microenterprise, to improve their competitiveness. For the most part, however, these kinds of external factors are outside the control of an NGO such as ACRE.

A given NGO cannot influence all the factors tht could contribute to poverty reduction. It cannot even control for all the factors that impact upon a single antipoverty strategy, such as microenterprise development. Yet NGOs can play an important role in mediating some of the external factors that face local communities. ACRE, for example, has mediated the relationship between women artisans and external markets. ACRE cannot change the nature of external markets, as it cannot change many of the structural factors aggravating poverty. But it can help local people overcome obstacles to accessing these external markets, and thus to harness resources that would have otherwise remained out of reach.

7

The Transformation Side of Microenterprise

The Case of the Opportunity International Program in Honduras

Makonen Getu

Opportunity International (OI) has been operating as a microfinance institution since 1971. This chapter is devoted to giving a brief introduction to the organization, looking at its history, vision and mission, organizational setup, and programs.

OI is a global network of Christian microfinance organizations based in both developed and developing countries. The network is composed of eight autonomous supporting partners and forty-two implementing partners. The implementing partners (IPs), based in twenty-four less developed countries, implement the lending operations. The supporting partners (SPs), based in seven countries of the North (the United States, Canada, United Kingdom, Australia, Germany, New Zealand, and France), raise funding and provide technical assistance to the programs in the South.

The network has been formed voluntarily on the basis of a covenant of membership signed by all member organizations, committing them to:

- uphold the purpose and statements of the Opportunity International network;
- promote excellence and provide mutual accountability;
- share in mutual opportunities for delivering services and managing the network;
- provide leadership in governance that establishes a common direction; and
- present consistent communications.

The covenant was developed following a two-year intensive research and dialogue process facilitated by the design council and drawn up by a commission consisting of elected representatives from SPs and IPs as well as independent consultants.

OI's mission is to provide opportunities for people in chronic poverty to improve their overall well-being. Its strategy is to create jobs, stimulate small businesses, and strengthen communities among the poor. Its method consists of working through indigenous partner organizations that provide small business loans and other financial services, training, and counsel.

OI's core values draw on Christian principles and consist of respect (valuing and affirming each client's dignity and uniqueness), commitment to the poor (allowing services to be determined by clients' business needs and expectations), stewardship (exercising thoughtful and cost-effective use of resources), and integrity (walking the talk). Although OI is a Christian organization and is motivated by Jesus Christ's call to serve the poor, its commitment, both in theory and practice, is to provide credit, training, and other financial services to people in poverty without regard to race, gender, or religious affiliation.

The OI network is governed by an international board consisting of twelve members coming from both SPs and IPs. The international directors are elected by national and regional boards and serve a term of three years. The board meets on a quarterly basis to review achievements, challenges, opportunities, make appropriate decisions, and give direction. Each SP and IP has its own national board with one or two seats for representatives of other partner organizations.

The operational and administrative coordination is provided by the OI network office that is run by the CEO, the COO, and three vice presidents supported by the international management group. At the field level, the operations in Africa, Asia, Eastern Europe, and Latin America are overseen by regional directors with minimal administrative costs, based in Kumasi, Ghana; Manila, Philippines; Sydney, Australia; Oxford, United Kingdom; and Bogota, Colombia.

The three overarching goals of the OI network relate to outreach, quality, and impact. OI plans to increase its outreach from 200,000 in the year 2000 to 700,000 in 2005 and 2 million in 2010 (OI 2000a). It also aims to reduce arrears rates on loans to an average of 2 percent and portfolio at risk to 10 percent by the year 2005. Regarding impact, OI strives to enable clients to become agents of change in their communities: to transform their lives and become agents of transformational development (OI 1998).

This brings us to the presentation and discussion of OI's model of transformational development (TD).

OI's Transformational Development Model

The Premise

OI's understanding of poverty is that it is human made and not a natural phenomenon. Human beings are not born poor but become poor as a result of economic, social, political, and belief systems that deprive some people of the opportunity to lead decent lives. OI believes that people are not poor because they lack ability or intelligence but because they lack opportunity.

Poverty manifests itself in the deprivation of external rights and opportunities by human-made production and distribution systems and structures that constrain other human beings from unleashing their internal potential to achieve meaningful goals for themselves and others in society. OI believes that lack of access to credit and financial services is one of the critical opportunities the poor are deprived of.

Poverty is a grim phenomenon with a crushing and crippling effect on its victims whom it subjects to marginalization, loss of confidence, self-hatred, and hopelessness. In the words of an OI client in Moldova, "Poverty is pain; it feels like a disease. It attacks a person not only materially but also morally. It eats away one's dignity and drives one into total despair."

OI started participating in the fight to alleviate poverty through the provision of credit and related financial training services to people who are poor. To date, OI has helped more than 1 million people to alleviate their poverty through the creation of employment and the generation of income. While recognizing that this is important and has to continue, OI argues that focusing on money generation is only one small part of finding the way out of poverty. The alleviation of poverty is not only about having but also about being and becoming. Life does not consist of possessions alone, and poverty is not only about lack or deprivation of material resources. It is also about powerlessness, gender inequality, corruption, dishonesty, greed, moral decay, fear, environmental degradation, and dependency.

Human beings are economic, social, political, spiritual, and emotional by nature. Economic intervention alone does not come anywhere near to addressing the complex issues people face in life. Helping people who are poor to get their daily bread is good, but what matters most is what happens to them as human beings. The alleviation of poverty requires, therefore, a whole-person development approach to tackle the issues of life holistically. This is OI's basic premise for developing and applying the model of transformational development, or TD, because the model does just that.

Definition of Transformational Development

OI began to deliberately embark on the path of promoting financial excellence and transformation simultaneously in 1996. A team was formed to conduct research in four countries in different regions and to come up with a definition and a set of indicators that would help the network to understand and measure transformation (Horn et al. 1997). The long process of dialogue and discussions has resulted in the following definition of what TD involves:

> A deeply rooted change in people's economic, social, political, spiritual and behavioral conditions resulting in their enjoyment of wholeness of life under God's ordinances. (Opportunity Center for Transformation Studies [OCTS] 2000)

The composite meaning of the above definition relates to a profound, holistic, and deep change in the economic, political, social, spiritual, and behavioral realms of human life. TD is about dying to the old and living to the new—becoming a new individual, family, community, and nation. It is about people with insufficient economic resources attaining higher levels of abundance, empowerment, freedom, and independence.

The Components of the Model

The TD model consists of four major components: (a) abundance, (b) empowerment, (c) character, and (d) service.

Abundance

The overwhelming majority of the world's poverty is a result of the socio-economic systems operating at both global and local levels. These systems leave many people exploited, landless, homeless, unemployed, illiterate, and penniless. The poor are tilling the land and manufacturing goods and services for incomes at or below subsistence level because they have to sell their products under unfavorable terms of trade. As a consequence, they are continuously submerged into a condition of misery and degradation while those who own the land, capital, technology, and know-how are able to generate a high level of wealth accompanied by a high standard of living. The economic system simultaneously produces poverty at one end and prosperity at the other. The poor are victims of economic injustice characterized by the unequal distribution of national resources.

The task of development is therefore to enable the poor to achieve relative abundance through economic transformation that generates increased wealth and a fair and effective distribution of resources and benefits. It is about freeing the poor from the cruel grip of poverty and exploitation. The core of economic transformation is the creation of relative material abundance. This does not mean that the poor become millionaires. It simply means that poor people begin to earn more surplus income and go beyond subsistence level; they do not lack anything to meet their material and social needs. It is about the ability of the poor to be self-sufficient.

Thus, the poor move from a condition of suffering from scarcity to enjoying abundance. The poor begin to consume, save, and invest more. Improvements in food, housing, health, education, and communication take place. Technology progresses, productivity increases, and business expands to produce more wealth. Unemployment declines and wealth begins to be distributed more fairly. Their standard of living and quality of life begin to improve. Poverty ceases to exercise its crippling power. The gap between the poor and the rich begins to decline.

The abundance component of TD gives information about the extent to which the poverty cycle entangling the poor has been broken and the quality of life has improved as a result of an economic intervention such as microfinance. It is about breaking the bondage of material poverty, and measures the level of material ease/economic freedom attained by the poor. This does not look only at the immediate multiplication of choices and opportunities but also at the long-term perspectives of sustainability. Abundance deals with both the quantity and quality of life and is a fundamental factor in poverty eradication at all times. It is about attaining both more wealth and a better standard of living.

In establishing to what extent a microfinance intervention has helped the poor to attain relative abundance, the model looks at the levels of individual, household, and business incomes. This includes the standard of living relating to improvements in housing, food, education, health, and communication as well as the level of investments, including personal savings, technology, and innovation.

Empowerment

OI recognizes that in less-developed countries the poor are often subjected to despicable political injustice and atrocities. They are often marginalized and ignored, and hold a peripheral place in the policy- and decision-making systems and structures of their respective countries. In most cases they are restrained from exercising their basic democratic and human rights in meaningful ways. The poor do not often express their political and other views, and when they do, they often are not heard. Their sociopolitical participation is heavily constrained. Women in particular are among the most oppressed and subjugated social groups of any given developing society. Political oppression hinders the poor from fully unleashing their creativity. It has a stifling and impoverishing effect on human and social development. The poor are compelled to lead a life that draws not on power but powerlessness.

The empowerment component of the TD model is about enabling the poor to be in charge of their own destiny through active engagement in current sociopolitical affairs. This in turn requires a political transformation that addresses injustice and inequality issues and creates a favorable and nonthreatening environment for all citizens. It is about freeing and enabling the poor, especially women, to influence the political affairs that affect their destiny. This relates to the recognition and respect of their freedom to form or join political parties and or groups (associations, trade unions, etc.), elect and be elected to local and national political positions, express views and opinions, own and inherit property, and move and work without any restrictions. Empowerment is about creating a system that offers justice, equality, security, and stability for the poor, men and women alike, to fully participate in policy- and decision-making processes at all levels.

In other words, empowerment is about gaining political freedom and breaking loose from the trap of powerlessness, deprivation, and despair. This means that the poor are enabled to express their rights and carry out their responsibilities, exert effective pressure on local and national authorities, have self-worth, take initiatives and risks, and participate more actively in the affairs of their communities.

The TD model holds that on its own, the relative abundance achieved by the poor takes them nowhere in their holistic development in the absence of democratic rights, gender equity, and justice. Genuine TD requires that the bonds of material poverty and powerlessness are simultaneously broken. To indicate whether and to what extent the clients have been empowered, the model considers areas such as the level of selfconfidence, political participation, influence, and gender equity experienced by participating clients.

Character

The poor do not only suffer from material shortage and powerlessness. They also suffer from internal and external inadequacies related to their habits, values, traditional practices, belief systems, and ways of thinking. Relative abundance and empowerment will achieve little if no change is made in terms of their character. The term character as applied here does not imply that poor people have "poor character." It refers, rather, to positive changes in their values, attitudes, belief systems, and practices. For TD to happen, the model requires that the poor must experience positive character change alongside relative abundance and empowerment.

Relative abundance and empowerment are mainly about having. Character on the other hand is about being. As a Christian NGO, OI believes that the poor experience newness of life in their being when they experience religious conversion and live accordingly. When the poor know God's laws and standards of life and practice them in their own lives, new values and habits take shape and old ones give way. Mutual trust, mutual care, mutual respect, honesty, peace, reconciliation, and unity among the poor are enhanced. The poor value themselves and others and view their traditions, belief systems, and environment in new and more positive ways.

The character component of the TD model is about breaking free from the bondage of bad, old habits, and provides information about the nature of the new values, attitudes, and practices clients are experiencing and developing as a result of OI's microfinance intervention. These are manifested by their relationships with God, one another, themselves, and their environment. The component answers the central question of whether the clients are enabled to become better people in regard to their values and practices.

The basic thrust of this component is that the issue of relationship holds a pivotal place in life. Relationships are influenced by what goes on inside individual human beings in the relationship equation. The internal and external factors in the lives of human beings are dialectically interrelated, reinforcing or counteracting each other. When clients internalize good external values and practices, good beings are enhanced, which in turn produces good externals (fruits) leading to better human families, communities, and nations. Character and relationship go hand in hand. Our values determine our character, and that in turn determines our relationships with God, our neighbors, and our environment. OI's view is that changing the human heart and changing human society are inseparable parts of a holistic development.

Some of the specific areas that the TD model looks at to establish whether and to what extent the clients' character has changed include increased faith, giving and sharing, family ties, integrity, stewardship, and peace and reconciliation among clients and their communities.

Service

The service component of the TD model refers to the significant difference that the clients have been able to make in serving their communities. It provides information about the role OI clients have played as agents of change in their communities, and seeks to demonstrate the specific areas to which they have contributed. This component measures the economic, social, political, and spiritual changes brought about by the clients in their respective communities.

Most of the communities where the poor live suffer from an inadequate supply of healthcare, education, water, sanitation, and communication facilities. Unemployment and crime rates are often rampant. The poor are often at the receiving end waiting for donors and government authorities to provide the services they need. The level of dependency is high and weighs heavily, and the waiting time for the arrival of services is long. The service component looks at two aspects: (a) the type and extent of shift clients have made in moving away from a receiving to a giving position, and (b) the type and extent of abundance, empowerment, and character improvements experienced by the remaining community members.

When clients use part of their newly generated relative abundance, time, and energy to respond to community needs, such as working to provide water supplies, building school facilities, cleaning up their streets, building public toilets, and caring for needy children in the form of voluntary contributions or investment, they demonstrate a willingness and ability to be socially responsible. They show that they want to be not only receivers but also givers. They do not want to enjoy the fruits of their businesses for their own good alone but also for the common good of their fellow citizens in the community. The move from a position of being "recipients" to a position of being "givers," or from dependency to independence is a tremendous indicator of holistic transformation.

Some of the specific areas used to establish whether and to what extent clients have made a difference at community level, include the level of employment their businesses have created, the number of service facilities they have contributed to, and overall economic growth achieved by their communities.

Summary

In the transformational development (TD) model, poverty is not about lack of ability or intelligence. It is about deprivation of economic, political, social, and spiritual opportunities to unleash internal potential. Abundance, empowerment, character, and service are all important indicators of holistic transformational development. Of the four, what matters most is character. The other three are basically about quantitative improvements. They deal with *having* and involve external changes. Character, on the other hand, is about being and becoming, and deals with changes that take place inside us. Opportunity International's TD model is therefore concerned with establishing a balance between the material and nonmaterial parts of people's lives, as life does not consist of possessions alone.

This model posits that our character, as the principal component in change, determines the level, type, management, and utilization of our relative abundance. Our character also determines how we manage and utilize the empowerment that comes with it. Good character means that we become good stewards, compassionate, givers, just, and followers of Christ. Spiritual transformation has a positive correlation with all the other components of TD, influencing them progressively. The proposition here is that spiritual transformation helps microentrepreneurs to work harder; take initiatives and risks; develop self-discipline; be free, hopeful, honest, good stewards, fair, reliable, and compassionate. In other words, increased spiritual transformation helps microentrepreneurs to generate more wealth and to lead a better quality of life (abundance), become more active citizens in society (empowerment), become honest and God-fearing (character), and to be more committed to one another (service).

That said, it must be pointed out here that this does not mean that OI's main microfinance mission is to convert people to Christianity. In fact, OI serves people with different religious backgrounds and does not impose its faith on its clients. There are many cases where both Moslems and Christians, for example, form groups and work together harmoniously. However, in contrast to non-Christian microfinance service providers, OI engages Christian staff members, who express Christian values through their deeds and lifestyles as they interact with clients in the lending process. OI's policy is to address the problems relating to the development of the whole person, including spiritual poverty.

Opportunity International in Honduras

This section of the chapter is devoted to describing the nature and impact of the OI program in Honduras and examining to what extent it has contributed to poverty alleviation there, in the context of the TD model outlined in the previous section. This section begins with a brief overview of the microfinance industry in Latin America in general and Honduras in particular.

Overview

In the form in which it is currently understood and practiced, microcredit or microfinance was started by the NGO community. In Latin America, microcredit originated in Bolivia. It was also in this country that the first commercialized microcredit services were delivered by an NGO when PRODEM (Fundación de Promoción y Desassollo de la Microempresa/ Microenterprise Promotion and Development Foundation) was granted a full banking license in 1993 (Christen 2000, 12).

According to a study carried out by the World Bank's Consultative Group to Assist the Poorest (CGAP), about 38 percent of the NGO credit service providers in Latin America currently operate as regulated microfinance institutions (MFIs). Together with commercial banks (29 percent) and other specially licensed financial intermediaries, these institutions account for 74 percent of the active loans given and for 53 percent of the active clients in Latin America (CGAP cited in Christen 2000, 5, 9).

The 1999 CGAP study shows that about 205 regulated and unregulated MFIs serve about 1.52 million active clients in Latin America. Christen estimates that microcredit reaches more than 25 percent of the potential market in thirteen Latin American countries, and as much as 50 percent in some other countries. He also estimates that there are more than 10 million potential microcredit clients still to be reached. About 7 million of these live in Argentina, Brazil, Mexico, Uruguay, and Venezuela, where best-practice microlending is practically nonexistent. Ninety percent of the current microcredit clients in Latin America are estimated to live in countries representing only 31 percent of potential demand (CGAP cited in Christen 2000, 9, 10).

Another feature of the Latin American microcredit industry is its domination by internationally affiliated organizations based mainly in North America. According to a market survey carried out by the Katalysis Partnership in 2000, among ninety-six organizations in Nicaragua, El Salvador, Honduras, and Guatemala, such organizations account for 66 percent of the total number of active clients (360,000) and 50 percent of the total service providers in those countries. Furthermore, only five internationally affiliated networks, including OI, are responsible for 51 percent of the total credit market (Katalysis Partnership 2001, 52). This means that over half of the total credit market in the four central American countries is in the hands of five internationally affiliated networks.

Honduras has a total population of just over 6 million in an area of 112 square kilometers. The population is growing at 2.9 percent and the population density is 57 per square kilometer, with a GNP per capita of $760. Honduras has been rapidly urbanizing; its urban population grew from 35 percent in 1980 to 56 percent in 1999. Women make up about 31 percent of the total labor force and 66 percent of employment in the service sector (UNDP 2000). The gross domestic product in 1999 in Honduras stood at $5.4 billion: 18 percent agriculture, 30 percent industry, 18 percent manufacturing, and 52 percent services. Honduras' external debt service was 6.8 percent of the GDP and official development assistance was 15.2 percent of the GDP in 1999 (UNDP 2000).

Although there has been overall improvement during the past decade, Honduras is still a poor country, with 41 percent of the population earning one dollar or less a day. Under-five child mortality rate is about 46 per 1,000, illiteracy rate is 27 percent, and population without access to safe water, 24 percent (UNDP 2000).

As in any other developing economy, the informal/microenterprise sector plays a significant role in the economy and social life of Honduras, and has become increasingly important since Hurricane Mitch hit in November 1998. The economy was devastated by this natural disaster, putting tens of thousands out of work and bringing the unemployment rate to about 42 percent in the formal sector and 80 percent in some of the rural areas. This in turn caused a growing number of people, especially the poor, to resort to the informal microenterprise sector as a source of livelihood. In most cases, microenterprise has been used as a survival mechanism and its relevance in the economy has increased ever since (OI Canada 1999).

Aided directly or indirectly by technical donors, particularly the U.S. Agency for International Development (USAID), the Honduran government has also supported microenterprise programs as part of its poverty alleviation program. Both local and international organizations have been and are participating in the implementation of microenterprise programs in collaboration with both the national government and international donors. There are about nineteen major organizations providing microcredit services in Honduras. Half of these are purely microfinance providers and the remaining half provide a range of other services. Together they serve a total population of 97,000 active clients (Katalysis Partnership 2001, 27–28).

Urban areas have remained the major points of concentration. Almost all the MFIs run more than 95 percent of their lending operations in urban areas, causing market saturation and stiff competition in the client market. This has been because of the difficulty and lack of experience in agricultural lending and the strong role that the service industry plays in the Honduran economy compared to agriculture. The demand for microcredit is much stronger in the former than in the latter. However, it is likely that the future trend will change in favor of the rural market as donor pressure to do so is increasing, and microfinance service providers are developing increasing confidence in handling rural challenges related to agricultural lending (Katalysis Partnership 2001, 32).

Some of the major microcredit service providers in Honduras are international microfinance organizations that work in collaboration with local affiliates. OI is one of these international networks, and the Instituto para el Desarrollo Hondureño (IDH), or Honduran Development Institute, is its partner. The following section is devoted to outlining the nature and impact of the OI and IDH (here after denoted as OI-IDH) partnership and their program.

The OI-IDH Program

The first OI program in Latin America was initiated in Colombia in 1971. Today OI serves the poor in six countries of the region through collaboration with seven implementing partners, including IDH in Honduras. The other countries include Nicaragua, Costa Rica, the Dominican Republic, and Peru.

The IDH was founded more than two decades ago, obtaining legal status in 1979. The vision of IDH is to assist the economic and social transformation of its clients, their families, and communities. Its mission is to contribute to the socioeconomic development of Honduras through the provision of credit and technical assistance to microentrepreneurs.

IDH has been a member of the OI network for about ten years and operates under the organizational covenant of 1997. Like any other OI member, IDH is committed to promote transformational development by implementing the network's three core goals: outreach, quality, and impact. This section considers the outreach and quality of the OI-IDH program and describes its current methodology and future plans. The following section will address the impact of this program on poverty alleviation.

Outreach

The concept of outreach has been articulated by OI-IDH to mean two things: The first relates to the size or number of poor people and poor geographical areas served by the OI-IDH microcredit program (breadth of outreach). The objective is to reach out to the largest possible number at a given time and with given amounts of available resources. The second aspect relates to reaching out to the poorest of the poor, particularly women (depth of outreach).

Having disbursed a total of more than 9,000 loans in 2000, IDH is the third largest OI partner in Latin America, after AGAPE in Colombia with 21,000 loans and ASODENIC in Nicaragua with 15,000 loans (OI 2000b, 7). At the moment, IDH operates in five urban and periurban areas, including Juticalpa, Tegucigalpa (head office), Siguatepeque, Danli, and Ceiba. Table 7.1 provides more detailed information about the trend of the OI-IDH program over the three years covering the period from 1998 (last two quarters) to 2001 (first two quarters).

As will be noted from the data in Table 7.1, an average of 87 percent of the total number of loans made and 82 percent of the total value of those loans went to female clients during the period covered. Women are among the most disadvantaged social groups in terms of access to credit, and the OI-IDH outreach focus is on the poorest of the poor. The average loan was about US$129. Geographically the program covered about five major poor

Table 7.1

IDH Client Outreach and Loan Portfolio Growth, 1998–2001

	1998	1999	2000	2001
Total clients outstanding	6,143	8,136	14,476	9,966
Total portfolio outstanding	14,117,672	17,505,584	25,406,337	1,853,758
Average portfolio per client	2,295	2,174	1,794	1,870
Total number of loans made	2,254	3,469	9,156	8,371
Percent to women	90	93	86	85
Total value of loans made	7,391,260	10,226,570	19,614,472	13,809,350
Percent to women	80	84	82	80
Average loan size	3,298	3,143	2,265	1,716

Source: OI Network Partnership Reporting System, OI Network Office, August 2001.
Notes: The financial amounts are in lempira, the Honduran currency; the exchange rate is approximately 16 lempira/US$1.

areas, including rural areas often neglected by other players because of transportation problems and the high levels of operational costs involved (OI Canada 2001, 4).

The total number of loans made in the first two quarters of 2001 was almost four times greater than the last two quarters of 1998. In the same way, the total number of clients outstanding increased by over 60 percent. There was a sharp decline toward the end of 1999 and early 2000 as clients faced marketing problems because of poor national economic performance resulting from the international slump in coffee prices, the hurricane disaster, and closure of some tobacco factories. Overall, however, the program experienced a steady growth in outreach.

Quality and Sustainability

The concept of quality as articulated by OI-IDH refers to portfolio management and cost efficiency. The OI network's objective is to reach a global average arrears rate of 2 percent and a 10 percent rate of portfolio at risk. There is a high level of commitment to financial excellence.

Financial excellence, in terms of portfolio quality, goes hand in hand with sustainability. The better an organization manages its portfolio, the stronger the chances are for it to reach financial and organizational sustainability and vice versa. Lower arrears, portfolio-at-risk and cost rates are part of good quality financial management and hence the basis for sustainability.

Table 7.2 shows the portfolio quality, cost efficiency, and sustainability rates achieved by OI-IDH during the period from 1998 (last two quarters) to 2001 (first two quarters).

Table 7.2

Trends of OI-IDH Portfolio Quality, Cost Efficiency, and Sustainability, 1998–2001

Item	1998	1999	2000	2001
Portfolio quality				
Percent arrears > 30 days	26	6.5	5	5
Percent at risk > 30 days	30	10.6	5.5	12.5
Efficiency				
Cost per loan made	865.76	1,427.55	479.45	327.13
Cost per unit of money lent	0.26	0.45	0.21	0.20
Sustainability (in percent)				
MED operational	75.44	62.26	93.48	92.80
MED financial	79.31	70.33	75.47	73.48
Organizational operation	79.65	51.56	69.74	72.13
Organizational financial	83.78	55.48	59.32	61.16

Source: OI Partnership Reporting Systems, OI Network Office, August 2001.
Note: MED = Microenterprise Development

The data in Table 7.2 show that the portfolio quality hugely improved between 1998 and 2001, with a steady decline in the delinquency rate. The arrears greater than thirty days fell from 26 percent in 1998 to 5 percent in 2001, while the portfolio at risk greater than thirty days fell from 30 percent to 12.5 percent—although in the latter case the figure was higher than in 1999 and 2000. The cost per loan made dropped almost three times, while the cost per unit of money lent declined from 0.26 to 0.20. The high cost in 1999 was due to the general economic slump caused by Hurricane Mitch and the decline in world coffee prices. The cost per loan is calculated by dividing operating costs by the total number of loans made. It provides an indication of the cost of providing credit based on the number of loans made. Cost per unit of money lent, on the other hand, is calculated by dividing operating costs by total amount disbursed. It highlights the efficiency of the loan disbursement system (SEEP [Small Enterprise Education and Promotion Network] 1995, 29–30).

Operational sustainability ratios (see Table 7.2) measure the extent to which income earned from interest and fees is sufficient to cover operational and actual financial costs of running a microfinance institution. Financial sustainability ratios, on the other hand, measure the extent to which the institution is profitable and can cover all costs, including an adjustment for inflation and the real costs of all liabilities. Both types of ratios are often referred to, with 100 percent being the target to indicate that break-even self-sufficiency has been reached (SEEP 1995, 28–29). For OI-IDH, both operational and financial sustainability ratios declined in 1999 then rose in 2000 and 2001, but with the exception of MED operational sustainability, they were still below the 1998 levels.

OI-IDH is taking corrective measures to improve portfolio quality and sustainability ratios in the immediate future. The most critical measure to be taken includes the installation and implementation of "eMerge": a portfolio management, accounting and information software system developed by the OI network with the ability to be adjusted to suit local contexts. The purpose is to improve the quality of loan tracking and administration and data collection for making informed policy decisions (OI 2001a).

Lending Methodology

The Katalysis Partnership study shows that about 70 percent of the microcredit market in Central America is dedicated to group lending activities. Village banks account for 57 percent and solidarity groups for 12 percent, leaving individual lending at 31 percent (Katalysis Partnership 2001, 32).

The core of the OI-IDH lending program is no exception to this trend. Although IDH practiced individual lending as its main methodology in much of its early history, group lending has become predominant in recent years. During the second quarter of 2001, for example, OI-IDH had 619 individual clients, compared with 4,682 group lending clients (both trust bank and solidarity group). There were 131 new individual clients as opposed to 1,029 new trust bank clients (OI 2001a).

The group lending methodology applied by OI-IDH is a modified variation of the village bank model practiced by other microfinance players, including Americans for Community Cooperation in other Nations (ACCION) and the Foundation for International Community Assistance (FINCA). It was developed by the Women's Opportunity Fund (WOF), an affiliate of OI; Kabalikat para sa Maunlad na Buhay, Inc. (KMBI), an OI implementing partner in the Philippines, was the main source and collaborator. The core characteristics of the trust bank model include the following:

1. Trust banks (TBs) focus on the poorest of the economically active population, and especially on women. TBs are formed over a period of eight to ten weeks during which time members are given orientation sessions. TBs are composed of twenty-five to forty self-selected members, and are divided into subgroups of five to seven members each. TBs develop their own constitution and democratically elect leaders to manage them from among the leaders of the subgroups, usually a chair, vice chair, secretary, and treasurer. They hold weekly meetings for the duration of the loan cycles.

2. Operationally, TBs are formed by the clients in cooperation with loan officers and community leaders. Once the TB has been established, loan applications are assessed and loan amounts recommended by the TB leaders for approval by the TB members in collaboration with loan officers. The members coguarantee all loans and collateral is not required. The members receive small initial loans simultaneously and pay interest at the market rate. The loan terms are often four to six months and loan repayments are made on a weekly basis. The leaders are responsible for receiving, depositing, and monitoring loan repayments. Loans are renewed with a continuous, gradually increasing "line of credit" following successful repayments. The members are required to save regularly in a group savings account. Leaders provide reports to the loan officers on a regular basis.

3. TBs do not only manage financial operations. They also pursue social, spiritual, environmental, and other common goals. Under normal circumstances, one loan officer oversees about ten TBs and ensures that the TBs' leaders receive adequate leadership training. The training of TB leaders takes place at or outside of the weekly meetings. It is also during these weekly meetings that clients are trained in important aspects of transformational development, including basic business management and personal and community development (WOF 1998).

OI-IDH resorted to implementing trust banks more aggressively in 1999 in the aftermath of Hurricane Mitch. This was done in the belief that TBs would enable the program to have deeper outreach in the sense of serving the poorest of the poor in a more comprehensive and holistic way, commensurate with its mission to promote transformational development. The TBs were found to be an effective avenue for promoting both economic and noneconomic activities that would impact the lives of member clients and their communities in holistic and lasting ways. While this was the primary purpose, OI-IDH also thought that using TBs for microfinance service delivery would decrease operational costs and increase the quality and delivery of services (IDH 2000).

Although the emphasis is on trust banks as its core lending methodology, OI-IDH also applies the individual and solidarity group lending methodologies. These clients receive relatively higher loan amounts with longer terms of repayment. They often run slightly bigger businesses than the ones run by TB clients. When TB members want to expand their businesses and find that the loans permitted through the TBs will not allow the expansion, they are "graduated" to solidarity groups or become individual clients. This is a development that clients aspire to achieve in their business progression and is a strong motivating factor in keeping a good repayment record. The solidarity group methodology is less popular than individual loans. It represents a very insignificant portion of the OI-IDH program and might be phased out fully in due course.

Trust Banks in Practice

The OI-IDH transformation program launched in 2000 integrated the trust bank lending methodology and aimed at promoting:

- Business growth, including increased profits and greater stability;
- Strong family relations, including marital and parent-child relationships;
- Personal development, including spiritual growth, leadership skills, business capability, and self-esteem; and
- Community service, extending spiritual and material blessing to others in the same and surrounding neighborhoods.

The program was implemented at both staff and client levels. Staff members, particularly loan officers, were trained in facilitation, empowerment, adult education, planning, and microfinance management skills, and were provided with counseling sessions to deal with their own emotional and spiritual needs. The purpose was to equip and enable loan officers to become effective agents of change among the clients (Stickney 2000).

Regarding the clients themselves, the project aimed at developing ways of initiating and participating in community projects. Trust bank members were encouraged to "share the blessing" with other community members outside their groups by keeping communities clean, promoting healthy activities for the youth, reaching out to those in need, and so forth. The project also aimed at producing training curricula and modules in basic bookkeeping, marketing, pricing, quality control, family relations, forgiveness, self-esteem, and family planning to promote business development and personal growth among clients (Stickney 2000).

Leadership Development

In addition to client training, which takes place primarily through the trust banks, the OI-IDH program also invests in leadership development at organizational governance, management, and staff levels as part of its transformational development model. OI's overall investment in leadership seems to have increased in relation to the pace of program growth in size and complexity, with a view to coping with the new challenges more effectively.

Recognizing the critical role of boards of directors as the guardians of organizational vision, mission, values, and direction, OI established a center in 1998 to develop tools and techniques for effective governance. Two volumes of tools: *Governance with Policy* and *Board Self-Assessment* were developed in 1999 (Bussau, et al. 1999). A series of training workshops were conducted to equip board members and senior managers with the tools contained in those volumes. Board members and senior managers are also trained during quarterly meetings, annual retreats, regional meetings, and global conferences. In many cases, exposure visits to successful programs both within and outside the OI network and donor headquarters are organized. Such visits have helped the directors and managers to broaden their knowledge and experience and gain new insights.

The three-year Poverty Alleviation in Central America Project, funded by a U.K. National Lottery and Charities Board grant from 1997/98, was one initiative that enabled training for board members, management, and staff of OI's implementing partners (IPs). This project involved the organization of regional conferences and retreats; training in leadership, governance, management information systems (MIS), and impact evaluation; a "training of trainers" course for loan officers, and a focus on other skills and resources that would enable the IPs to increase their outreach, conduct baseline surveys, and develop impact monitoring system (OI United Kingdom 2001).

For OI's Honduran partner IDH, the Lottery Grant Project Evaluation Report of 2001 indicated that during 2000 IDH recognized the critical role of loan officers as well as their economic and emotional needs, and focused on fostering their personal growth and transformation so as to enable them to serve the clients as effective agents for change. This emphasis was made as a result of IDH's realization that effective client transformation would require enhanced skills development among both loan officers and clients (OI United Kingdom 2001).

The Latin American regional office of OI also initiated "The Group of Twelve" leadership development program in 2000, specifically targeting board members. The program covers "twelve directors from six countries in the region that have demonstrated in their work and in their lives that they embrace the concept of the servant leader and clearly identify with the vision of trying to lift the poor out of economic, social and spiritual poverty" (LARO [Latin America Regional Office] 2000). The overall goal of the program has been to train the twelve directors in the areas of servant leadership, stewardship, governance, and microcredit best practices with the aim that they will in turn train the other board members in their respective countries. The skills gained through this training program are intended to enable the board members to understand, distinguish, and discharge their roles and responsibilities effectively by focusing more on long-term issues and planning, and less on day-to-day operations.

Future Plans

The OI network facilitated a strategic planning process in January 2001, through which a great number of its implementing partners identified critical initiatives that they plan to undertake during the coming three years. IDH identified the following list of capacity development activities as part of its three-year strategic plan:

- Open new branch offices in four zones of low penetration to increase portfolio growth;
- Revise and redefine the trust bank methodology to adjust operations to serve the target population in a better way;
- Promote business services development and incorporate formal technical assistance into the individual credit program according to the needs of individual clients;
- Expand existing operations by maximizing the capacity of existing offices as part of the overall expansion plan;
- Develop new product design to launch a credit program that will help dynamic entrepreneurs surpass the level of subsistence businesses;
- Define transformation and develop a clear implementation plan;
- Develop impact evaluation tools;
- Revisit and redefine organizational vision, mission, values, and policies (OI 2001a).

Impact: The Role of OI-IDH in Poverty Alleviation

Impact is one of the three main goals of the OI network. The other two (outreach and quality/sustainability) have been discussed above. In line with its treatment of poverty as being composed of both material and nonmaterial aspects as described in its transformational development (TD) model, the OI network defines its goal for impact as "enabling the poor to become agents of change in their communities" (OI 1998).

This subsection is devoted to examining the impact that the OI-IDH program has made in Honduras. In doing so, the discussion will make reference to the four components of the TD model: abundance, empowerment, character, and service. Reference will also be made to individual clients that have experienced positive change as a result of their participation in the OI-IDH microlending operations.

Abundance

As outlined in OI's TD model, the alleviation of material poverty is, under normal conditions, correlated with the generation of relative abundance, as

Table 7.3

OI Network Outreach by Region, 2000

Region	Loans made	U.S. dollars loaned
Africa	69,233	6,966,354
Asia	187,647	24,102,939
Eastern Europe	17,003	23,710,138
Latin America	49,192	8,168,794
Global Impact	323,075	62,948,225

Source: OI Annual Report 2000.

increased wealth enables people to improve the quality of their living conditions. What has OI-IDH achieved in this regard?

Before answering that question, a brief description of OI's worldwide impact is given as a general background. Table 7.3 shows the number and amounts of loans made in each of the regions where OI operated during the year 2000.

As shown in Table 7.3 above, the OI network made a total of 323,075 loans to both existing and new businesses, amounting to nearly US$63 million in the year 2000 alone. These loans went to 243,654 clients creating a total number of 430,270 jobs. (Job creation is often calculated at an approximate average of 1.5 jobs per loan.) During the period 1996–2000, the OI network loaned a total of about US$229 million and created 1,111,926 jobs across the globe (OI 2001a). Assuming that one job supports an average of five people, the jobs that have been created through OI lending operations have helped over 5.6 million individuals in Africa, Asia, Eastern Europe, and Latin America.

In Latin America the total number of loans given in the year 2000 represents about 12 percent of OI's global outreach. In Honduras, 9,156 loans amounting to more than US$1.3 million were made to 4,680 clients. This represented about 10 percent of the loans made in the region. The experiences of individual OI-IDH clients below serve to illustrate in more concrete terms the impact that these loans have had.

Filomena Sanchez Martinez belongs to a trust bank called Nuestra Ayuda Viene del Señor (Our Help Comes from the Lord) located in the rural community of Lepaterique. She sells fruits and vegetables. She received a loan of about US$65, which she invested in more varieties of vegetables. The increased profits have allowed her not only to pay the school fees for her three children, but also to save. Filomena says that, "for the first time in my life, I have been able to save."

Esmeralda Castanos was running a small store in a little town called San Mateus, when she received her first two loans through her trust bank. In eight months her profits doubled and her savings increased from US$30 to US$130. She needed to expand her business and got an individual loan of US$640. With this loan she was able to expand her pulpería (small store) into a super market, with a comedor (small restaurant) and a freezer.

Armando Mairena is fifty years old and a member of the Fuente de Vida Eterna (Source of Eternal Life) trust bank in Danli. He lives in a very poor neighborhood in a dirt-floored home and sells spices for a living. Despite running his business for fifteen years, Armando was unable to save even a cent. After two loans he has managed to save US$64 and plans on putting a cement floor in his house.

Georgina Almendarez started her business in tailoring with just herself and her treadle sewing machine. She used to make an average of US$2.90 a day. With her first loan of US$96, she purchased her second sewing machine. She bought two more machines with her second loan of US$144. She now owns a shop where she not only sews but also trains others in tailoring, charging a tuition fee of US$3.20 a month. She makes a profit of US$12.80 each day—four times higher than what she was making before her participation in the OI-IDH program.

Victoria García, seventy years old and member of the Shema trust bank, is a potter who makes clay jugs, bowls, and a griddle called a *comal*. She also makes pots, children's piggy banks, and tortilla grills, and she bakes bread. She lives with five of her nine children. Victoria sells her products in the local market in Ojonjona. Her house and outdoor oven (kiln) were destroyed when Hurricane Mitch hit Honduras in 1998. With her first loan of US$34, Victoria rebuilt her kiln. With her second loan of US$87, she built a second kiln to fire ceramic items, including animal figures and decorative plaques made in molds. She is now able to employ her thirty-year-old son to work with her. She has also diversified her activity by adding a new product line of baked bread, which she makes using her second kiln. Reflecting on her business, her life, and her family's situation, Victoria remarks, "I can see my life has changed. We are all better off. I am excited about the savings because I will have something for the future for the first time."

Suyapa Guillen, treasurer of the New Eden trust bank, is in the shoe making business. Before receiving her loan she worked in a shoe factory as a casual worker and was paid for piecework. Suyapa gained her skills in shoe making by learning from her coworkers. She is currently on her fourth loan. She invested US$25.60 of her second loan into buying a machine, and with her third and fourth loans she bought leather, soles, grommets, and laces in bulk. She repairs her own machines and figured out a way to adapt one machine to make perforated designs in the shoes. Suyapa says that the increased income from her business has helped her to improve her family's living conditions. She was, for example, able to buy Christmas gifts for her children and adequate food for a big celebration for the first time in her life. And she is determined to ensure that her two children enter into higher education. "Even if they have to walk to the university, they will get there," she says.

Martha Mendoza runs a small grocery store selling basic grains, bread, snacks, and soda beverages. She began her business in her dirt-floored house that is no bigger than a garden shed. She had no running water, no electricity, and no money to increase her inventory of materials. With four children and no husband, Martha survived on a daily profit of less than US$1.28. With a loan of US$77, Martha bought a secondhand machine, and as a result she has been able to double her production efforts leading to a huge increase in profit. She was able to repay her loan within four months, with enough left over to start buying materials in bulk.

The Amazon trust bank outside Danli consists of twenty-one women and three men engaged in a variety of businesses ranging from bakeries to village stores and tortilla making. These businesses had an average business net worth of US$101 at the time of their first loan. The group's total accumulated savings was under US$12.80. After three loan cycles (one year), the average net worth had increased by 71 percent to about $173.

The above stories demonstrate that the OI program in Honduras has enabled its clients to create and sustain employment, expand and diversify their businesses, generate increased income, and improve their standard of living through investment in better nutrition, education, health, and housing.

Empowerment

The concept of empowerment relates to the ability to participate in and influence decision-making processes. The following discussion will consider two aspects: general client empowerment and gender empowerment.

The poor are often at the periphery of decision-making processes for various reasons. In some cases, authorities wrongly fail to appreciate the resourcefulness of the poor in decision- and policy-making processes. They then tend to sideline or ignore them with no or little effort to consult, involve, and listen to what they have to say. So national, regional, and local decisions that affect the poor are made with no substantial grassroots participation, resulting in their exclusion. The authorities also tend to deliberately leave the poor out of the equation because of politically motivated and/or economic reasons. In the latter case, consultation processes are conceived as time consuming and costly to finance. In other cases, the poor do not make an effort to participate and influence decision- and policy-making processes because of their limited awareness of their rights and responsibilities, caused by lack of opportunities and cultural barriers.

OI-IDH has taken the opposite approach. It recognizes the resourcefulness of the poor in decision making and equip them to unleash or translate their potential into tangible outcomes so that they can play their legitimate role in shaping the course of development in a way that is relevant and meaningful to them.

The first critical aspect of empowerment has been the confidence OI-IDH offers to clients. The commitment to and mutual respect for the poor demonstrated by OI-IDH directors, managers, loan officers, and donors have been empowering to the clients. The clients have not felt threatened or disrespected by any of those involved in the OI-IDH programs. On the contrary, they have felt that they have been cared for, loved, respected, supported, consulted, and listened/attended to. This has made them feel valued and appreciated, boosting their self-confidence. This in turn has helped them to speak to and negotiate with local authorities.

Moreover, the provision of credit on the basis of trust and not collateral has been another source of empowerment, as often the only attitude the poor have experienced has been one of mistrust and rejection. The other aspect of empowerment attached to the provision of credit is that it is not a "handout." The poor feel empowered when they borrow and pay back their loans with interest, rather than when they receive them as a charity (Getu 1996). They don't see themselves as "beggars" but as equal business partners. OI-IDH has deliberately treated its relationship with the poor as partnership, and the clients have found that empowering in itself. By involving them in the shaping of OI-IDH services through impact assessment, client satisfaction research, and other forms of dialogue, OI-IDH has promoted a participatory tradition among the clients that is being passed on into social practices outside the OI-IDH program.

The discussions in training events and weekly trust bank meetings have increased the flow of information and general knowledge of the clients about their rights, roles, and responsibilities, as well as available resources. As a result of this, the poor have begun to break free from the bondage of fear and to take the constructive initiatives and risks necessary to expand their businesses and promote community development. In short, the overall level of self-confidence, participation, and influence exerted by the poor in businesses and communities has increased as a result of their participation in the OI-IDH microlending program. The days of silence and insignificance are being consigned to the past.

The other aspect of empowerment relates to gender equity, and principally to the empowerment of women. Like any other developing country, women have been and are at the center of production, but are at the periphery when it comes to benefits. In most cases women have been deprived of all relevant rights including formal education, access to and control over resources, credit opportunities, the right to vote and to be voted into office, the right to choose her spouse, and the right to say "no" when appropriate.

OI-IDH believes that any genuine holistic and sustainable development should put women's issues at the center. With this in mind, about 89 percent of OI-IDH loans were to women from the second half of 1998 to the first half of 2001. As a result of the OI-IDH program, poor women have been able to overcome the obstacle that blocked them from getting access to credit to create employment and generate income for themselves, their families, and their communities. With their businesses, they need not be confined to domestic work but can play a wider role in society. They have been enabled to run profitable businesses, earn income, make savings, and manage/control resources. These changes have enabled them to move from the role of housewives only, to the role of business managers/planners, employers, and providers.

As a result of the leadership and other noneconomic training provided to clients, and the self-confidence gained, a good number of women clients have also emerged as leaders in their own groups as chairs, secretaries, and treasurers. Some have even taken steps to contest elections for local leadership positions, thereby breaking the tradition of powerlessness. For instance, Esmeralda Castanos, a former trust bank leader, ran for mayor in her town, San Mateus.

These are good demonstrations of how women have been enabled to appreciate themselves and their overall ability more positively, and to reject society's conventional perception of women that undermined their ability and confidence and restricted them from unleashing their potential. Increased knowledge and increased income have helped them to exercise independence, see their own self-worth, restore their self-esteem, build their dignity, realize their potential, and establish gender equity. Working together in groups, they have seen that they are able and have the right to do all that has traditionally been "for men only."

The OI-IDH gender training provided through the trust banks has often included spouses, and the lending procedure made the spouse of the borrower coresponsible and supportive of the other. As a result, men have also been helped to build a more positive understanding of gender relations and have a positive appreciation of the socioeconomic relevance of women's participation in productive activities outside the home. This in itself was another aspect of gender empowerment.

In societies like Honduras, where gender bias is strong, female children are traditionally the most disadvantaged when it comes to school. They are either not sent to school or are taken out of school in times of economic difficulties, as families often tend to give priority to their sons. This has served as a basis for gender inequality as participation in society through employment or otherwise has been determined by the level of education and formal skills. The clients that participated in the OI-IDH program, however, have been able to send both their sons and daughters to school, thus forming the basis for future gender equity.

Character

The change in character has been a difficult area to detect. Specific client cases, however, give some indication that the OI-IDH clients have experienced some positive changes in their values, behavior, and attitudes.

To begin with, the clients' faith has been strengthened following the religious education that they have received through their trust banks' weekly meetings. Very often, religious educational events are organized by the trust bank leaders themselves in collaboration with local churches, and focus on biblical studies. Issues related to business ethics, integrity, and stewardship are also covered. The events are not conducted as a mandatory requirement for a trust bank; they are optional and done as and when the trust banks choose or find the exercise relevant. These events have helped trust bank members to develop new values and ethics regarding giving, sharing, integrity, and stewardship.

As pointed out in the section below, the level of mutual care and love among the trust bank members and other community members has improved, in that they help one another in times of social and economic crises. It is also believed that OI-IDH's clients have become more honest in their business dealings and relationships with one another as they internalize the concept that dishonest gain, corruption, and nepotism are ethically wrong. Family relationships have also been strengthened as a result of increased mutual respect.

Service

Due to the relative material abundance, increased empowerment, and changed character (values and behavior), OI-IDH clients have been enabled not only to support other members of the group but also to contribute, both financially and practically, to socioeconomic activities that have benefited their communities as a whole.

First of, all by creating and sustaining employment, the program has helped people to become more productive to themselves and their communities. Many have been enabled to move from being a community liability to being a community asset. This also helped to mitigate the rate of migration from rural to urban areas where unemployment is already high (OI Canada 2001).

Profits from businesses may be channeled to meet community needs. The Esmeralda trust bank, for example, bought a first-aid kit and, with their president as the neighborhood nurse, provides treatment for minor injuries to its members and their families. People do not have to travel long distances for such treatment or suffer because they cannot travel. As a result there has been a marked reduction in incidences of infection.

The trust banks become support networks through which members show mutual care in times of need and pool resources to meet common goals. When one of the members of the Lazos de Amistad trust bank outside Juticalpa lost her daughter in a car accident, the members paid for all the burial expenses she incurred and covered her three remaining loan repayments. When Maria Calix, another trust bank member in Juticalpa, was diagnosed with uterine cancer, she was told that removing the cancer would involve an operation that would cost her US$1,920. Maria's trust bank members contacted other trust bank members to raise the required funding. Through raffles, the sale of special items, and their own contributions, they raised US$960 within two weeks. The hospital agreed to do the operation with what was raised with the agreement that the rest would be paid on completion of the treatment.

Similarly, the New Eden trust bank members established a common building fund amounting to US$3,840 for the purpose of buying land from the government. The goal is to use the land as collateral for a bank loan so that they can build houses for their families. About 50 percent of the fund has been raised and the money is kept in a joint savings account.

The clients' knowledge and positive attitudes toward environmental control have also increased. OI-IDH clients have begun planting trees and cleaning up streets and compounds in their neighborhood. Garbage collection in connection with weekly meetings has become a common activity that trust bank clients undertake to serve themselves and their communities.

Summary

The global, regional, and Honduran national impact data presented above show how OI microlending programs, using the TD approach, have helped millions of people to break loose from their chains of economic, social, political, and spiritual poverty and to lead more meaningful and purposeful lives. The jobs created and sustained have enabled the poor to increase their household income, to eat more healthily, to improve their health and housing conditions, and to send their children to schools. They have also been able to invest more to diversify and expand their businesses and to save more for the future and buy insurance to protect against emergencies.

Through their increased wealth, improved quality of life, and successful businesses, a growing number of poor people have earned increased recognition and influence in their communities. Their voices have begun to receive attention from the authorities and their participation in decision-making processes has seen significant improvement. The clients have also experienced improved moral and ethical values: mutual respect, mutual care, integrity, stewardship, and environmental control; and commitment to giving, sharing, and enhancing their community service. They have begun to emerge as a bold, risk-taking, and innovative social force playing their rightful role in community development and nation building.

However, it must be said that although poverty seems to have ceased to exercise its crushing power on a good number of the OI-IDH clients, many are still struggling. Most businesses are still at survival level and far from making profits that ensure full self-sufficiency. Many are still constrained by capital, technology, and market problems. Lack of formal and business literacy are other limiting factors. Even legal factors seem to hinder the smooth promotion of microenterprises, negatively affecting expansion and sustainability. A more detailed discussion of the institutional and client challenges is advanced in the following section.

Implications and Challenges

With reference to the general and specific findings related to the Latin American and Honduran contexts as well as the OI-IDH programs, this section will discuss some of the major implications of these and challenges for the future.

Competitiveness

The microfinance industry is a fast-growing industry. The competition in the capital and client markets in both Latin America as a region and in Honduras specifically, is becoming stiffer by the day. The number of service providers is increasing at a fast rate while the number of traditional capital sources has remained the same. The budget allocated to microfinance by the main donors has begun to shrink following economic recession. In some cases donors restrict their assistance to certain countries for geopolitical reasons. Donor money is not available in all places or all of the time. In Honduras the major source of technical grants for microfinance-related programs is USAID. Service providers also borrow from the IDB (Inter-American Development Bank) for on-lending to clients.

The increasing number of both local and international microfinance service providers in the poorer countries of Latin America, including Honduras, is causing market saturation in the client market, particularly in the urban areas. Provided they don't "double dip," this scenario is likely to be good for the clients as it will offer them options and hopefully lead to lower costs and better service. For the service providers, however, it means less outreach and less business, and hence less propensity to sustain themselves.

The competition among the MFIs has been exacerbated by the commercial banks increasingly entering the market. In the early days of the microfinance industry, commercial banks showed little interest in providing credit services to poor entrepreneurs on the basis that they were high risk and high cost. That view has been proven wrong by the successful experiences of NGO MFIs over the years. The result has been the participation of formal financial institutions in the industry through direct and indirect interventions. With their long experience and widespread infrastructure, a full-scale participation in the sector by these institutions is likely to take a large share of the market.

Regarding competition in the capital and client markets, OI seems to be taking timely initiatives. In the first case, it is encouraging its local partners to consolidate and become formal financial institutions. In fact the first Opportunity Microfinance Bank was established in the Philippines in August 2001 and many more partners are in the process of establishing formal financial institutions (OI 2001b). This is likely to enable OI and its partners to depend less on grants and more on private capital mobilized through investment and public savings, including the savings of the poor themselves. In his study, Koenraad Verhagen argues that the poor have a higher demand for savings services than credit services (Verhagen 2000). By going the banking way, OI will not only be able to remain competitive, but also to provide much needed and often neglected savings services to the poor.

In the second case, OI-IDH is increasingly and systematically expanding its programs from urban areas into periurban and rural areas. This will require new systems and skills and will be a challenge. OI-IDH is also committed to high level of client satisfaction, client care, and consultation; the special investment in quality service and client transformation constitute a strong comparative advantage. Moreover, OI is also looking into moving to parts of the unreached market in the lager economies by initiating new programs in Brazil and New Mexico (OI 2001a).

OI-IDH also faces competition in relation to the labor market. Most managers and staff members do not have formal microfinance qualifications. The skills that staff members possess have, in most cases, been developed on the job. Those who come with some solid background are the ones currently working in the financial market. Very often these staff members are very costly, as they have to leave current employment and require more attractive packages. As the labor market does not offer much, service providers "poach" personnel from one another by offering more. This has made retaining staff very difficult and recruitment very expensive; turnover is costly. It has also caused discontinuity and instability in many instances, disturbing the pace of implementation as a result of falling morale and the departure of trained personnel.

This implies that OI-IDH will be required to invest more in staff and leadership development, to continuously offer a competitive working environment, to enhance its transformational servant leadership style, and to hold fast to its core values of integrity and stewardship. This will help OI-IDH to lessen the consequences of staff/management instability.

Triple Bottom-Line Approach

During the past year or two, OI has been committed to forming microfinance banks. There have been two main reasons: for the provision of needed savings services to the poor, and for the mobilization of increased loan capital so as to reach out to more poor people. Banks will be formed where appropriate by privatizing current NGO microfinance programs and converting their assets into venture capital. This undertaking will take place only if the bank to be established will (a) serve the poorest of the poor, (b) ensure sustainability, and (c) promote transformation as evidenced by an in-depth feasibility study and analysis. This is the "triple bottom line" for bank formation.

At least two challenges emerge here. On one hand, OI has to deal with local macroeconomic policies and meet the necessary legal requirements. This is a long, costly, and painstaking process. On the other hand, OI has to raise the necessary venture capital, both local and foreign, and, once the bank is in place, make sure that the triple bottom-line approach works: The poorest of the poor are served, and sustainability and transformation go hand in hand.

Clients increasingly want to grow their businesses beyond the survival level by taking bigger loans on an individual basis. That is one of the reasons that solidarity group lending is becoming less and less popular. The desire and commitment to transform microenterprises from survival level to a sustainable means of livelihood is a development intervention that is long-term in nature, and that involves providing a wide range of loan amounts simultaneously according to different clients' needs. The promotion of productivity, quality, cost efficiency, and transformation will have to be done as an integral part of OI's whole-person development model. This, in turn, will require putting in place a sophisticated management and information system to track loans effectively and to make informed decisions. It will also require the placement of highly qualified personnel with banking knowledge and experience, who have commitment to transformation and the ability to promote it.

OI has responded to this need by forming an international MIS team that is tasked with developing and installing contextualized management and information systems to help implementing partners (IPs) improve their data collection and loan-tracking and decision-making processes.

Moreover, with varied investors in the microfinance banks and the split of IPs into formal financial institutions and NGOs, OI will be challenged with the management of different levels of commitment to spiritual transformation, which might render the keeping and advancing of its original vision and mission difficult. Managing the risks of drifting from the original mission will constitute a critical challenge.

Dialogue

This chapter has shown how OI's model of transformational development treats poverty and its solution as holistic. The model advances the concept that relative material abundance, empowerment, good character, and commitment to common service constitute parts of the poverty solution. In other words, OI's model draws on the assertion that the poor will not be well-off if they have increased their wealth but are powerless, separated from one another and God, and constantly looking outward for solutions. They must be well in all the other areas of their lives simultaneously.

What makes OI's approach distinctive from all other microfinance approaches is its consideration and treatment of spiritual factors as inseparable parts of a holistic development effort. While the mainstream development approach sidelines and puts spiritual factors outside the development equation, OI's model sees and treats them as indispensable parts of the poverty alleviation effort. The claim here is that the poor suffer from spiritual poverty as much as they suffer from material and political poverty and will not be made well with solutions to only part of the problems that they face. Hence, the focus on whole-person development: transformation.

OI holds that its ultimate purpose is not only enabling the poor to have more possessions, but also to become better people and better citizens, making their world a better place to live in. In its work, OI treats microfinance as its means, and transformation as its end. OI is in dialogue with both secular and faith-based microfinance institutions, sharing its perspectives and learning from theirs. Through collaboration with important microfinance organizations such as SEEP, Assessing the Impact of Microenterprise Services

(AIMS), Consultative Group to Assist the Poorest (CGAP), Microcredit Summit (MCS), ImpAct, and Christian Microenterprise Development (CMED), OI has developed policies and tools and delivered workshops and papers to discuss the issues of defining, measuring/assessing, and promoting transformation as well as impact (Reed and Cheston 1999).

While OI needs to keep on with the important progress it has made in articulating and discussing the cause and solution of poverty holistically with other MFIs, initiating a similar move in the donor community remains a highly desirable development. The continuous failure of the mainstream development effort to address the issues of poverty during the last five decades has prompted even secular thinkers and donors to question the validity of the conventional development paradigm that focused on one main part of development: economic growth measured in quantitative terms.

The search for meaningful development has been intensified and this has led secular thinkers and donors to be either accommodative or supportive of spiritual factors. The dismissing of such factors as unimportant or private matters seems no longer to be the case. Development has entered an era where noneconomic factors, including spiritual ones, are given more and more of a role to play.

The need to engage in dialogue with the academic community is even more important for two reasons. On one hand, academia is generally "reluctant" to acknowledge the causal significance of a religious worldview on economic life and is slow to admit religion's influence on political life (Sherman 1999, 78). On the other hand, academia serves as the "think tank" for the donor community in the area of training, consulting, and policy formulation.

As a leading Christian microfinance institution, OI would make a vital contribution to a more balanced and healthy microenterprise development perspective in Latin America if it held a systematic dialogue with the secular donor community and academia. This would require that OI participate in academic seminars and symposia and produce well-researched publications to inform the academic community with credibility about the positive correlations between spiritual transformation and holistic development. This is another challenge for OI.

Gender and Development

This chapter has shown that 85 to 90 percent of the microfinance clients served by OI-IDH are women. It has also shown that through increased access to and control of resources as a result of their participation in OI-IDH microfinance programs, women have begun to experience some degree of social, economic, political, and spiritual empowerment. OI has developed an international gender policy and formed a task force to oversee its implementation. Although this is a major breakthrough in addressing gender issues both at organizational and client levels, a lot remains to be done in effectively tackling the myriad gender problems that are complex in nature and vary from one cultural context to another. Women still suffer from heavy workloads and cultural as well as social barriers.

To enhance gender empowerment and ensure gender equity for the benefit of women and society as a whole, OI-IDH will need to:

1. Have an organizational gender policy that is developed and implemented with grassroots participation and ownership, with the necessary resources to implement it in the context of the unequivocal principle (value) of equal opportunity. The present international gender policy and gender task force will need to be reinforced to ensure full realization.
2. Strengthen the trust banks in such a way that they become effective channels for educating clients about gender issues. The gender education should be given to men and youth as well. Outside the trust banks, boards of directors, managers, loan officers, and other staff members should also receive systematic gender education.
3. Ensure that women are given leading positions both at board and management levels. It will be important to recruit men who have gender awareness and positive attitudes toward women's leadership.
4. Develop tools that enhance gender equity and well-being. The current microfinance tools are focused on financial operations and tend to do very little in addressing the noneconomic needs of women. Such tools might include literacy, health, family planning, AIDS, and political and spiritual education. OI-IDH conducts training in these areas, but more needs to be done. These tools will help anti-women cultural values to change.

Advocacy

Client businesses can be affected by national macroeconomic policies, economic performance, national disasters (such as Hurricane Mitch) and international trends. Clients are also faced with domestic and foreign competition, lack of market for their products, lack of premises, high tax rates, lack of good infrastructure facilities, inadequate or irregular supplies of inputs, and so forth.

Moreover, the regulatory and control systems put in place by local governments are not, in most cases, conducive to the promotion of the microfinance sector. The policies are not straightforward and often tend to be restrictive. Although the overwhelming majority of microfinance clients are women, the policies and practices that many governments have are not women friendly and remain as the major constraints to gender empowerment.

These situations threaten to weaken the microfinance sector as a vehicle for poverty alleviation and need to be addressed effectively. This calls for all MFIs to forge strategic alliances and lobby at national, regional, and international levels for clearer microfinance policies, for women-friendly policies, and for more conducive macroeconomic environments both for the clients and the service providers. OI-IDH should play a more active advocacy role in the region.

Conclusion

The premise of OI's microfinance program is that poverty is multidimensional in nature, that it exists in the form of economic, social, political, and spiritual deprivations, and that it can be alleviated or solved only in a holistic way. By developing its transformational development approach, OI has used microfinance as a means of promoting relative abundance, empowerment, good character, and community service among the poor. Although there is a lot more that needs to be done for the poor to reach full self-sufficiency and independence, OI's program has shown that microfinance can be used to address poverty holistically and in a sustainable way to diminish clients' material, social, political, and spiritual poverty.

Poverty is widespread in Latin America and still exercises strong power on millions of people. There are many countries, especially the larger economies (Brazil, Mexico, Chile, Argentina, and Venezuela) where very few microfinance services are available. Even in those countries where there is a good concentration of service providers, many rural and periurban areas have not yet been reached.

In other words, although much has been done by MFIs including OI and IDH to address poverty in Latin America through microcredit, there is a lot more to be done, both to serve existing clients more effectively and to reach out to others. To play its antipoverty role in Latin America and other regions more effectively, OI will need to remain competitive in the capital, labor, and client markets; develop tools and capacity to successfully implement its triple bottom-line approach; enhance its mutual learning through dialogue with the relevant players; put in place and practice value-driven gender policy; and lobby and advocate for a conducive macroeconomic environment at international, regional, and national levels in collaboration with other players. Herein lie OI's future challenges and prospects.

8

Awakening

Campesino Families, Development Institutions, and the Process of Socioeconomic Change

Ana María Condori

This chapter is the result of the process of working with *campesino*[1] families who participate in economic organizations, and of the reflection and discussion among members of the technical team of the Uñatatawi Foundation about their experiences.

Worldwide, the central theme is the millions of people who live in extreme poverty. The majority of the poor live in rural areas, but urban poverty grows faster because of constant migration, especially in Latin America. This article presents the lived experiences of the author and of the team as a whole. It focuses on the real-life situations of campesino families and of women in particular, and of our attempt to build upon these experiences to create an organization that supports the neediest families in their attempts to overcome economic crisis. I begin with my personal experiences and then move on to describe the work of the Uñatatawi Foundation which I founded in 1988.

Biography of an Altiplano Woman:
"My Awakening" (*Uñatatawi*)

In March of 1987 I wrote a book about my life. In this way I set out upon the work of transmitting to the women and men of my country my reflections and experiences as a woman of the Bolivian altiplano, a migrant domestic worker, and a colonizer of the Alto Beni region.

I was born in 1954 in an indigenous, Aymara-speaking community called Choquecota, located in Carangas province of the department of Oruro, in the altiplano of western Bolivia. As for my educational level, I am self-taught. Girls in rural Bolivia have household responsibilities from the age of five: they look after the animals, help to care for younger brothers and sisters, and, when there are many children, they must seek outside work, obviously with the support of their parents.

At the age of nine I went to work in the city of Oruro as a domestic worker, and for eleven years I lived in the harsh and discriminative conditions of domestic service, seeking work from door to door. This is a common situation for women and men from the countryside, particularly young people; they migrate to the cities in search of work and opportunities, and suffer discrimination as campesino migrants. Often, because of poor living conditions and being undervalued in their home communities, youths go to work in the cities without any incentives or support structures.

When I was twenty I moved to the north of La Paz department, to the tropical zone of the Alto Beni, because my father had migrated there some years before as part of the Aymara and Quechua colonization of this region. Due to family circumstances, I became responsible for my father's agricultural land and participated as a member of the farmers' syndicate and the cooperative. The fundamental objective of the cooperative was to collect and commercialize cocoa beans in the Alto Beni region. This experience allowed me to know and understand the situation of women colonizers who must face harsh conditions in agricultural production that are sharply different from those in the Bolivian altiplano. The tools are different, the food is different, there are flies and heat—but nevertheless, we survived and have become accustomed to this hot but welcoming climate.

Meanwhile, institutions such as NGOs have begun to introduce training projects, especially in production, focused on social goals, and development or "promotion" projects for women. Some of these institutions have covered necessities such as the training of leaders, and thanks to this, sustainable syndicates, associations, and cooperatives exist. Others have been "assistentialist," for instance, institutions that distribute food, creating a situation of dependency in rural communities and in poor urban neighborhoods.

Reflections on the Work of Nongovernmental Organizations

Beginning in the decade of the seventies in Latin America and Bolivia, NGOs intervened widely to develop research, training, health, and educational services for low-income populations. In the 1980s, women became an important focus of development efforts; in the 1990s, food security and women's participation in political, management, and executive positions were key themes; and in the new millennium, alternative development for the poor was offered with the direct participation of civil society.

Nevertheless, both private and state institutions have always done their thinking at desk level, unaware of the potential and initiatives of poor people themselves, and above all, ignorant of their real interests and expectations. How can we think on behalf of people or elaborate abstract proposals—as if it were possible to save the poor with a stroke of a pen?

While the campesino economy is basically one of subsistence, many families in certain eco-zones are able to accumulate surplus and generate employment. Yet the Bolivian government does not invest in these regions to build their potential.

The poor family's household economy is characterized by diversification of economic activities: agriculture, herding, handicrafts, commerce, and casual wage labor. Under their own initiative, people have developed socioeconomic relationships that have allowed them to survive major climactic disasters, adverse government policies, and so forth; they also have the ability to adapt to fluctuations in the country's economic system.[2]

All people have to organize themselves to face problems and other circumstances. For this reason, poor families—both campesinos living in rural areas and emigrants to the cities—have syndicate organizations to give them a political voice and, parallel to these, economic organizations such as associations, cooperatives, and so forth. The reaction of a community to any given circumstance is conditioned by the character and temperament of the families that make up these organizations. In NGOs, this is something that has been difficult to understand or that NGO staff have preferred to ignore: we have not wanted to recognize these psychosocial characteristics and take into account each community's idiosyncrasies. For this reason, we have been unable to understand their problems and needs, and they have not understood our ways of thinking and acting.

The imposition of certain programs and projects by funding and implementing organizations has meant that the majority of antipoverty investment has failed. Examples abound: creating dependence upon gifts, offering training without clear criteria, transferring Green Revolution technology to the Bolivian altiplano with negative results, and so forth. To effect technology transfer, some institutions performed their well-known "diagnostics" and thought they understood the issues facing poor people and how to improve their living conditions. But in recent years the scene has shifted: many professionals and other people working in rural development are seeing the situation from a different point of view.

My colleagues and I combined our past experiences working in non-governmental institutions to convert the Uñatatawi Foundation into an institution with a different focus, making use of the good and the bad results of the past. Our reflection was that when we speak of *poor campesinos*, we are speaking of a family group that acts out their own development activities based in a socioeconomic unit that has incredible capacity for subsistence. We recognize that poor families have sufficient organizational capability and that many institutions have provided useful support.

Institutional Vision and Action

The Uñatatawi Foundation began work in 1988 as a team dedicated to development and training for campesinos, motivated by the publication of my book *Nayan Uñatatawi* ("My Awakening").[3] In April of 1994 the Uñatatawi Foundation was finally constituted formally as a private development institution, with the goal of contributing to the well-being and sustainable human security of families, working through their economic organizations (agricultural and artisan organizations) to raise the productive capacity of rural and periurban areas.

The Uñatatawi Foundation sees these economic organizations as the principal actors because their membership comprises the neediest people in rural and periurban areas. The foundation offers services to these organizations in the areas of technical assistance, specialized training, product transformation, and commercialization. Technical assistance focuses on natural and ecological production, because of its higher aggregate value. Training encompasses both production techniques and business management. Commercialization of products and marketing is handled through a consortium of enterprises.

Our work is focused on the northern zone of La Paz department, in subtropical, valley, and altiplano areas belonging to four municipal government areas: Caranavi, Irupana, Laja, and Charaña. These municipalities have signed formal agreements with Uñatatawi and contribute 10 to 15 percent toward the cost of projects.

Our clients are families ranging from three to ten people, depending on the number of children; we refer to them as clients because they should be able to negotiate on equal footing with the foundation. Currently the Uñatatawi Foundation works with 139 families; 62 percent of clients are women and 38 percent are men. These families all belong to economic organizations such as associations, cooperatives, and the Regional Corporation of Campesino Producers (CORACAS).

The Uñatatawi Foundation works with already-existing economic organizations or those that organize themselves; we do not impose organizations upon people. These organizations apply to the Uñatatawi Foundation to obtain the services it offers. If a person does not belong to any organization, they need to join their community's economic organization in order to receive the requested services; it is very difficult to reach families individually.

The intent is for each person to feel ownership in all current and upcoming projects. We aim for the relationships with our clients to be centered on negotiation, in which discrimination is avoided, meetings take account of all viewpoints, and each party is able to comply with its commitments. The foundation signs formal agreements with each organization according to the organization's requests, prioritizing problems and needs, taking into account the potential of the region and of each family, and assuring that this potential is incorporated into the development of the projects.

The Causes of Poverty and the Process of Socioeconomic Change

Poverty has many causes. The Bolivian government has an alternative development program called Plan for the Poor (*Plan para los Pobres*), but in practice this plan does not reach people directly. There are no opportunities for training or education, nor are situations such as natural disasters and environmental contamination, land tenancy, and lack of market information addressed. The government does not motivate national enterprises. Meanwhile, NGO personnel who are not involved in party politics have difficulty accessing social development projects.

Uñatatawi is not exempt from socioeconomic problems and national political difficulties, but we are working to attack the causes of poverty. Seed capital funds from the Trickle Up Program[4] have been useful for families to begin or expand productive activities and other small businesses. While supporting and following up these activities, we have developed strategies for sustainable resource use based on a prioritization of problems and necessities, and have used these in our negotiations with state and private funding organizations.

Our focus is on increasing productive capacity. Many NGOs work with social themes such as health and education, which are both important and necessary for poor people. But, as long as poor families do not have sufficient income, they cannot access medical centers, buy medicines, obtain good nutrition, and so forth, and their education and health centers will remain underequipped and unable to cover the costs of serving the poor.

Many NGOs, both financing and implementing organizations, say that they are contributing toward reducing the flow of migrants from countryside to city, but how can people continue to live where they have no basic services and no opportunities for improving the socioeconomic situation for their children? We know that in these conditions, it is difficult to prevent migration and NGOs alone cannot solve the problem, nevertheless the theorizing continues. In recent years cities have grown and there is more poverty, but people still find opportunities there, especially opportunities for their children. Education is a key opportunity: in the city, children can receive an education, even if the family's daily diet is nothing but bread and coffee-husk tea.

For Uñatatawi our work is difficult but not impossible. It is easy to plan sitting at a desk; on the ground is where one has to take into account all the components: environmental, cultural, social, economic, and political, which affect how poor families are involved in production and commercialization and whether they obtain good returns. Achieving this is obviously a process, something that happens over the long term and requires a lot of dedication. In this process it is important not to overlook the training of human resources; financial resources are of no use if there are no people capable of administering them.

Bolivia has seen negative experiences in the past, such as the investment of millions of dollars with no positive results while poor people stay poor. There have also been positive experiences, such as that of the El Ceibo Agro-Industrial Cooperative.[5] This cooperative, with the support of a volunteer from the German institution DED, Deutscher Entwicklungsdienst (German Development Services) grew incredibly. Human resources training was a priority and El Ceibo is now an enterprise administered by the poor campesinos themselves and by their children who have studied and become professionals. Uñatatawi is working so that the economic organizations of our clients also become enterprises under campesino control.

Conclusion

Since 1999, the Uñatatawi Foundation has had technical staff to support its activities. The impact of the foundation's work has not yet been seen at national levels; nevertheless, one impact of our work has been the contacts established with national and international markets for all of our alternative products (for instance, alpaca textiles, herbs, and native grains). The signing of agreements with municipal authorities has been another achievement, for Uñatatawi was one of the first institutions to coordinate its activities with local governments. The municipalities offer direct support to families through their economic organizations for the purchase of seeds, and this program enjoys significant demand.

Living in different worlds of Bolivian society has provided the opportunity to reflect upon Bolivia's social reality and the work of NGOs in rural communities and periurban neighborhoods. Experience has shown that poor people must reflect on their situation and seek resolutions to their families' economic problems themselves. People organize themselves to meet their needs, and the resulting organizations are a key part of community life. Development institutions must understand people's on-the-ground realities and the many interrelated factors that influence poor families' activities. Out of this real-life understanding, organizations can develop negotiated working relationships with the poor to provide key services and awaken families' and regions' potentials.

9

NGOs and Ecotourism in Ecuador's Amazon

Frank Hutchins

To get the authentic experience of living for several days with the Quichua Indians of Ecuador's Upper Amazon, you might try going through an environmental organization that has its roots in the Missouri Botanical Gardens. Once you arrive in an authentic rainforest community, you can rest up in cabins financed by a Spanish NGO. Your authentic meals will be prepared by locals trained through a grant generously provided by an NGO that survives through Greek, Dutch, and U.S. funding. As you tour, don't be surprised to run across other travelers who arranged their visits through a Swiss NGO. And if you thoroughly enjoy your authentic Amazonian experience, send your hosts a "thank you" by e-mail; they were recently checking their messages at the local office of a German NGO.

Nongovernmental organizations, like ecotourists, have crowded into the Amazon rainforest to design, organize, finance, and provide technical advice on countless projects aimed at sustainable development and environmental protection. Many of these projects in Ecuador involve indigenous communities, making NGOs important actors among a variety of others who have influence over the lives of Quichua, Cofan, Huaorani, Siona-Secoya, Shuar, and Achuar peoples. The meeting grounds on which outsiders and locals come together are filled with acts of communication—signs, symbols, translations, motions, dances. From these come the understandings and misunderstandings that define and make meaningful the encounter. This is also a space in which people wield power, that determines how the benefits and costs of tourism are divided, how culture and nature are presented as attractions, and how destination sites are integrated into larger economic and political structures.

My objective in this chapter is to look at a particular indigenous organization in Ecuador's Amazon region which, although it emerged out of a regional Quichua federation, now functions much like a grassroots support organization as described by Fisher and Markowitz (Fisher 1998; Markowitz 2001). Such groups act as mediators for community-based organizations, channeling funds and facilitating development projects. The organization I have worked with in the Ecuadorian Amazon is called the Red Indígena de Comunidades del Alto Napo para la Convivencia Intercultural y el Ecoturismo (RICANCIE), and it coordinates tourism activities for a network of ten Quichua communities in Napo province.

In the following sections I use theoretical tools from anthropology and human geography to examine how a locally based organization, intimately connected to the communities it is committed to serve, helps expand the knowledge base and skills of community members. This involves much more than the accumulation of facts and abilities. Most important, it leads to a better understanding of how such communities are connected to, and affected by, discourses, decisions, and actions that influence community life. For example, understanding why tourists visit the Amazon, how the industry organizes and controls tourism, and the various ways that governments promote and regulate these activities can lead to community empowerment. I refer to these insights as *perspectives*—or positions of awareness and reflexivity—that I think are key to true sustainable development. Perspectives, as Sack theorizes them, are "those views that are complex, consciously formed, and presented by a culture as a way of viewing the world" (Sack 1997, 153).

As perspectives become more broad and elevated, they enhance the ability to comprehend one's place in a changing world—to see the connections between cause and effect, between power and subordination. They are important in areas such as the Amazon because relative isolation is daily penetrated by global forces. For example, the destruction of coca plants initiated by Plan Colombia is causing significant human movements in southern Colombia, pushing both peasants and guerrillas into northern Ecuador. Lawlessness and overtaxed services are the norm in many of the towns of Sucumbíos, Napo, and Orellana provinces in the Ecuadorian Amazon. Coffee prices plummeted from up to ten dollars per hundred pounds in early 2001 to around one dollar by mid-year as local people, directly affected by the upheavals, were no longer able to buy such a luxury item.[1] Timber and mining companies are also busy scouring the Amazon for resources, while oil companies for decades have dumped residue into rivers and lakes, polluting waters that for many are the only sources from which to drink and in which to bathe and do laundry (Kimerling 1991). Appreciating the breadth of sources behind these changes and understanding the power plays involved require particular skills and knowledge acquired beyond community borders.

The Ecuadorian government has historically treated the "oriente" region as outpost and frontier, ignoring it in what Vickers calls a "de facto policy of neglect" (Vickers 1984, 9–10). With eroding faith in national governments, and growing interest in Latin America by environmental and development organizations, NGOs have stepped in to fill many economic and social functions in the region (Tulchin and Espach 2001); Ecuador is no exception to this trend. As in much of Latin America, non-state actors—and the mainstream Western values they often promote—have increasing influence in places such as the Amazon.

Actors act, and in so doing engage in place-making and place-altering activities. With regard to NGOs, these activities—most commonly carried out through projects—can be measured statistically by amount spent, number of families assisted, growth in local income, and so forth. But if sustainable development is to have any truly future-enhancing possibilities, I believe that impact statements and evaluations should also encompass factors such as the broadening of perspectives and consideration of moral questions surrounding the use of place. For example, is an ecotourism project that generates income for some families, while making a spectacle of local culture, truly sustainable? Are community members simply display items, or are they integrated into tourism activities as decision makers and meaningful benefactors? As Sack maintains, places have the power to transform reality, and any attempt to influence place includes an assumption about what "ought" to happen there.

> Creating places to create a new reality, or to keep it as it is, or to return it to what we think it once was, invokes moral issues from the very beginning. Even creating the smallest place is a moral act for it involves not only creating but also destroying, and including and excluding. (Sack 2001b)

Ecotourism projects can attempt to create new realities, keep current conditions as they are, or return places to some Edenic notion of what they used to be. They do so not only by building infrastructures and imposing restrictions, but also by introducing new meanings and conceptions of nature, and by adjusting social relations. For example, environmentalist discourse influences discussions about and designs for the Amazon, and it often includes the concept of "ecologically noble savages" (Conklin and Graham 1995; Peluso 1993; Redford 1990) and pristine, paradisiacal rainforests (Cleary 1991; Slater 1996). Ecotourist literature is full of such references, which introduce new meanings to those people and places that transport, feed, entertain, and host the tourist. With regard to environmentalist discourse, I have noticed an emerging dichotomy between a disillusioned, degraded, drug- and crime-filled West and a native Amazonian world of wisdom, guardianship, and reciprocity. In Napo province, I've seen the prefix "eco" or the adjective "ecological" attached to schools, diesel trucks, a road slicing through the rainforest, and a bar sign advertising, in English, "Ecologic Cold Beer." Ecotourism guides and project managers talk about protecting the "lungs of the earth" for those visitors who have escaped their own contaminated environs. A complex world appears molded to fit a formula clearly defining culprits, saviors, problems, and solutions.

In communities where I have worked, social relations are also altered as visitors seek out the authenticity of particular indigenous figures, such as shamans, Tarzan-like guides, and craftsmen. Money paid for their services is usually welcomed and needed, but it also creates or exacerbates economic and status differences. Real or perceived disparities in benefits derived from tourism led to many disputes in communities where I worked, and have split up communities in other parts of the Ecuadorian Amazon.[2]

My basic argument is that organizations involved in promoting ecotourism should be aware in the broadest sense of their place-altering activities. This includes an analysis of how new meanings are introduced through tourism, and how they complement or clash with extant meanings. Hannerz encourages us to think of "habitats of meaning," which relate coherent sets of meaning to particular institutional and social contexts that continually expand or contract as meanings change (Hannerz 1996). Quichua habitats of meaning change when the first tourists arrive, when development projects introduce new conceptions of health care or education, and when government officials initiate land reform. Any analysis of how culture is affected by these changes should include consideration of the moral dimensions of intervention and reflexivity over particular project decisions that involve value judgments about what is proper, good, and beneficial for local communities.

I elaborate on this position by first examining the growth of NGOs, with particular reference to Ecuador. I next describe in more detail place and space theory that informs my position, and follow this with details about the specific project (RICANCIE) that I researched. My conclusion is that grassroots organizations such as RICANCIE, which draws its administrators from communities with which it works and bases its project design on community input, come closest to meeting ecotourism's goals of environmental protection, sustainable development, and cultural valorization.

NGOs on a Global Scale

Julie Fisher separates NGOs working in developing countries into two major groups: grassroots organizations (GROs), which are based in local communities, and grassroots support organizations (GRSOs), which are regionally or nationally based development assistance organizations (Fisher 1998, 4). Both GROs and GRSOs have expanded dramatically in developing countries as civil society takes on more of the responsibilities for social and economic development that states are unable or unwilling to assume. Fisher says these NGOs, individually or cooperatively, aim to empower local groups, while also serving to link these groups with, and protect them from, the outside world (1998, 8). In this role, GRSOs concentrate primarily on sustainable development that reduces poverty and protects the environment. Designing and implementing projects that target these goals insert both GRSOs and GROs between the for-profit and nonprofit sectors of civil society. In promoting microenterprise development, these organizations also help spread out the ownership of capital through the devolution of income-generating activities (1998, 16). With regard to tourism, one can measure this process as community-based projects mature and stake a claim to ecotourism benefits traditionally controlled by established operators.

Fisher for the most part discusses the potential roles NGOs can play in creating constructive and dialogic space for civil society. But these organizations also emerge from certain philosophies and experiences that determine how development problems are evaluated and addressed. From a macro perspective, one can see the NGO network as a primary carrier of particular meanings within what Boli and Thomas refer to as a "world polity" (Boli and Thomas 1999). International NGOs, according to Boli and Thomas, are transnational bodies that promote certain world-cultural principles via "rational voluntarism." "They employ limited resources to make rules, set standards, propagate principles, and broadly represent 'humanity' vis-à-vis states and other actors" (1999, 14). The themes that underlie this process—universalism, individualism, rational voluntaristic authority, the dialectics of rationalizing progress, and world citizenship (1999, 35)—characterize the activities of many NGOs dedicated to environmental protection and development.

The ecosystem model that informs much environmental action, for example, rationalizes—and thus desacralizes—nature by placing it within a discourse that evaluates the natural on principles of progress, economics, and science. The discourse on biodiversity frames nature as a source of value that fits neatly into the capitalist system of production. Both nature and culture fall victim to a "semiotic conquest," as development arrives to save environmental riches from abuse at the hands of the Third World poor (Escobar 1995, 203). A recent editorial by Ecuador's former minister of the environment, Yolanda Kakabadse Navarro, captures this rationalization process quite well: "Latin America, and therefore Ecuador, are characterized as having an exceptional natural capital. We have forests, rivers, fertile soils, fruits, fish, oil, mines, and a biological diversity that constitutes a current and future source of pharmaceuticals, foods and chemicals for industry, that can contribute to satisfying current needs of the region and the world, and so doing strengthening the economy of our country."[3]

Within this discourse, culture is also commodified, as the tourism industry packages and sells "ethnic" and "heritage" tours. Once these elements have been established as having an economic value, NGOs involved in sustainable development and environmental protection help circulate the meanings associated with culture-as-commodity. Do NGOs promoting ecotourism projects ultimately serve the interests of the powers that generate "world polity" discourse and action? Or do they indeed open up spaces where that discourse and action can be challenged and reconfigured to benefit those often left out of modernizing development projects? Does this debate simply boil down to economics, or are there other, less tangible, benefits that should be considered as well?

My conclusion indicates that there are identifiable discourses about nature and sustainability that are extended by NGO activities, but that these messages flow into local currents and countercurrents. Where NGOs demand strict adherence to certain philosophical and practical positions, there is certain to be local resistance. But where there is a measurable degree of respect for local input, there is also likely to be more of a middle-ground space created where the terms of development can be negotiated and modified to suit particular needs. This is the opening necessary for the free flow of ideas between different habitats of meaning that leads to better communication and understanding.

NGOs in Ecuador

The history of NGOs in Ecuador has been divided into three stages (Cabrera and Vallejo 1997). The first stage, in the early decades of the twentieth century, generally involved philanthropic and charity organizations. According to Segarra, these were initiated by the Catholic Church, with some secular NGOs emerging to offer technical support to the beneficiaries of Ecuador's first land reform carried out in 1964 (Segarra 1997, 11). In the second stage, during the 1960s and 1970s, development NGOs spread through Ecuador. Segarra says this second generation of NGOs, responding to the military regime's rapid expansion of social services in the 1970s, focused on social analysis and policy research (1997, 12). With the return to democracy, these NGOs underwent a reevaluation of their roles within changing political conditions. The third stage, beginning in the 1980s, saw NGOs significantly expand projects related to small business, the environment, women, children, and human rights.

In Ecuador, as in other developing countries, this expansion was due to decentralization of government and the erosion of the state as social benefactor, as well as the globalization of political and economic activities. Where the government stepped out, civil society stepped in to fill the void in health and education services (43 percent of NGO projects in 1996); production and income generation (22 percent); and environmental protection (17 percent) (Segarra 1997, 41). This third stage of NGO evolution also saw a dramatic increase in the numbers of organizations working in Ecuador, growing from 250 registered NGOs to over 1,000 by the end of the decade (1997, 13).

Ecotourism grew up during the third stage of NGO expansion, and has been incorporated into development projects that seek a balance between conservation and economic and cultural sustainability for local populations. This type of tourism, defined by the Ecotourism Society as "responsible travel to natural areas that conserves the environment and sustains the well-being of local people" (Wood 1998, 10), has been promoted in Ecuador by a number of environmental NGOs. Nongovernmental organizations are involved in tourism activities in the Amazon both directly and indirectly. Since ecotourism is seen as a sustainable development alternative that helps preserve the environment, support local economies, and reinforce cultural values, NGOs committed to one or more of these goals may offer technical assistance or funding for tourism-related projects.

The rationalization process discussed above comes into play as various components of sustainable development projects are defined, measured, and evaluated by NGOs for their potential contribution to project goals. The CARE project at Añangu, a Quichua community along the Napo River, "appraised" certain cultural elements with a point system based on potential contribution to ecotourism. Thus "spiritual culture" gets a "bad" rating, "material culture" gets a "good" rating, and "geographic habitat" gets an "excellent" rating. So that cultural survival isn't threatened by outside influences carried into Añangu by ecotourists, a plan of "mitigation" calls for "studies and talks that aim to recuperate ancestral forms of life of the indigenous. . . ." This corrective is mentioned directly above a suggestion for controlling pests by using rat and mouse traps, acquiring a cat, and utilizing boric acid for cockroaches.[4]

When placed within project formulas such as these, culture is presented as something that can be manipulated, enhanced, and drawn from a deep well of reserves in the service of economic development. The evidence here indicates to me the pitfalls that arise when the habitats of meaning that define the philosophy and practice of an institution are impervious to the flow of ideas and meanings from other realms in other places. The degree to which locals and outsiders share knowledge is constrained by limits on the flows of ideas and meanings that can enter into and inform or challenge extant meanings. As Sack maintains, the development of awareness "requires institutions that allow the flow of ideas, so that people can share perspectives and check each others' views" (Sack 1997, 163).

Place Making and Perspectives

I have alluded to "places," "meanings," and "realms" in the above section. It is now time to more clearly explain my usage of these terms. Much of my understanding of space, place, and landscape theory comes from human geography, but anthropologists are becoming increasingly interested in these areas as well (Appadurai 1991, 1996; Auge 1995; Clifford 1997; Escobar 2001; Hirsch and O'Hanlon 1995; Marcus 1998; Olwig and Hastrup 1997; Tsing 2000). With regard to environmental and development issues, Brosius encourages anthropologists to look closely at how actual and metaphorical spaces are produced, and how particular people are situated in those spaces (Brosius 1999). This brings up again the question of "ought": who *ought* to live in the rainforest and how *should* they live? Who *ought* to determine use, wise-use, or no-use policies for biospheres, parks, and other "environmentally sensitive" areas? In short, who has the *right* or *responsibility* to determine place rules of inclusion and exclusion?

The answers to these questions may become clearer if we first understand the dynamics of place and space. I begin with Sack's broad definition of *place* as "humanly bounded and constructed areas of space" (Sack 1999, 26), but with boundaries that are porous in terms of the regular flows of meanings that move in, through, and beyond. Places have certain rules and regulations about what can and cannot happen there. J.E. Malpas says "place" is where people have their grounding, where they act and are acted upon in specific ways (Malpas 1999, 37). Olwig makes the point that even in a globalized world of movements, many people have places where they regularly touch down and return to, and from which they get sustenance and meaning (Olwig and Hastrup 1997). In attempting to overcome the modernist notion of place as bounded and static, without abstracting places into nonexistence, Dirlik distinguishes between place-based and place-bound. The former is grounded in local topography and meanings, but is also characterized by porosity, while the latter is firmly rooted, essential, and timeless (Dirlik 2001).

In Sack's theoretical framework, *space* is open, unfettered nature that has yet to be altered by any form of human agency. But when it gains a name, boundaries, and regulations—even rudimentary signs of human intent—it becomes place. Place draws nature and culture together in a circumscribed area. The home, schools, parks, and ecotourism cabins are places. As geographical entities, places occupy physical space and incorporate elements of nature, from the flora and fauna of a rainforest park to the conditioned air and human bodies of a ministerial office. As cultural entities, places also harbor meaning (ideas) and social relations.

These three realms (meaning, social relations, and nature) overlap and influence one another in varying degrees. The result is a "place" that has its own dynamics, as the elements in these three realms mix in different ways. Nature may appear the predominant realm in a park, but meanings influence how that nature is understood and used, while social relations often determine who may use the park, and under what terms. National parks in the United States, for example, were rhetorically and literally emptied of native inhabitants and eventually, as Patin reveals, became sites for the construction of national identity (Patin 1999, 58). With regard to the Amazon, a wealth of material has been produced in the past few decades that indicates how the rainforest is politicized, commodified, and appropriated for a variety of purposes (Cleary 1991; Conklin and Graham 1995; Hecht and Cockburn 1990; Kane 1995; Kimerling 1991; Nugent 1993; Peluso 1993; Ruiz 1993; Santos-Granero 1996; Schmink and Wood 1992; Slater 1996; Smith 1993; Sponsel 1995).

Other characteristics of place concern the depth of meanings and the breadth of activities that are allowed—explicitly or implicitly—within that place. This is what Sack refers to as the "thickness" or "thinness" of place. In the lowland Quichua communities of Amazonian Ecuador, places tend to be thick with cultural meaning. In the predawn hours, the significance of that night's dreams may be discussed over *huayusa* tea. In the same space, cooking, weaving, and informal education may fill the hours as the day progresses. Thick places, says Sack, contain interwoven layers of elements from the three realms. Thin places, however, are made so by differentiation of activities associated generally with modernization: each activity—education, work, eating—in its respective place. The result is segmentation and specialization—what some experience as liberation, and others feel as alienation.

Ecotourism, in many ways, promotes an artificial thickness of place that often obscures indigenous reality. In Ecuador, indigenous communities that host visitors are encouraged at every turn to retain cultural "authenticity" and hide signs of change that suggest that real indigenous life has been thinned out by cultural pollution. For the tourism industry, real Amazonian Indians are timelessly bound to place, living out the unaltered lives of the primitive.

These messages—that successful tourism requires an appropriate cultural showcase—are most visibly received in communities where tourism is controlled by outside operators. But even in indigenous-run projects, special efforts are made to create a curtain between lived existence and the romanticized ideals of tourism. I traveled to a Quichua community with a group of college students who spent an evening learning how to weave baskets and shoot darts from a blowgun. Their day ended with men in palm skirts dancing around a fire. That same weekend, the indigenous head of the tourism project had given an impassioned speech at a province-wide forum in which he explained the pressing needs of his people with regard to education, health services, and economic opportunities. These "real" Quichua dilemmas, even though they revealed much about indigenous life in the 1990s, had no part in tourism activities. The growing complexity of indigenous habitats of meaning, and the related thinning out of their living spaces, creates problems for those in search of purity and stasis.

Such an experience suggests the division of space in tourism destinations into front and back regions, with the latter being the locus of authenticity. As described by MacCannell, the front region is where hosts offer a "staged reality" to guests, while in the back region, beyond the eyes of guests, real life is lived (MacCannell 1973). In the example mentioned above, I stayed in the community after the student tourists had gone. That evening, the fourteen-inch Goldstar television and Cinemaster VCR were hooked to a generator, and everyone enjoyed a couple of Japanese martial arts movies. In the community of Capirona, the structured tourism program I was observing ended when the German tourists were carried away by motorized canoe. What seemed to me a truly rich cultural scene then unfolded as a communal work project (*minga*) began. Men and women gathered to put the final touches on a canoe hollowed from a single tree. Nearby, women began to cook plantains and smoked *paca* for lunch as the captain of the work party passed around shots of liquor. The community shaman performed a cleansing on a small girl with a respiratory problem, chanting, blowing smoke, and brushing the patient with a bundle of branches.

In the staged version of local life, the thinning out of place is masked with artificial layers of thickness. This condensed and preserved culture is the commercial product of tourism. Quichua places have in reality been thinned out by a variety of processes, from missionary incursions to growing inclusion in a capitalist economy to expanded educational opportunities. Ecotourism, for all its efforts to do otherwise, also thins out place as community space is redefined to accommodate cabins, kitchens, and cultural programs. Sacred waterfalls, caves, and trees that are traditional homes to forest spirits (*supay*) are also sites of great interest to tourists. Taboos are regularly broken as visitors swim in once-prohibited waters, shine flashlights into once-feared caves, and gather around giant ceiba trees that are also spirit dwellings. These places of thicker meaning, and social relations that regulate interaction with such places, thin out with tourism. The irony is that this happens as tourists search for sites of more cultural depth—the hearths of a more primal life.

NGOs and Place

Whether their objectives are to vaccinate children, teach farmers how to raise fish, strengthen civil society, or protect threatened areas, NGOs are involved in place-altering and place-making activities that influence the locations and conditions in which people live. These activities are at the heart of what Sack refers to as "the geographic problematic." He explains this problematic in three stages: The first is that as humans, we cannot accept reality as it is, and thus are always in the process of transforming it; the second is that this transformation involves constructing places with boundaries and rules, which allow us to undertake projects; the third is that we engage in this process because we imagine what reality should be, and act accordingly. Since this process is filled with ideas of what *ought* to be done or not done in a particular place, it is replete with moral issues (Sack 2001a). Cresswell argues that these "expectations about behavior in place" directly influence the construction and maintenance of ideological values (Cresswell 1996, 4).

With regard to ecotourism, moral issues arise in the conscious or unconscious attempts to preserve thickness of place, which is reflected in terms such as "authenticity" and "tradition." If we agree that culture is forever changing and adapting, then by what measure is authenticity determined, and who decides what is and isn't authentic? Whose voices and power are exercised in the valorization of local culture? For most anthropologists, questions of morality mark the borders of a danger zone. But for applied anthropologists, and other practitioners working with NGOs, they represent the core of questions that should be asked and, if at all possible, answered.

Intervention of almost any sort is place altering, and should be evaluated not merely on the instrumentality of concrete project goals, but also on intangibles such as perspective and awareness that allow people to see how their home and work places are affected by other people and places. The meanings and social relations affected by interventions should foster creativity and release cultural energy, rather than mask them with an insistence on tradition and authenticity—or stifle them by pushing unquestioned technology. People who have to deal with the extraordinary or mundane consequences of change should be managing the thinning and thickening processes that affect their communities. When they don't, normative geographies and social settings are prescribed from without, and sustainability becomes nothing more than a catchword.

In the final section, I bring these arguments to the ground by returning to the RICANCIE project and the impacts of ecotourism in the Ecuadorian Amazon. I offer specific examples of where I see opportunities for the development of perspectives and awareness realized, or squelched.

Community-Based Ecotourism and the Power of Place

Tourism in the Ecuadorian Amazon started with a few lodges that opened in the 1960s. With the rising interest in the rainforest and its inhabitants, the number of lodges and camps has grown dramatically. Only in the past decade, however, have indigenous communities begun to play a significant role in tourist activities beyond being mere attractions. In a guide to ecotourism in the Ecuadorian Amazon, Wesche and Drumm focus on community-based ecotourism projects, which they define as "enterprises which are located in indigenous territories and which are owned and/or operated by indigenous people" (Wesche and Drumm 1999, 15). One such community-based project, RICANCIE, was the focus of field research in 1997 and 1998.

The RICANCIE project began in 1993 with a group of Quichua communities in the Tena-Archidona area of Ecuador's Napo province. The Quichua indigenous federation in Napo, reacting to the success of the community of Capirona in starting its own tourism project, agreed to form an ecotourism network as an economic alternative to oil and timber development, and as a way to valorize local culture. RICANCIE currently has ten member communities, each with its own ecotourism project. A central office in Tena helps develop tourism infrastructures in the communities, channels tourists, and serves as a facilitator between the network and governmental and nongovernmental organizations.

Funding that targets ecotourism and other development projects is usually channeled through several layers of nongovernmental structure. RICANCIE is at the bottom of this structure, and represents a base organization that works directly with communities. While RICANCIE was born beneath the guidance and support of the Federación de Organizaciones Indígenas del Napo, it has gradually gained a degree of autonomy. Thus, as a network that aggregates community-based groups, such as village councils and local tourism projects, and ties them into various development organizations, RICANCIE takes on the functions of a GRSO that provides both horizontal and vertical linkages. The Tena-based office solicits technical assistance, loans, and tourism contacts nationally and internationally, then works through local governance structures to develop ecotourism projects.

While RICANCIE is truly Quichua owned and operated, it has come together with the guidance and financial support of a number of NGOs. Managing this process involves grant writing; planning and design of infrastructures; training of guides, cooks, accountants, and administrators; and communicating with tour operators, various levels of government, and the hundreds of tourists that visit network communities each year. It also means identifying and marketing products that are attractive to tourists.

The flora and fauna of the rainforest are of obvious interest to travelers visiting the Amazon. But so are the indigenous cultures that have lived there for thousands of years. When these cultures become part of commercial ventures, they are treated like any other product that must be packaged and promoted if it is to sell. Commercial tour operators have traditionally done much of the packaging of the Amazon, but in the past decade indigenous individuals, organizations, and communities have also become directly involved in tourism. Their involvement, often mediated by NGOs interested in environmental protection and sustainable development, has both challenged and extended the discourse that defines Amazonian cultures as tourism products. This affects how indigenous people see themselves, and how they are seen by others.

The apparent cultural hodgepodge that is ecotourism actually unfolds in particular "places," where at least some rules govern the encounter. RICANCIE has worked out a list of regulations and suggestions for tourists to save embarrassment and confusion on both sides of the encounter. A separate set of guidelines applies to community members working in the tourism project. Beyond these explicit rules, guides or other intermediaries can help sort through problems. The point is that tourism is carried out in specific "places," and it is the characteristics of these places that determine how habitats of meaning overlap and intersect.

A key to understanding the dynamics of each realm in Sack's model, and thus to understanding the dynamics of place, is to map the flows of elements as they enter, and travel through, specific places. The Quichua communities in the Tena-Archidona area are places into which distinct flows of these elements have mixed. The intrusions of oil and timber companies into community lands brought new meanings to resource use (the realm of nature) and group resistance (the realm of social relations). The identity politics of indigenous federations has stirred the realm of meanings, leading to new leadership roles (social relations) and ethnicity-based mobilizations. Ecotourism has also led to changes in those communities that host visitors.

The Edenic narrative in Amazonian ecotourism generates an environmental discourse that, to varying degrees, leads to reflection on the use-value of the rainforest. The insistence on cultural authenticity puts a heavy emphasis on those aspects of local life that can be presented for tourist consumption. And the skill development and pay scales associated with tourism project managers, treasurers, guides, cooks, dancers, and canoeists means local social relations are shuffled. These impacts and changes vary from place to place, determined not just by the local content of the three realms identified by Sack, but also how they overlap, and how porous their borders are with regard to the entrance of new meanings, ideas, and relationships.

The degree to which NGOs contribute to local-level empowerment and sustainable development is related to the quality of relationships and communication. For meanings and social relations within an NGO to be adaptable and responsive to needs emanating from communities, there has to be an unobstructed flow of ideas from the bottom up. In the Amazon, NGOs and government organizations often promote a stereotypical indigenous community as a way of marketing tourism. Responding to a long history that describes a culturally or ecologically noble savage, these organizations push notions of authenticity and purity in the making of indigenous tourism sites.

An environmental NGO that supports the RICANCIE project thus compiled a long list of suggestions for improving services and making communities presentable: Don't use animal hides or dead birds as cabin adornments (plants are better); place gardens in cabin areas; make paths in areas where tourists can see the most forest; develop rest stops in areas where certain plants or insects can be discussed; revive traditional games and stories for tourists to enjoy; and display traditional indigenous skills such as using blowguns, weaving baskets, and setting traps. RICANCIE has its own list of guidelines for maintaining "authenticity": Guides should use the native *shigra* bag, made of palm fiber, rather than backpacks. They should avoid wearing sunglasses and T-shirts with drawings and foreign phrases, and opt for native hats rather than caps with foreign words. In constructing cabins, care should be taken in the use of cement, blocks, wire, and tin bought in the city. Traditional materials are preferable. In the kitchen, build a good fireplace, and use the gas stove only when necessary. For lighting, use candles and reduce reliance on generators. When music is played, do so on traditional instruments, and eliminate stereo systems.

What new "habitats of meaning" might intersect at the local level via these flows of meaning? Certainly, the discourse of sustainable development and environmental protection is circulated much more thoroughly than before through the Quichua communities that make up RICANCIE, as they are tied to funding sources that promote these values. The technicians in the central office, all Quichua, have attended various workshops and courses, both nationally and internationally. They communicate information gathered during these experiences to member communities. For example, the plan of operations for 1997 includes the strategy of turning the ecotourism project into "an alternative for insertion into the market," which requires strengthening skills and technical capabilities. The plan calls for three-day workshops in each RICANCIE community to "reorganize the administrative system." Plans for the following year call for similar workshops to develop management and business skills.[5] RICANCIE reports mention these "general strategies" as part of the organization's efforts to promote "reflection and capacity building" among member communities.

In the "General Strategy of the Project," outlined in the 1997 report mentioned above, RICANCIE specifically mentions the development of capabilities and awareness of new challenges and possibilities as ultimate goals:

> If the management of ecotourism appears as the primary motivator of the organization, then this has an integral perspective that considers three fundamental points of action: the conservation and sustainable management of natural resources in the productive arena; the development of technical skills and the realization of their own capacities by the population that allows them to confront their conditions; and the social and organizational strengthening of the base.

This involves changing habitats of meaning with regard to how people see themselves and their relationships with outside organizations. As Emilio Grefa, RICANCIE's head of community development, stated in an interview in 1998, the objective is to "gradually eliminate paternalism" that comes with outright grants. "Now we're going to cut the grants, and we're going to provide credit, so they themselves can become responsible for care of the cabins, all the materials. . . . Considering that they have many needs, we're controlling, or putting the brakes on, so that they become more aware, and are more responsible to care for things."

What evidence is there that RICANCIE's activities promote the development of perspectives, or an enhanced sense of their place and potentials within the tourism industry? I think this question can be answered in part by analyzing the discourse and actions of community members and administrators that make up the RICANCIE network. In interviews that I conducted during fieldwork, in meetings I attended, and in documents I reviewed in the RICANCIE office, I got the distinct impression that activities are geared toward building on democratic principles traditionally valued by lowland Quichua, while also expanding awareness through formal education and experiential learning. A regular cycle of meetings, workshops, and community visits leads to continuous planning, evaluation, and modification of project goals. It is through this process of direct community involvement that the negative impacts of ecotourism can be mitigated, and the potential for economic and social benefits can be realized.

In a 1998 interview, Samuel Grefa, a guide in the RICANCIE community of Río Blanco, indicated that money earned from ecotourism was used to educate his children. He wanted to push the community to open bank accounts in Tena so a percentage of earnings could be saved to meet future needs of the ecotourism project, and also for investment in other productive activities. It was clear that the less tangible dimensions of awareness, perspectives, and self-respect were also important. In the following quote, Samuel suggests how Quichua people might respond to the power that outsiders have historically exercised in representing and controlling indigenous peoples.

> If we are owners of the Amazon, we have to work with tourism. . . . Maybe write a book saying we are the ones who have lived here in the Amazon. The Quichua people haven't been able to have our people trained as technicians, such as anthropologists, lawyers. Maybe we could get together with all the anthropologists, to sit and discuss, to write a good book about the Amazon—to say that we are the ones who have lived here, not those who come from outside.

Documents from RICANCIE meetings are also filled with the debates, arguments, ideas, and adjustments that I believe constitute the growth of perspectives through a process of laborious reflection. For example, the minutes from an early meeting of RICANCIE's general assembly of administrators and community representatives (August 30, 1994), indicate discussion of a number of issues affecting the well-being of Quichua communities. In addition to discussing ecotourism activities and ways to improve the project, assembly members also debated a protracted fight with oil companies; the development of various courses in cooking, guiding, accounting, and community organization; and the expenditure and management of project funds, which included calculations on how to take advantage of exchange rates between the sucre and the dollar. A long list of "various issues" discussed at the end of the meeting included a reprimand of community members who drink liquor during tourism programs ("This will bring grave problems to our programs"); a protest against an NGO that had sent researchers studying medicinal plants and shamanism to Río Blanco without community permission; and the suggestion that visitors pay a fee to support both the community visited and the provincial indigenous organization.

Taquino Tapuy, a Quichua leader who helped found, and is director of, RICANCIE, is convinced that the organization's efforts have helped these indigenous communities accumulate important social capital. When asked about this during a 1998 interview, he pointed to the growing confidence and capabilities of Cesar Andi, the manager of the tourism project in RICANCIE's cornerstone community of Capirona, and Augustine Grefa, the guide in Río Blanco. "We don't have money saved up in the bank, but we have Cesar, we have Augustine, we have other colleagues in the communities who now will help you plan, who now will push you, who now will criticize you, who now will question you—who in general help us to generate ideas, to improve things. . . ." The skills and knowledge that appear to be developing through RICANCIE's intervention are applicable not only to tourism-related activities, but also to a variety of other economic, political, and cultural endeavors.

How does the expanded vision developing within RICANCIE affect the communities that make up the network? One way is through an emphasis on education. The organization devotes part of the money it receives from funding sources and tourism profits to scholarships for students from member communities. It also empowers communities to make their own decisions about how to distribute tourism income. The community of Capirona uses ecotourism profits to hire schoolteachers, invest in a communal health care policy, and provide low- and no-interest loans to members. Through its centralized organizational and administrative functions, RICANCIE also facilitates the flow of ideas and experiences between member communities and other indigenous groups. In regular assemblies and workshops, people elected by member communities discuss and make policies that affect not only the tourism projects themselves, but also the manner in which those projects affect other aspects of community life.

Meetings that drag on into the morning hours, the presence of RICANCIE community members in that organization's administrative structure, a built-in flexibility that allows communities autonomy over important financial and cultural issues, and a home-grown sense of democracy are all important elements of a reflexive and responsive institution. Such an institution, I believe, encourages truly sustainable development through which perspectives can be elevated, and the important moral issues of place-making debated. This requires an intimate understanding of local and extra-local habitats of meaning, and regular evaluation of the changes taking place when those habitats intersect.

Projects based on a more paternalistic sense of doing good for the downtrodden, rather than allowing a local sense of what is good and proper to emerge, may meet short-term instrumental goals, but fall short of truly sustainable development. If the sometimes inefficient processes of negotiation, debate, and consensus are allowed to run their course, then project beneficiaries might work out hybrid arrangements informed by an expanding knowledge of how their capabilities can benefit from, and contribute to, exchanges with other peoples and places.

10

Disencumbering Development

Alleviating Poverty Through
Autonomy in Chiapas

Jeanne Simonelli and Duncan Earle

Indians do not seem mysterious or poetic to me.
What happens is that they live in atrocious poverty.

—*Rosario Castellanos*

The people of Cerro Verde are poor. They lack capital resources, though not spirit or potential. They explain this fact to foreigners who happen to visit their enclave at the edge of the jungle in southern Chiapas, on the chance that some NGO or donor will take interest in their plight. At times they are hungry, subsisting on black beans and corn tortillas in an environment where the corn they grow only lasts three months and the coffee they produce sells for two or three pesos a pound. Acculturated Tojolobal Mayas, they are neither mysterious nor poetic, yet while they live in economic poverty, they would be the first to describe the relative richness and strength of their community life.

For the past four years the people of Cerro Verde have been the recipients of various forms of outside aid, initiated by IDEFEM, a UN-funded NGO, and continued through contacts with foundations, facilitated by the authors. This process has constituted a ongoing discussion between community members, NGO staff, anthropologists, and students. Its course has generated reflection and analysis on the part of all parties, including the NGO, as well as stimulating a long-term dialogue between the community and ourselves. In the following pages, we use this experience to examine the relationship between NGOs and community development, to reflect upon the community's own definition of poverty and well-being, critique the NGO enterprise itself, and offer up a model for change.

Community Development in a Conflict Zone

Chiapas, an agrarian and primary-resource state in southern Mexico, has experienced escalating political tension and violent strife for decades, culminating in the Zapatista uprising on January 1, 1994. Coinciding with the signing of the North American Free Trade Agreement (NAFTA), the rebellion responded to long-standing patterns of exploitation and discrimination in this region of rich land and poor people, and the failure of more peaceable methods to effect change (Earle 1994; Ross 1995).

The fall in the price of oil in 1982, the subsequent collapse of the peso, and the international financial bailout that followed, laid the groundwork for a decline in living standards for the indigenous and *campesino* (rural) peoples of Chiapas. As the Mexican government sought more foreign loans in the beginning of 1986, they agreed to remove food subsidies and to retreat from social programs in order to comply with economic reforms mandated for continued international funding. Declines in social programs paralleled the escalation and expression of guerilla activity in the most marginal areas of the state, eventually coalescing at the moment of the signing of NAFTA.

The purpose of NAFTA was to open economic borders between the United States, Mexico, and Canada through "free trade." Though free trade should benefit all levels of producers in Chiapas, it has allowed foreign and national businesses to bypass local governments in decisions concerning use or sale of resources. A precursor to NAFTA was the reform of Article 27 of the Mexican Constitution, which allowed for the private sale of communally held *ejido* land. This and other constitutional changes erode and betray the agrarian reforms of the Mexican revolution. They were changes dictated from the top without consultation with those impacted at the bottom.

The Zapatista uprising began with ten days of fighting in 1994, followed by a cease-fire that led to stillborn peace accords inked in 1996. Since that time, low intensity warfare has continued, notoriously exemplified by the massacre of forty-seven women, children, and men in the village of Acteal in December 1997. A massive military presence, the support for irregular military forces in rural communities, and a harassment policy against foreign scholars and activists have characterized the war.

In July 2000, Vicente Fox defeated the candidate of the *Partido Revolucionario Institucional* (PRI) becoming the first opposition president of Mexico in seventy-one years. One month later, the PRI was also defeated in Chiapas as a coalition candidate was elected governor. Though Fox vowed to end the war in Chiapas "in fifteen minutes" and the Zapatistas traveled to Mexico City in March 2001 to address the Mexican Congress with the intent of reactivating the moribund peace process, little has been accomplished. A new indigenous law was approved by a majority of Mexican states in July 2001, but Chiapas and other states with high indigenous populations refused to ratify the document. The full peace agreement has not been honored and the law does not recognize indigenous autonomy, as the previously negoti- ated versions of the peace accords had done (Coordinadora 2001). In spite of the continuing conflict and yet another failure of the political culture at the top of the structures of power in Mexico, in the countryside non-Zapatista and Zapatista communities-in-resistance in several areas of the state try to live peacefully and autonomously. Many, like those in Cerro Verde, feel that they are in the eye of a storm, planting seeds of peace in the fields of war, as they struggle to develop their communities using their own models for change.

Our assessment of NGO involvement with community development in Chiapas continues in this political environment. It builds on two decades of work with community development among Maya and other rural communi- ties, and recent intensive research in the Río Chayote region of the state.[1] The Río Chayote is a frontier region colonized in the 1950s by Mayas exiled from other areas by politics, religion, and demography. Some of these were highland people in search of land where they could grow coffee for sale and corn for survival. Others were Mayas whose parents spoke the Tojolobal language, but who rapidly lost their linguistic heritage. Adding to this com- plex mix, beginning in the 1980s, refugees from the Guatemalan violence settled in the area. During this same period, the internal conflict in Chiapas deepened, and public sector social provisioning declined as a result of struc- tural adjustments associated with neoliberal reforms.

In response to the influx of refugees, aid agencies began to promote com- munity development. These included local NGOs, Mexican government pro- grams, and massive international aid. Most programs reflected donor agency policy and concerns, targeting Guatemalans and not Mexicans; women and children rather than families; production, but not marketing. Social, economic, and political upheaval in the area intensified after 1994. Refugee communi- ties exceeded 120 settlements with some 150,000 inhabitants at their peak (Verillo and Earle 1993, 228). Zapatista supporters declared the area autono- mous, and the government established a formidable military presence. Though often divided politically, all settlements faced common problems, including economic uncertainty from having limited land (made more intractable by the official termination of agrarian reform) and constrained access to mar- kets. In addition, settlements also dealt with political uncertainty and anxiety stemming from efforts to steer between the parties in conflict. They attempted to maintain a viable community organization, while negotiating complex relations with each other and a variety of outsiders.

The village[2] of Cerro Verde was one of the earliest settlements established in the region and had at its heart an ejido, or cooperative landholding group, founded by Maya and non-Maya settlers. In 1993, the Cerro Verde community faction began a process of reflection, which led to a declaration of resistance in the ejido's communitary assembly. The community faction established its own school and health clinic, being careful at the same time to honor their commitment to provide cooperative agricultural labor and other legally stipulated services to the larger ejido.

In 1997, Simonelli began working with IDEFEM, a United Nations–funded NGO, whose official charge was to work with Guatemalan refugee communities in the Chayote region. IDEFEM proposed and initiated numerous microproduction projects, and, like so many other aid agencies in the area, their failures outnumbered their successes. Cerro Verde was one of the communities included in this NGO's programs. Duncan Earle contributes a historical perspective and comparative data, drawing on his twenty-five years of research in the region, which focused on a community (Ojo de Agua) with a very different social and political profile.[3]

As a community-in-resistance, Cerro Verde has made continued efforts to coexist with those on the other side of the conflict. Using legal and peaceful means, community members have met challenges to their continued participation in the ejido that they helped found. They have well-formed and carefully considered ideas about the shape they would like development to take in their community and in the region. In the face of a devastating decline in coffee prices, the community is attempting to find avenues of peaceful and sustainable market development. Further, by embracing an alternative process by which they govern their community and educate a new generation through their alternative vision of schooling, they seek to take control over this process of "guided change" we have often called community development (CD).

NGOs and Development

In Chiapas, as elsewhere, NGOs often promote development initiatives that compensate for the decline in national public sector programs or provide international humanitarian aid. Ranging from well-endowed and familiar organizations like Save The Children to poorly financed local or regional programs, they bring diverse agendas and visions to their efforts (Black 1999, 85–89; Edwards and Hulme 1996).

While some see NGO projects as a panacea for myriad development short-comings (Bauzon 1992), others view their activities as just extensions of the neoliberal program. At one extreme, many NGOs internalize the notion that their programs are short-term bridges on the long road to privatization, promoting economic opportunities that are seen as part of the process of liberalization (Duffield 1997, 174; Hackenberg 1999; Warren 1998, 4; World Bank/ NGOs 2000). At the other extreme, the organizations act as spokespersons for civil society in rebellion, seeing their alternative development initiatives as ways to subvert and circumvent the system (Burgerman 1998; Nash 2001, 228–31). Orlove (1999, 199) notes that "social movements have an affinity to NGOs that can promote them and channel their efforts." Given this diverse and skewed set of perceptions, what "good" do NGOs actually do? What role, if any, should social scientists take (Gardner and Lewis 1996, 160–68)?

The results of studies that examine specific projects and organizations highlight barriers to efficacious programs at all levels of action and involvement. Focusing on the relationship between organizational philosophy and program efficacy in Senegal, Roberts notes that success on the local level was linked to the ways in which NGO staff replicated donor ideals in actual programs (2000, 159–71). However, Gezon cites the exclusion of targeted people from project design as a difficulty in going from ideals to structure (2000, 200). She also notes that while some NGO projects undertake needs assessments with communities, these results are often ignored or used only to legitimize organizational undertakings (2000, 203–4). While including the target population and indigenous knowledge in program planning is a recent and frequent exhortation (Sillitoe 1998; Gezon 2000, 208), Loker (2000) points out that determining who speaks for which community interest may not be easy. This echoes Long's (1992, 5) observation that when working with projects and the numerous stakeholders involved with them, we are dealing with "multiple realities."

Moreover, while paying lip service to the need to consult with those who are to be aid recipients, donor organizations are still unable to translate that insight into program definition. In a video conference between World Bank representatives and members of a Chiapas weaving cooperative, designed to get local input into bank planning, the bank was unable to envision a project that functioned outside of a preconceived model of how development should take place (Wake Forest 2000; see also Hines 2000, 186–89). Such inflexibility in both ideology and practice can undermine projects from the outset. This is particularly true with those programs involved in humanitarian aid, where organizations are unable or unwilling to underwrite long periods of integrated analysis and capacity building (Earle and Simonelli 2000, 118; Rew 1997, 101–2).

The patterns of problems identified in these and other individual studies indicate that there are generalizations to be made concerning what works and what doesn't in community development, and these generalizations provide a series of metaphors that define NGO practices. Although it has been suggested that there are too many exceptions to be able to create a rule, we maintain that the questions raised by studies of a specific NGO are those of all NGOs. Moreover, in this case, outlining the problems of a particular NGO leads us to consider the interface between the NGO and the community, and what this interaction tells us about NGOs and community development.

Consequently, our contribution as anthropologists comes from examining both the developers and the recipients, assessing the economic processes, the political economy, the cultural logics, and the social landscape of rural communities, as well as those of the NGOs tasked to help them. As social scientists, it is important for us to clarify the process of NGO intervention in the development endeavor, while allowing analytic space for the subjects to speak to the same issue. At the same time, we avoid the naive notion that attention to indigenous knowledge and bottom-up decision making can, of itself, lead to positive change in previously underempowered communities (Sillitoe 1998, 233).

Converting Poverty to Prosperity

As practicing anthropologists, it is our experience in the field rather than the library that forces us to confront, both for ourselves and for those who work in the collection of disciplines concerned with community development, what is meant by poverty and prosperity. In achieving the latter, material gain itself is not a solution, for this says nothing about whether it is employed to ends that are sustainable, equitable, or even responsible. Most discussions of poverty alleviation will easily accede that we are not talking about individual progress or gain. The community, or at least some significant sector of it, must benefit in order to affirm that poverty has been somehow reduced. Moreover, the absence of resources must be overcome on a long-term basis, if it is to be called overcoming poverty. What, then, would provide reliable indicators of increased well-being for a particular social group or formation? How can we even address the question of whether or not NGOs alleviate poverty if we are unclear about the nature of the disease, and what its cure would look like? In this section, we attempt to refine a definition of poverty, eventually returning to a discussion of whether NGOs can effectively help to convert poverty to prosperity.

At this point in the history of development initiatives, *sustainability* is a term with a pedigree, and despite its many interpretations, the concept does introduce the notion of time-depth and continuity. Clearly, it is not the size of the feast but its frequency and regularity that concerns us when discussing the well-being of those who have little. Contrary to the fiscal-year thinking of corporate and institutional cultures, short-term solutions to long-term problems are a poor fit, and may in fact do harm in the long run. It is safe to say, then, that the alleviation of poverty must be achieved in some sustained form over time.

A sustainable cash flow, equitably distributed to our social unit—the venerable community—is a tempting way to go about defining prosperity, and thereby what poverty is not. The problem with this approach is that it dwells on the outcome, not the process, and it is the process that will determine the sustainability and equitable distribution of the outcome. A focus on process shifts the discussion to questions about *how* resources are secured and distributed in a sustainable fashion. If they are to be secured locally, how can they be gathered in a way that assures the process of doing so does not undermine the future ability to do the same? If gathered through interactions with the outside economy, regional or global, how can these relations remain sustainable in the context of the inevitable and often perplexing fluctuations in the market demand, price, and costs? And beyond this material definition of prosperity and well-being, how can we parsimoniously express what, from the perspective of the people we are attempting to help, this well-being should look like (see Powers 2001, 87–109)?

In our fieldwork we have learned that long-term community welfare cannot always be reduced to project goals, measurable results, or sector-specific successes. Determining development effectiveness requires an in-depth understanding of people's subjective assessments of the benefits they derive, benefits that go beyond monetary or material concerns to measure their internal and external "well-being." Well-being is at its best when people desire less than they have, and feel secure that they will continue to have it in the future, for themselves, for those they care for, and for those upon whom they depend. Increased well-being also ties into the amount people feel in control of their lives, which is their ability to reliably expect future well-being.

If development can provide conditions, systems, technologies, or knowledge that will help people gain a greater well-being on their own terms, then there will have been a development success. This success must be judged on the basis of its sustainability at the time of intervention and afterwards. It must be observable by objective means and assessable by people's subjective reports. There is a complicated algebra by which participants in community development assess their own well-being, a complex balance between material and social value.

Consequently, another approach to the problem is to discuss poverty as lack or loss of control. Prosperity, or *positive* CD, can then be defined as the process of gaining control, especially over those factors determining the well-being of those for whom one is responsible. A shift to the issue of control frees us from consideration of material indicators, be they last year's income, current nutritional biometric indicators, or any other concrete measurement of people's possessions and health status. Using control as a proxy leads to considerations of power, information, and its management, and the responsive flexibility of social and economic arrangements.

For the people we are learning from in the field, control over one's personal and community life is *the* community development issue. It is from this starting point that the alleviation of poverty, and equitable and sustainable prosperity of the community is seen to flow. By examining NGO operations in the Río Chayote region from this perspective, it is evident that well-meaning efforts have failed to address control issues, and by this avenue have betrayed the process of poverty alleviation.

IDEFEM: Metaphors for Mistakes

> At the end of these years the story of the development of [IDEFEM's] projects has been a list of good guesses and errors, an intense reflection concerning our work with indigenous women, as designed and implemented by mestiza women. (Duran Duran 2001, 2)

Claudia Duran Duran, the most recent director of IDEFEM, died unexpectedly on June 18, 2001. Her death at the age of thirty-seven was a tragedy, not just for her family and friends, but also for the communities with whom she worked. In her final year guiding the NGO, as the organization struggled, downsized, and searched for funding, Claudia had begun to grow in both practical and theoretical insight concerning the role of IDEFEM in particular and NGOs in general. Perhaps the greatest example of her development as an emerging applied social scientist was the paper she presented just one month earlier at the annual meeting of the Society for Applied Anthropology in Merida, Mexico.[4] Her analysis of IDEFEM's mistakes illustrates the metaphors that best describe NGO shortcomings in their relationship with both communities and donor agencies.

The Missionary Position

Funding organizations define their areas of interest and concern in formal mission statements that also encapsulate their ideologies of aid. That their stated mission directs them to provide financial aid under certain circumstances presupposes a belief that they can and should use that aid to promote change. They seek out situations that allow them to fulfill that mission: generic domains of need, or fields of opportunity that seem to call out for intervention. This expresses a subtle type of paternalism that says that a mission of intervention can be efficacious in the first place.

As intermediaries or ombudsmen, NGOs like IDEFEM solicit resources and implement programs that derive from the interface of the NGO's own mission and the donor's stated intent. The ideas and plans of larger funding agencies and donors are translated into actual programs in diverse cultural and geographical settings, regardless of the particular conditions of each specific place and point in time.

As a woman-focused NGO, IDEFEM was selected to implement programs of the United Nations High Commission for Refugees (UNHCR) because of a perceived goodness of fit between the stated missions of the two groups. UNHCR's mission includes the statement that "UNHCR pays particular attention to the needs of children and seeks to promote equal rights of women and girls" (UNHCR 2001, 2). In like manner, IDEFEM's work was always presented through the perspective of gender, looking to find a way to make the relations between men and women more equitable. With these goals in mind, the funds the NGO received were earmarked for specific types of programs, and there was little wiggle room in terms of project design. As Duran Duran notes:

> The design of the projects was subject to the vision not just of the implementers, but in a greater part to that of the financiers. In our case, this was the United Nations High Commission for Refugees. Planning excluded those who were recipients of the programs, for which we received serious criticism from the women and communities. (2001, 2)

IDEFEM's projects were aimed at diminishing poverty through specific activities designed for a specific sector of the population. Targeting women and children, interventions were devised using the perspective of urban feminism, which focused on individualism at the expense of the community. Yet those working for IDEFEM soon realized that there were serious differences between the notions of gender held by both the donor and the implementing NGO, and that of groups with whom they worked. According to Duran Duran, "these [ideas] developed from an analysis of socioeconomic and cultural conditions radically different from those that develop in an indigenous, rural environment" (2001, 2).

Realizing that the financial agents were trying to impose work schemes that did not correspond to the "Maya cosmovision," IDEFEM eventually diverted designated funds into projects that were a better fit with the cultural and political logic of the region. Needless to say, they quickly ran into problems with their donors (Earle and Simonelli 2000).

IDEFEM's initial years of work, carried out according to their own mission and that of UNHRC, became the field analysis that should have taken place prior to any work at all with and in the communities. Duran Duran concluded that finding methods to alleviate poverty under the difficult conditions of the Chiapas conflict required an analysis of the social and political barriers to alternative development (2001, 5). Yet there are few funding agencies willing to finance this type of microlevel study of a particular group of people responding to a specific set of circumstances that, *in general*, fit the mission of the organization. A belief in *proyectismo* (projectism), or the project as object, excludes the possibility of developing from below. It leaves communities stuck in a missionary position: where assuming the validity of the mission silences the voices of the people.

McDevelopment

As noted earlier, there are few funding agencies that do not at least pay lip service to the notion that communities should be involved in decisions concerning the nature of donor/NGO sponsored projects. According to the UNHCR mission statement, "UNHCR is committed to the principle of participation by consulting refugees on decisions that affect their lives" (UNHCR 2001, Part 2). Often, this is manifested in a fast-food model of community involvement in its own development decisions. For IDEFEM, the model involved a process of action-reflection-action. They offered women's groups a limited menu of possible projects, for instance a choice between a selection of small-scale productive activities, including hens, horticulture, or rabbits (action). The women retired to discuss these possibilities (reflection). Later, they would "decide to accept" one of the proffered activities (action). Thus, the illusion that grassroots decision making led to the acceptance of a project was preserved for all.

Since a donor's overall mission gives rise to particular areas of aid, NGOs often struggle to come up with projects that correspond to foundation assessments of what they see as the poverties of local life. According to IDEFEM, all their productive projects were intended to respond to set objectives, both social and economic. Thus, mission-determined McDevelopment limited the form a project might take, and ultimately short-circuited any realistic and practical ideas the community might have concerning the alleviation of their own poverty. NGO projects were directed at the production of commodities for local consumption, particularly products to improve the immediate nutrition of women and children. Community groups, on the other hand, were more interested in converting these activities into something that might be commercialized, with long-term benefit for all. For them, social transformation without economic outcome was useless. Economic outcome with culturally inappropriate social transformation was also unacceptable. But in spite of the contradictions, group after group chose to eat from IDEFEM's fastfood menu of projects. As we learned from IDEFEM's experiences, communities will agree to participate in NGO projects even if they are determined to be useless by all the stakeholders if the NGO is seen to control access to other valued resources, including information.

Sustainabullity[5]

IDEFEM, like other NGOs, has a continuing interest in its own longevity as an organization. Continued funding is usually contingent on the ability to claim success in project development and implementation, which provides the ultimate justification for sustaining the program's infrastructure. Successes are presented to the donor in an annual report, a positive portrayal of the results of the previous year's work. In short, the organization that has the best line of bull concerning program success is most likely to sustain the organization.

IDEFEM was born out of a split with a sister NGO and brought into its own mission that group's goals: to promote projects with refugee women to help overcome existing gender inequalities between men and women (Mama Maquin-CIAM 1994, 16). Yet IDEFEM's years of fieldwork eventually brought into question both of those foci. To work only with refugees in an area where everyone was poor and struggling seemed unethical. To work only with women and children was divisive. As the conflict in Chiapas deepened after 1997, the idea of provisioning one group of communities at the expense of another seemed like a really bad plan (Earle and Simonelli 2000, 109–11). Moreover, while their annual reports described the widespread acceptance of IDEFEM projects, in actuality the hens had been eaten, and the home gardens were covered with weeds (IDEFEM 1998).

Emerging from the NGO's own reflection was a series of conclusions and solutions. These included changing the paternalistic and protective attitude toward the communities, supporting communities' efforts at designing their own programs, making programs inclusive rather than exclusive on all levels, and limiting the duration of involvement of the NGO in a particular project or community (Duran Duran 2001, 6). All this added up to the same thing. To continue to receive funding meant to write reports that included the obfuscation of the actual results.

Paralleling IDEFEM's reanalysis of their own shortcomings, project beneficiaries also provided a critique of the pitfalls of sustainabullity. They saw themselves as pawns in a process by which NGO staff wrote reports ensuring their own continued employment at the expense of viable community projects. On yet another level, the competition between NGOs for limited funding also meant that sharing information about project success or failure with each other was also out of the question. NGOs working in the same circumscribed geographical region sometimes replicated each other's failed projects, since to make this information public might undermine their efforts to sustain funding.

As the last Guatemalans returned to their country or became Mexican citizens, the NGO's life cycle as a provider of aid to refugees was coming to an end. Nevertheless, IDEFEM could have continued to be a viable avenue for women-focused projects. Instead, the group attempted to change their organizational focus to a unit of investigation that was not "politically correct." This included work in politically divided villages, and within these, with families as a whole rather than women and children. This stance became the kiss of death for the NGO.

Ethnographic Poverty: With Whom Are We Dealing?

A defining characteristic of anthropology as an academic discipline has been the use of in-depth ethnography as a means of learning about other cultural traditions. One unfortunate artifact of the division of labor within our broad field is that the detailed, comprehensive ethnographic studies of traditional ethnologists typically do not produce knowledge for applied ends. Rarely do we see in print lengthy tomes discussing the testing of applied anthropology concepts in specific communities by means of participant-observation techniques. This is truly unfortunate, for how can we know the specifics of what we must do to affect positive change if we do not know the community?

If we are to attempt to increase control over the CD process by the community and its leadership, we must know who the players are, what their social relations are, and what constitute the obstacles, resources, challenges, and possibilities. This is the kind of information that does not usually emerge from a brief visit or a hit-and-run survey methodology, in spite of what our colleagues in applied anthropology have written in the past (Schensul 2000, 21–23). The lack of such information is one more field-derived example of what NGOs should consider in their encounters with communities in need. It might be called the "poverty of ethnography."

This process of doing in-depth ethnographic analysis is not simple or easy, any more than say, learning a Mayan language to talk with the Mayas. While we are not saying we must all learn the indigenous languages of the people with whom we work, we are suggesting that ethnographic field work should be considered as a precursor to action in any community culturally, socially, economically, politically, and/or ecologically distinct from our own. Otherwise, we may not be able to understand what people mean by what they are saying; or worse, we may think we know and yet do not. Local people may even facilitate our misunderstandings, lacking the ability or motivation to disabuse us of our misconceptions; concerned, as many are, that if they do not reinforce our false understandings, they may lose resources in the end. This becomes their own expression of sustainabullity (Simonelli 2002).

Our years of work in the field lead us to conclude that there is no substitute, no adequate quick-fix alternative, to solid knowledge of the community in which interventions of any sort are to be attempted. We invite those who say there is not sufficient time to look at the decades of failure, for which there seems to have been plenty of time. For those who complain about expense, we submit that ethnography is inexpensive, and it frequently represents huge savings in terms of project and program failures averted. For those who say NGOs do not have the skills to carry it out, we answer, hire ethnographers, they are less costly than most NGO consultants in the more technical fields, and they are superabundant and underemployed (see Escobar 1998, 508).[6]

Rarely has ethnography been employed as an integral part of the preplanning stage of an NGO intervention, and as a way of establishing interactive, ongoing dialogue with the community. The reasons, we believe, have less to do with the issues mentioned above regarding time and expense, and more to do with NGO and donor culture, ideology, and institutionalization. In Table 10.1 we contrast this orientation with the ethnographic orientation of anthropology as we embrace it.

Autonomy as a Measure of Control over Life

For the indigenous and poor campesinos all over Mexico, March 2001 was a time of excitement and hope. The Zapatistas, accompanied by their spokesperson, Subcomandante Marcos, made a triumphant journey to Mexico City. Ultimately, representatives of the Zapatista leadership addressed the Mexican congress. Hopes were high that the *ley indígena*, the Indigenous Law, codifying much of that which had been negotiated in the San Andres peace accords, would finally be enacted. In Cerro Verde, four-year-old Marta looked at the photograph on the cover of *Proceso*, a Mexican news magazine. It showed a teeming and packed central plaza in Mexico City, as citizens of the capital came out to welcome the cadres of masked Zapatistas.

"Who are those people, Mommy?" Marta asked her mother.

"*Son nuestra gente . . .* they are our people," her mother answered proudly.

Table 10.1

Different Approaches to Work with Communities

Most NGOs and donors	Ethnographic/Anthropology
Sectoral/topical focus	Holistic/integrated
Monological	Dialogical
(prior conceptualizations)	(concepts from interaction)
Synchronic (current problems, crisis)	Diachronic (long view, over time)
Outcome orientation	Process and relational orientation
"Apolitical" or cause politics	Politicized neutrality
Surface knowledge of recipients	In-depth knowledge of community
Interaction focused on aided	Interaction with all sectors
Segregate intervention/lifestyle	Integrate research, daily life
Prefigured plan of action	Reconfigured, evolving action plan
Responsible to funders, institutions	Responsible to community, profession

In spite of these moments of pride and optimism, spring ended, the summer rains arrived, and still the Indigenous Law had not been passed. Vicente Fox met with George Bush and Central American leaders, eventually disclosing the details of Plan Puebla Panama, a *maquila* (factory)-based model for the development of the poverty stricken areas of Mexico (see Aubry 2002, 8). In Chiapas, Fox continued to court the NGOs as mediators and implementers of his development plans, a process he had begun even prior to his inauguration as president (Melel 2000a; 2000b).

In early July a modified indigenous law was sent out from the congress for ratification. While on the surface it seemed little changed from what the Zapatistas had demanded from the early days of the rebellion, subtle differences made the two documents worlds apart. The history of these negotiations and dialogue form a major piece of the history of the Zapatista rebellion and are documented elsewhere (see Ross 2000).

The central spirit of both the San Andres accords and the ley indígena as proposed to the congress was indigenous autonomy, not just in Chiapas, but all of Mexico. While recognizing culture, democracy, justice, and women's rights, an important piece of the Zapatista demands also focused on autonomy in development, and deriving from this, the autonomy to use their own perceptions of well-being as a measure of prosperity. This autonomy would allow indigenous groups to make their own decisions concerning natural and biological resources. In contrast, in Plan Puebla Panama, transnational interests supercede these concerns. Consequently, in the law modified by the congress and ultimately ratified by seventeen of twenty-nine Mexican states, notions of indigenous autonomy were weakened and the law made impotent.

While the ratified indigenous law recognizes the right to autonomy in thought, it does not recognize indigenous territory, as apart from national lands. While the law recognizes the use of resources in a collective form, it does not allow for the collective management of those resources, since the only type of ownership recognized is individual. While the San Andres accords stated that local laws, or "uses and customs" *must* be recognized in the management of collectively held resources, the law as ratified changed the word *must* to *can*, thereby changing an obligation for total recognition of autonomy in development to an option. In short, the law permits autonomy, but doesn't allow it to work. Twelve Mexican states, representing the bulk of the indigenous population of Mexico, refused to ratify the indigenous law (Coordinadora 2001). Without the constitutional right to autonomy in the practice of development, the road to prosperity, as defined by communities and the larger autonomous municipalities, was cut.

By 2002, thirty-six autonomous *municipios* existed in Chiapas. In the years following the Zapatista uprising, the PRI government made repeated efforts to short-circuit autonomy by disbanding autonomous governments, including that of Tierra y Libertad, where Cerro Verde is located (see Speed and Collier 2000, 896–900). The Fox government, shying away from military solutions, has used judicial and administrative means to accomplish the same ends. The message was clear. In any form, the Zapatista rebellion was about autonomy. Autonomy, or the right to take control over the administration of everything from rights to resources, was revolutionary. When the Mexican senate modified the San Andres peace accords, removing language they felt was threatening; it was again reiterating the state's fears about granting recognition of local autonomy. When the military destroyed the facilities and arrested the members of the Tierra y Libertad municipality in 1998, it was a reaction to efforts toward effective municipal autonomy (Ross 2000, 216; see also Nash 2001). It was this same exercise of autonomy that the community of Cerro Verde had been working through in its relationship with IDEFEM and subsequent development projects.

Over a year ago, we had taken a development proposal from the community to a small church-related foundation in rural New York. The proposal had been funded; we arrived with the money, and turned over full control to a Cerro Verde committee comprised of two women and two men. The very act of turning over the money had startled the community, used to paternalistic NGO control that doled out project funds like a teenager's weekly allowance.

"What do we do now?" they had asked, taking the zip-lock bag filled with cash.

"It's not our problem," we said, happy to be relieved of the burden of keeping a substantial number of pesos secure.

The community spent months reflecting over the most effective and efficient way to deploy their funds. They rejected the original proposal, a bakery co-op to be run by the women, in the interest of investing in ways to make their coffee crop marketable. They traded bread for coffee; internal markets for external markets. Presenting their findings to us six months later, the women defended the decision.

"Coffee is not just a men's thing, Juanita," said Luz, as if she could hear the criticisms of our San Cristobal feminist friends drifting in on the selva wind. "Coffee is something of the entire family. And we have already invested twenty years in its production. The bread would be something new, taking our energies."

Bread for coffee. Limits for options. Luz braced herself, as if expecting a fight.

"Fine," we said. "It's your project."

With each consecutive visit, the project moved slowly toward realization. The community purchased a coffee dryer and roaster, bought the lumber to build a small structure to house it. They told us about each step shyly, as though still expecting The Patron to emerge from somewhere within our rented Volkswagen Beetle. At the same time, as they determined the exact shape of the project, they were hungry for the information that we could provide for them concerning the logistics and aesthetics of marketing coffee to the world beyond the selva. They were, after all, a community-in-resistance, working to encounter globalism on its own terms, not just counter it with rhetoric, slogans, and epithets.

In the summer of 2001, we visited again, on another project. It was drizzling when we gathered in Cerro Verde, the dense mists of the late rainy season dripping off the edges of a lamina roof. The orange glow of a single light bulb cut through the night, attached to a ragged cord spliced into the electric line that supplied the entire enclave. In the open air ramada a colorful array of notebooks, crayons, pens, pencils, and other school supplies were laid out on a rough wooden table, surrounded by the children and adults of Cerro Verde, Chiapas, and the anthropologists and students of the Maya Summer Program. We came to the community for a four-day stay, arriving in the small red truck belonging to IDEFEM. We carried with us not just school supplies, but also a small sum of donated money, with which we expected to rebuild the group's autonomous school.

We presented the supplies, and bid farewell to sixteen-year-old Ramon, off to complete a six-month teacher's training in the Zapatista stronghold of Realidad. As we did, we learned that we were about to enter into a round of late night dialogue concerning the shape of community development not just in Cerro Verde but also in the autonomous municipality of which it is part. Rather than the ethnographic encounter and designated social service that we anticipated, we would begin discussions with representatives of this municipality, now clandestine and mobile, with whom we would have to negotiate the future of our relationship to the people there.

"Tenemos que hablar . . ."

"Tenemos que hablar, tenemos que consultar entre todos," said Rodrigo, for the third time in one day. We must speak, we have to consult with everyone.

These meetings became a pivotal activity. During an encounter with the elusive representative of the municipio of Tierra y Libertad (Land and Freedom), it became clear that the two entities, the community and the municipality, were negotiating with each other and with us, regarding where the limits of autonomy of a group should lie, and what kind of obligations need arise between the entities involved. We were seen as representatives of potential development resources, whether direct or from a sister city relationship, as they initially proposed. What was taking place in the meetings was the fine-tuning of the daily details of autonomy, how it is "operationalized" as a concept in the face of the need for communication, compromise, and consensus. We were privy to a community development process in which the community struggled even with its most proximate political allies for the right to negotiate their lives on their own. It was all about control.

In an earlier visit to Cerro Verde, the majority of the men had closed themselves up for yet another meeting, this one private. We hung out waiting, where else, but in the kitchen? Most of the women were either there or arrived shortly afterward, and before we knew it there was a meeting happening, to the sound of tortilla making and gurgling babies. The meeting was very animated, everyone opined.

"Is the other meeting in the house just for the men?" asked Duncan.

Luz, one of the leaders, responded casually,

"Yes, they have a meeting with themselves now, and we have ours too; and then, later we meet together. Everyone has a chance to speak of how they see things."

We realized then how we had jumped to conclusions about gender inequality, not respecting the indigenous idea about complementary opposition that precedes the dynamic union, how both segregating and integrating are part of their process of consensus, a part of how they practice autonomy. Through meetings they plumb the sensibility of the whole, in steps and stages, starting with the most familiar issues. Everyone learns to speak.

Their meetings, their desire to consult and dialogue, were key to how they worked so well together, as a conscious community, a community that had arrived at partial self-governance through this process of consultation with all adults (and not a few youths). Self-governance is only partial because they recognize they must still follow the agrarian rules, laid out in the constitution, that dictate obligations to the whole of the ejido community by all its members. So it is a balancing act between larger community obligations that are still acceptable and those that are not, particularly in education and health issues. As we were gradually learning, those were forms and obligations they were developing for themselves, with help from the Zapatista rebels in the form of training. In this, the Zapatistas are an alternative NGO, that, if we can accept the claims they make about themselves, *manda obediciendo* (leads by obeying). They attempt to serve their supporters with practical training in education and health, among other things, providing them with the raw materials for autonomy.

On the road to Cerro Verde, we passed through a military checkpoint bristling with eager officers and their frightened followers. The sign says it is a place of "control," and the officer explained that "we are controlling people on this road." Just as a struggle for control of political space in the development process was to emerge from within the meeting context we had witnessed, so it seemed the forces of the state were trying also to gain control, to win back the development process from the rebels, to reestablish their dominance. Once again, it became clear that autonomy, local ability to gain greater control over one's own life and the lives of those people for whom one feels responsible, is an essential part of the community development equation.

A challenge of NGO work is how to manage an aid organization on one hand, and allow the group being helped to maintain autonomy and control over their lives (and, ideally, gain more of it in the CD process), on the other. Even when people have no clue how they might safely improve their situation, they want to have some control over the process of other people's efforts to help them. This was certainly true of the representative of the autonomous municipality. One of his chief concerns, as he explained it, was that NGOs and others can use their contacts with communities to raise funds that don't reach the community in the end: in essence exploiting the rebels to run an organization and pay outsiders.

"We need to monitor resources that don't get to the people who need them, but are resources which are raised in their name. We need to know who is doing what, and where."

This sounded so familiar. Who controls CD, after all, when NGOs deploy their projects? For the municipality, it was a form of foreign policy.

"We also want to make certain that the truly remote communities are not neglected."

This also sounded familiar. Favoritism, divisionism, was bad development. For the municipality, it was also a form of fiscal policy.

Discussions continued, and a few meetings later, the quick-fix project of rebuilding the school was replaced with the long-range goal of funding education. We became part of a continuing process of consultation and reflection in the construction and evolution of aid initiatives. It was this transition from a defined project to general funding, from external to internal control that was to provide part of the answer to how NGOs can alleviate poverty.

Information: Turning Knowledge into Power

Claudia Duran Duran's frank assessment of IDEFEM's field-based learning experience, coupled with our own work with the same communities, provides us with a ground-level description of that NGO's interactions with communities. These assessments, in conjunction with the Cerro Verde community's own commentary on NGO behaviors, provide the metaphors for mistakes that plague many development initiatives. Yet more than just a set of cute phrases that allow the authors to critique NGO behavior, these descriptions are a road map for change.

Reversing the Missionary Position

The missionary position described above is the ideological inheritance of a crusader orientation. It dictates that we have the problem defined and the solutions sketched out prior to any serious dialogue with the communities we engage, since, as always, father knows best. This represents the gravest obstacle to NGO CD success, because how can we truly listen if the answers preceded the questions, if the plans (and the assumptions that underpin them) preceded the dialogue? If we reject this epistemological hegemony for a more dialogical approach, where doers and recipients negotiate mutually the nature of the relationship, the problems, and the projects, then the discourse must develop some common ground and have mutually informed negotiators. In short, it needs "deep mutual translation" (Earle and Simonelli 2000; Briggs 1986).

Reversing the missionary position means alleviating the poverty of ethnography. Any NGO activity in an area should begin with development ethnography, which, to our minds, differs from traditional ethnological research models because it is symmetrical. Not only are we learning about the regions and the communities we propose to work in, but our "subjects" are able to learn all they need to know about us and our world. Consequently, an initial piece of helping a community to tell us what projects best suit their needs is demystifying the rapidly globalizing world. Only when they have the information that they need to make informed decisions about how they can interface with the world beyond their own boundaries can we begin to talk about project design. Moreover, while we know enough to back away from the blatant paternalism of 1950s and 1960s applied anthropological projects, we must also recognize our tendency to be "maternalistic": to try to protect communities from making the same mistakes our own society has made as it "developed."

Reversing the missionary position also means actually beginning community development with the community. IDEFEM's mission-directed paradigm of action-reflection-action begins the process of community development work at the wrong point in the sequence. Moreover, envisioning the development endeavor in a linear fashion guarantees that nobody gets to learn. By using a circular or cyclical model, with the point of entry as reflection, communities and NGOs are able to construct and deconstruct projects in a fashion that better reflects their own needs.

The participatory action-research models that many social scientists working in community development espouse do not go far enough to produce truly sustainable, long-term prosperity (see Ervin 2000, 199–211). Those proposed by international development agencies like the World Bank do even less (see World Bank 2001). Both the Maya and Zapatista models of decision making, however, provide a template for NGO and anthropologist roles in community development. The consensus-based decision-making process that derives from a lengthy sequence of consultation and dialogue provides a good avenue for deciding community development needs. In this, the NGO worker should act as facilitator, as communities author their own programs armed with the information that we, as conduits to the outside world, can provide for them. Moreover, as the project cycle proceeds, we have a continuing role in the provision of evaluative feedback.

As we learned in our lengthy negotiation with the Cerro Verde community and the autonomous leadership of the Tierra y Libertad municipality, this type of program planning is not amenable to a quick-and-dirty model of involvement. Yet by engaging in ethnographic dialogue, knowledge becomes a source of power for all involved. Our years of working with indigenous communities have made us painfully familiar with the slow but effective process of consensus decision making. Our interactions with the Zapatista model introduced the notion of *manda obediciendo*, to lead by obeying. This seems to be a good metaphor for a role that NGOs and anthropologists could take in development work.[7]

Turning Fast Food Into Gourmet Fare

One of the great contradictions between NGOs and communities of need is that the NGO is almost never in a position of unrestricted giving; yet our thesis is that restrictions are impositions and we must make it possible for communities to be the authors of their own programs. We have seen how this works, and we have seen how this could work. For example, IDEFEM received funding because of a proposal to improve the nutrition of women and children using a fast-food selection of microproduction programs. These not only failed, but also divided the community along gender lines in the process. An alternative to this might be to fund an NGO that is trusted by a community to do the groundwork to develop a program that would ultimately lead to improved nutrition.

This summer in Cerro Verde, a lengthy discussion between Maya program students interested in maize agriculture (*milpa*) and coffee production yielded unexpected information concerning the importance of women in a work area frequently seen as inherently male. As such, it was often excluded from funding by donors with a gender focus. But when conversation turned to using organic fertilizers rather than chemical fertilizers, the men deferred to the women. We learned that women actually play a key role: Cerro Verde women produce all the organic fertilizers through composting. Because agricultural goods, including coffee and corn, get processed close to home, their residue is easily available for the women to use in a complex, layer cake system of composting that is later used in both the milpas and the *cafetales*. According to both the men and women, use of organic fertilizers increased yields in the long run, thus leading to better nutrition (more corn and beans to eat, more coffee to sell) for everyone, not just the women and children. Recognizing the importance of women in production areas seen as male controlled could allow gender-focused NGOs to support projects in a sector previously neglected because of a narrow donor mission.

In like manner, though we arrived with funds to be used to purchase lumber and materials to rebuild the school, it became clear within a few days that there was a far greater need to finance education in general. We quickly transformed a specific category into a broad range of possible activities, as a means of alleviating educational poverty. Thus, the community will get to devise its own recipe out of available ingredients: information, skills, needs, money, and so forth. In this case, broadening the category from "school" to "education," from the specific to the general, from fixed objective to ongoing process, made it possible to underwrite other parts of the overall well-being of the community. Some of the money was used immediately to help pay the costs of sending Ramon to teacher training: directly educational. In addition, some money also went to pay for training and supplies for the community's health care worker. Even broader, the funds helped the community to feed two other young teachers who stayed with them during their practicum assignment, and who were unable to return to their own distant communities. Thus, in the end, our school funds became an investment in human infrastructure, not just for the community of Cerro Verde, but also for the municipality as a whole. This arrangement was therefore beneficial to Cerro Verde in another way, as it sought to fill its obligations to the larger polity. With these diversified actions, significant needs of the social whole were addressed simultaneously.

The Truth Shall Set You Free?

When we left Chiapas in mid-August 2001, IDEFEM had moved into a small office in the home of one of its long-time members. The NGO was still receiving funding for the informational radio programs that they broadcast once a week in four Mayan languages and Spanish. As a means of getting information to a huge geographical area of listeners who remain outside of the realm of television, the programs were moderately successful, but underutilized. Beyond the radio programs, Claudia had little success generating support for IDEFEM's continued work. In part, this was because her paper at the Merida meetings was but one version of the soul-searching and honest reports that IDEFEM had written for their principle donors. The process of telling it like it was did not endear them to the organizations, who saw their pet projects described for what they were: long-run failures.

There is no profit for the nonprofit in telling it like it is, or was. Yet the only way to take the bull out of sustainabullity and replace it with truly sustainable, informed, and codesigned interventions is to report on the failures in a public forum, and use those failures as the building blocks of the next generation of programs. For IDEFEM, the truth has made them cease to be. For the communities, the failures have made them jaded and cynical.

Alleviating Poverty through Cultural Translation

It would be naive to propose that in the political economy of charity, aid might be distributed without any constraints at all. What we learned from all our meetings with the community, as we faced the contradiction between proyectismo and autonomy of action, is that it is best to maintain very broad categories of what will fit within designated areas like education, health, or production. We can go farther, to say: The only way that NGOs can relieve poverty in a way that makes sense to the community is to define sufficiently broad categories of "designated" aid to allow both donors and communities to be satisfied that the money is being properly spent.

By opening up the semantic fields of giving, which are the sectoral categories of specialized concern, and by taking the time needed to come to know the community of intervention, NGOs and the communities they serve can be freed from the tyranny of designated funds. By disencumbering resources, NGOs have a far better chance of alleviating poverty on the community's own terms. But communicating those terms to potential aid partners is not always easy.

That summer we attended both spontaneous and planned meetings, trying to agree on a template for collaboration. We also spent hours talking with the children and teachers at the tiny autonomous school. They explained their philosophy of education: teachers, other students, and parents assist each individual child as she moves at her own pace through levels of learning. Currently, the autonomous schools in Tierra y Libertad end at the equivalent of eighth grade. Schools at the next educational level will be developed, as the communities need them. Children can read and write poetry, do math, and have a good grasp of the history of the world and their relationship to it. They enjoy music and art. The system is compassionate and effective. Teachers are raised up from their own communities and, most important, return from training to share their skills.

Our encounters with the educational system, formal and informal, were part of the community's carefully crafted plan: part of a cultural translation process that guided us to seeing the wisdom of disencumbering the educational funds. The importance of this sensitizing process was made painfully clear after returning home, as we tried to communicate this view of education to a potential donor. Animated descriptions of the teacher-training programs and the children's proficiency with the 3 R's were not sufficient.

"What kind of jobs will they be able to get with that kind of education?" asked the donor. "Will that help them get out of poverty?"

We were not speaking the same language, nor was she measuring outcome with the same yardstick as the Cerro Verde community. She was seeing their education from the standpoint of formal standards, viewed as the only means to "getting ahead" professionally. By contrast, they look upon education as a way to learn what you need to know to be a contributing member of the community. Such radically different goals in education give rise to different methods and techniques of educating (see Friere 1970). Concomitantly, they also give rise to very different project designs and goals.

How, then, can we help donors and NGOs to give up hegemonic control over not just the purse strings, but also over philosophies of education, health, production, or gender relations? As Duran Duran noted when describing IDEFEM's failures, "we tried to translate to this reality concepts and structures of analysis in opposition to the perception of the reality of the indigenous women" (2001, 2; see also Eber 2001, 6). It simply didn't work.

In spite of this, communities continue to seek help. But although they seek help from NGOs and donors, they do not want patrons on either level. Imagine what a different world of community development it would be if those who receive aid became more informed consumers and participated in the global communication network. As a result of their global exposure communities might post their development queries on an Internet site, in help wanted ads, of a sort, soliciting donors to facilitate their proposed plans. Imagine a "Wanted: NGO Services" column, featuring the following, all actual development questions and situations we have encountered in Chiapas:

- Progovernment evangelical Mayan women seek help organizing a textile cooperative, no Saturday work;
- Jungleflower honey producers seek organic food supermarkets to purchase bulk honey, top grade;
- Ginger and sugarcane producers would like to develop candied ginger market;
- Autonomous municipio seeks investment in educational training programs for teachers, health care workers, and agricultural extension agents; also seeks to establish a supply center for consumer goods in an isolated region. Please make inquires through the Enlace Civil, Tuesday afternoons only;
- Highly organized Tzotzil-Maya ejido seeks enthusiastic archaeologist able to generate financial support for research and restoration of archaeological site inside ejido territory, can gain backing from Mexican institutions through cooperative arrangements and networking. Spanish, Tzotzil, English a must, French, German, also good.

There is a key role for NGOs in a development process that is not mission directed. It is a managerial position that involves helping a donor get funds to a particular project and making sure the project is monitored and documented, failures as well as successes. It includes managing the details of the plans worked out by the community, through consultation and dialogue. The relationship is less about telling and more about listening and learning. Good CD by good NGOs, if there is to be any, must come from learning, for failure becomes more and more expensive and unethical as time goes on. To test untried ideas and unresearched projects on the eager poor becomes immoral if better alternatives might result from inquiry and dialogue.

The NGO role is also a research position, since a donor-supported fact-finding, fact-disseminating phase is crucial to the project cycle. But for both of these tasks, NGO workers must learn to speak with the people. This requires knowledge of their habits of speaking, an attention far beyond that of the typical NGO expatriate, which enters into the arena of professional ethnography. We reiterate that adding ethnography is not costly. It costs so much less than the expense associated with failures. As for time, those in a rush should recall the time spent on failed projects, and reflect that part of sustainability is patience with the change process. Change will often be better, more sustainable, if it takes a little longer, especially if that time is used to ensure long-run sustainability. And that, in a development process of, by, and for the people, is what counts.

Effective community development and effective NGO participation in this process asks us to modify our world view and give up attempts to solve the world's problems in a way that conforms to our own views. Giving communities the autonomy to design programs that fit within broad categories asks that donors and NGOs give up their own control, a disorienting change in process. Alleviating poverty means turning NGOs into cultural translators, helping a donor to see the problem and collaborate on a solution. Better yet, borrowing another Zapatista model, NGOs would need to become development companions, crafting the relationship between their organization and communities using the notion of "compañerismo." Indeed, each of us, in our particular role in the development process, would accompany the community on its own slippery path to prosperity.

Notes

Notes to Introduction

1. Overseas Development Institute 1996. Between 10 percent and 15 percent of all aid to developing countries is channeled by or through nongovernmental organizations (NGOs).
2. See Fisher (1998) and Bebbington (1997).

Notes to Chapter 1

1. The population estimate for the upper Cañar region comes from an internal report prepared for the Cañar office of the Ecuadorian government rural development agency DRI (Desarrollo Rural Integral).
2. PROMUSTA was administratively considered an Ecuadorian national NGO, even though the national administration and project methodology came from CARE.
3. Average educational attainment in the study communities was three years of primary education (INEC 1990).

Note to Chapter 2

I express my gratitude to Ellie Brodie for help with the research in this chapter.

Notes to Chapter 3

This chapter was translated by the editor.

1. Many argue that NGOs rely on voluntary labor, and that the existence of paid labor signifies an economic enterprise—private business rather than civil-society organization.

2. *Con fines Sociales. Organizaciones de la Sociedad Civil de Promoción y Desarrollo de Argentina*, PNUD-GADIS (Grupo de análisis y desarrollo institucional y social), Buenos Aires, 2000.

3. Statistics on NGOs are difficult to obtain, and they are neither exhaustive nor representative of the universe of NGOs, which is very heterogeneous. On one hand, different groups work with different definitions; and on the other, the visibility of the organizations varies. These are different registries that do not reflect any numerical exactness, for example the *Centro Nacional de Organizaciones Comunitarias* or National Center for Community Organizations (CENOC) estimated in 1996 that there were around 40,000 NGOs in the country and CENOC had a registry of 2,410. The registry coordinated in 1997 by D. Filmus for FLASCO and the World Bank, *El perfil de las ongs en la Argentina* (Profile of NGOs in Argentina), on the other hand, constructed via a different database, counted 3,678 NGOs in the country.

4. Data from the National Statistics and Census Institute (Instituto Nacional de Estadísticas y Censos—INDEC), Household Survey in May of 2001, for the city of Buenos Aires and parts of the suburban area, where approximately 33 percent of the country's population is concentrated. Poverty line is defined as: household income sufficient to satisfy, through the purchase of goods and services, a basket of food and nonfood necessities considered essential. Extreme poverty (*Línea de indigencia*) is defined as: household income sufficient to cover a food basket capable of satisfying minimum energy and protein needs.

5. The UNDP study (PNUD-GADIS 2000) presented these data as reported by NGOs themselves. The categories of responses were not pre-defined, and some categories may overlap.

6. See, for example, D. Filmus 1997, 63.

7. See, for example, Asociación Civil Don Jaime de Nevares (Quilmes) 2000.

8. The outcomes of this workshop are described in the World Bank report, *Las voces de los pobres*, Feliu 2000.

9. The first national forum was held in the city of Buenos Aires in November of 1991 with the participation of between 174 and 300 NGOs (no exact register exists), and the second gathering was held in Río Ceballos Pcia. de Córdoba in December of 1992 with a smaller number of organizations. Six regional forums have also been held.

10. In 1984 a group of Latin American NGOs formed the NGO Working Group on the World Bank (*Grupo de Trabajo de Ongs sobre el Banco Mundial* [GTONG-BM]), with the purpose of maintaining a critical dialogue about the policies and projects of the World Bank, and maintaining absolute autonomy. In 1998 GTONG Argentina was created, a decentralized local level of the same network, which involves some fifty NGOs and networks in the country.

11. See, for example, Asociación Civil Don Jaime de Nevares (Quilmes) 2000, 13.

12. Informe Number 19992–AR, Spanish version, "Un Pueblo Pobre en un Pais Rico." Reducción de la pobreza y manejo económico, Región de América Latina y el Caribe. Banco Mundial, 23 March 2000.

13. "Estrategia de Asistencia País. Respuesta al proceso consultivo con la sociedad civil." World Bank. All of the World Bank documents mentioned here can be viewed through the Bank's Argentina Web site, www.bancomundial.org.ar.

14. See, for example, Eduardo Lozano 1996, 287–312.

Notes to Chapter 4

1. At the time when I was conducting field research, in 1996–97, Fundapaz worked primarily in Los Blancos, with a smaller program in the larger Wichí community in Embarcación. Since that time, the NGO has greatly expanded its work in Embarcación, with the installation of a permanent team there, and more recently has begun to work with Wichí communities in the Pilcomayo region, where land claims have stalled in a highly political, widely publicized, and extremely contentious process. While I do not consider this expansion and its ramifications here, I believe that this growth of the organization is logical and timely. Fundapaz's geographic extension is based on its experiences with the Wichí culture and people in the area around Los Blancos, its networks with other organizations in the Pilcomayo region, and a process of organizational growth.

2. In the Wichí community of Los Blancos, the carpentry workshop, built as a project by Fundapaz, has electricity; this is the only building in any of the Wichí communities in the region with power. In comparison, the criollo town of Los Blancos has power twenty-four hours and Page has a generator for three to four hours each evening. The more remote criollo settlements do not have electricity.

3. All figures are in U.S. dollars. The Argentine peso is fixed (1 : 1) to the U.S. dollar.

4. Such wage labor is generally only available to men. Wichí women have much more difficulty finding paid work. When they do find work doing laundry or other household chores, they are paid much less, about half of what men earn.

5. This meeting was part of the PPI, or Participación de los Pueblos Indígenas, a series of meetings intended to encourage indigenous communities to make recommendations to the national legislature on laws that directly affected indigenous peoples. The final document was presented to the national legislature in August 1997.

6. From the mid-1990s until the present, Argentina has been plagued by unemployment rates reaching up to 20 percent. In agricultural areas in the north, the real rate of unemployment is much higher.

7. The scarcity of paid labor for women in the villages means that these positions are coveted, and sometimes are the sources of disagreements. Women in one community responded by implementing a creative "job sharing" schedule that rotated work on a monthly basis among several women; OCLADE resisted this plan on the grounds that it did not provide enough consistency for children.

8. A *departamento* is an administrative district, similar to a county.

9. Argentina has undergone a series of neoliberal economic reforms, many of which have targeted social spending. For discussions of neoliberal economic policy in Argentina and its implications for NGOs, see Aguilar 1993, Jelin 1994.

10. In this section in particular, my views are heavily shaped by my own experiences with each organization and the role that I was able to take in each. With OCLADE, despite initial assurances of interest, I was seldom able to meet with administrative personnel, and had little access to meetings at the regional level. On a local level, although I was able to observe some meetings, I was not integrated into the regular work of the promoter. I had cordial relationships with OCLADE's field workers and volunteers, but the bulk of my data came from participant-observation and interviews with people in the community. With Fundapaz, in contrast, I was able to observe and

participate in as many of the regular team meetings as I wanted, and regularly and frequently attended meetings in the communities. I was very friendly with the team members, and had excellent personal and professional relationships with them. Near the end of my time in the region, I was able to participate in a two-day introspective meeting of the team, during which there was a great deal of reflexive thinking about the NGO's relationship with the community.

11. Including the anthropologist.

12. This is not to suggest that the Wichí are not adept at "politics"; in familiar contexts, some Wichí leaders can be shrewd politicians. This is a highly valued leadership skill, as is speaking well in public. There is, however, a lack of understanding of bureaucracies and a lack of familiarity with the ways things are done in a more bureaucratic society.

13. This particular idea is frustrating to the Fundapaz staff, who are well aware of it, as it often makes the NGO out to be stingy, capriciously holding back resources. During my stay, the NGO invited community leaders to travel to the city to buy materials for projects with staff members, in part to dispel the warehouse myth.

14. One of the team members speaks Wichí fluently; a couple of them understand it a bit.

15. In fact, government development agencies have a fairly low profile in the region, with no permanent offices and only sporadic projects.

16. In 1976, the prelature of Humahuaca was linked with a Spanish missionary order called the Misioneros de la Corazón de María, or Claretianos. This link represented an infusion of personnel and resources into the region, which had not previously had such an active Catholic presence. The clergy come from Spain, with the exception of a few recently ordained Kolla priests.

17. ENDEPA is the national Catholic NGO that is extremely active in indigenous rights issues and legislation; EPPREPA is the corresponding NGO in the prelature.

18. Although OCLADE does employ some Kollas in the community, their functions are quite limited, and do not include significant decision-making or leadership roles.

Notes to Chapter 5

1. Colloredo-Mansfeld (1999) offers a similar example for Otavalan indigenous peoples in Ecuador, and Chaterjee (1989, 1993) provides an insightful discussion of the importance of Indian women in the maintenance of traditional gender roles in nineteenth-century India.

2. Chicha is typically a fermented drink. In the Andean highlands, it is often made from corn. In many parts of Ecuador's Amazon, however, it is usually made from manioc and can either be served fresh or fermented. It is consumed as a staple drink among indigenous peoples throughout Ecuador's Amazon region.

3. Sinchi Sacha blamed the failures of the project on political disputes between Sinchi Sacha and the Unión Huacamayos. From Sinchi Sacha's point of view, the Unión's leaders were creating conflicts that undermined the efforts of the NGO in Santa Rita and elsewhere. From the Unión's point of view, it was acting to ensure that Sinchi Sacha did not take unfair advantage of the communities (see Wilson 2003).

Notes to Chapter 6

This chapter was translated by the editor.

1. Data from Bolivian National Statistics Institute (*Instituto Nacional de Estadísticas* [INE]) 1992 national census.
2. The Trickle Up Program, New York. Further information on this NGO can be found at www.trickleup.org.
3. See Human Development Report (2000), *Human Rights and Human Development*, "Gender-Related Development Index," p. 163; United Nations Development Programme, New York, available on the Internet at: www.undp.org/hdro (May 3, 2002).
4. Ibid.
5. (Editor's note) *Campesinos* are rural smallholders; in the Andes, campesinos are generally of indigenous Aymara or Quechua background.

Notes to Chapter 8

This chapter was translated by the editor.

1. (Editor's note) *Campesinos*: Rural smallholders; in the Andes campesinos are generally of indigenous Aymara or Quechua background.
2. (Editor's note) See Buechler, Hans C. and Judith-Maria Buechler, 1992. *Manufacturing Against the Odds: Small-Scale Producers in an Andean City*. Boulder, CO: Westview Press, for one interesting study of the adaptive ability of urban Bolivian households under conditions of economic crisis.
3. Published in La Paz, Bolivia in 1987; now out of print.
4. A New York–based NGO; further information is available at www.trickleup.org
5. (Editor's note) For more information on the El Ceibo cooperative, see Healy, Kevin, 1988, "Vertical Integration in Bolivia," in *Direct to the Poor, Grassroots Development in Latin America*, ed. S. Annis and P. Hakim, Boulder, CO: Lynne Rienner Publishers.

Notes to Chapter 9

1. From "Cuyabeno le hace frente a la crisis" in *El Comercio,* on-line article, "Ecuador" section, August 8, 2001. www.elcomercio.com.
2. The Siona-Secoya community of Puerto Bolivar was one of those that split into two separate communities, while others have split based on those that work with tourism and those that do not. Money is not always the decisive factor; some people simply do not want outsiders wandering regularly through their villages.
3. Comments in *El Comercio*, "Opinión" section, October 28, 2000.
4. From a report titled "Proyecto SUBIR: Inventario y Jerarquización de Atractivos Turísticos del Sitio Añangu," March 1993. CARE.
5. From RICANCIE report titled "Actividades: Periodo Noviembre–Abril 1998."

Notes to Chapter 10

The authors wish to thank the people of the study community, referred to here as Cerro Verde, for their infinite patience. Partial support for our work comes from the Archie Fund, the Pro Humanitate Fund, and the Mellon Foundation, facilitated by Wake Forest University. Some portions of this work appear in Earle and Simonelli 2000.

1. We use pseudonyms for the communities and river valley described here.

2. For purposes of this paper, *village* is the geographical entity that includes the entire population of Cerro Verde; the *ejido* refers to all those belonging to the land-holding corporate entity, and *community* is defined as a loose alliance of households, united by common identity or goal, who have come together in order to facilitate a transformation in socioeconomic or political status, in this case identifying themselves as a community-in-resistance.

3. For a complete description of these relationships see Earle and Simonelli 2000.

4. In March 2001, community members, NGO staff, and anthropologists working in Chiapas participated in a session titled "Workshop and Conversation: Building a Network of Cooperation for Chiapas" at the annual meeting of the Society for Applied Anthropology, Merida, Mexico.

5. Our thanks to Walter "Chip" Morris, whose many effective and cynical years working in development in Chiapas led him to coin the term "sustainabullity."

6. Reports by the American Anthropological Association concerning the employment of MA- and Ph.D.-level anthropologists are testimony to the fact that many do not secure permanent positions in the discipline.

7. Our thanks to Maya program student Beth Niehaus for pointing out the connection between the Zapatista model and community development.

References

References to Introduction

Annis, S. 1987. "Can Small-Scale Development be a Large-Scale Policy? The Case of Latin America." *World Development* 15 (Supplement): 129–34.
Bebbington, A. 1997. "Reinventing NGOs and Rethinking Alternatives in the Andes." *The Annals of the American Academy of Political and Social Science* 554 (November): 117–35.
Cameron, J. 2000. "Development Economics. The New Institutional Economics and NGOs." *Third World Quarterly* 21(4): 627–35.
Cernea, M. 1988. *Nongovernmental Organizations and Local Development.* World Bank Discussion Paper Number 40. Washington, DC: The World Bank.
Escobar, A. 1995. *Encountering Development: The Making and Unmaking of the Third World.* Princeton, NJ: Princeton University Press.
Esman, M., and N. Uphoff. 1984. *Local Organizations, Intermediaries in Rural Development.* Ithaca, NY: Cornell University Press.
Ferguson, J. 1990. *The Anti-Politics Machine: Development, Depoliticization, and Bureaucratic Power in Lesotho.* Cambridge, UK: Cambridge University Press.
Fisher, J. 1998. *NonGovernments: NGOs and the Political Development of the Third World.* West Hartford, CT: Kumarian Press.
Fowler, A. 1997. *Striking a Balance: A Guide to Enhancing the Effectiveness of Non-Governmental Organizations in International Development.* London: Earthscan Publications.
Freire, P. 1974. *Education for Critical Consciousness,* trans. M.B. Ramos, L. Bigwood, and M. Marshall. London: Sheed and Ward.
Hammergren, L. 1999. "The Development Wars: Analyzing Foreign Assistance Impact and Policy." *Latin American Research Review* 34(2): 179–97.
Hirschman, A. 1984. *Getting Ahead Collectively: Grassroots Experiences in Latin America.* Elmsford, NY: Pergamon Press.
Inter-American Development Bank (IADB). 1997. *Latin America after a Decade of*

Reforms: Economic and Social Progress, 1997 Report. Washington DC: The Inter-American Development Bank.

Inter-American Development Bank (IADB). 1999. *Facing Up to Inequality in Latin America*. Economic and Social Progress Report 1998/1999. Washington, DC. Inter-American Development Bank.

Inter-American Foundation (IAF). 1977. *They Know How: An Experiment in Development Assistance*. Rosslyn, VA: The Inter-American Foundation.

Kenyon, P., and A. Black, eds. 2001. *Small Town Renewal: Overview and Case Studies*. Canberra, Australia: Rural Industries Research and Development Corporation. Available at: www.rirdc.gov.au/reports/HCC/01–043.pdf.

Killick T. 1999. "Making Adjustment Work for the Poor." Overseas Development Institute (ODI) Poverty Briefing Paper Number 5 (May). London: Overseas Development Institute. Available at: www.odi.org.uk/briefing/pov5.html.

Lackey, A. et al. 1987. "Healthy Communities: The Goal of Community Development." *Journal of the Community Development Society* 18: 1–17.

Maxwell, S. 1999. "The Meaning and Measurement of Poverty," Overseas Development Institute (ODI) Poverty Briefing Paper Number 3 (February). London: Overseas Development Institute. Available at: www.odi.org.uk/briefing/pov3.html.

Maxwell, S., and P. Kenway. 2000. "New Thinking on Poverty in the UK: Any Lessons for the South?" Overseas Development Institute (ODI) Poverty Briefing Paper Number 9 (November). London: Overseas Development Institute. Available at: www.odi.org.uk/briefing/pov9.html.

Meyer, C. 1999. *The Economics and Politics of NGOs in Latin America*. Westport, CT: Praeger.

Narayan, D., with R. Patel, K. Schafft, A. Rademacher, and S. Koch-Schulte. 1999. *Can Anyone Hear Us? Voices from 47 Countries*, Voices of the Poor Reports Vol. 1, Poverty Group PREM. Washington, DC: The World Bank. Available at: www.worldbank.org/poverty/voices/reports/canany/vol1.pdf.

North, D. 1990. *Institutions, Institutional Change and Economic Performance*. Cambridge, UK: Cambridge University Press.

Nustad, K. 2000. "On the Theoretical Framework of the World Development Report." In *A Critical Review of the World Bank Report: World Development Report 2000/2001*: Attacking Poverty. (Published and established by CROP.) Comparative Research Programme on Poverty (CROP). Bergen, Norway. Available at: www.crop.org/publications/reports.cmf.

O'Connor, A. 1995. "Evaluating Comprehensive Community Initiatives: A View From History." In *New Approaches to Evaluating Community Initiatives*, ed. J. Connell et al., Washington, DC: The Aspen Institute. Available at: www.aspenroundtable.org/vol1/index.htm.

Overseas Development Institute (ODI) 1996. "The Impact Of NGO Development Projects." Overseas Development Institute (ODI) Briefing Paper (May). London: Overseas Development Institute. Available at: www.odi.org.uk/briefing/2_96.html.

Oyen, E. 2000. "Six Questions to the World Bank on the World Development Report 2000/2001: 'Attacking Poverty.'" In *A Critical Review of the World Bank Report: World Development Report 2000/2001: Attacking Poverty.* Comparative Research Programme on Poverty (CROP), Bergen, Norway. Available at: www.crop.org/publications/reports/cmf.

Sen, A. 1999. *Development as Freedom*. New York: Alfred A. Knopf.

———. 1981. *Poverty and Famines*. Oxford, UK: Clarendon Press.

United Nations Development Program (UNDP). 2000a. *Human Rights and Human Development, UNDP Human Development Report 2000*. United Nations. Available at: www.undp.org/hdr2000/home.html.

————. 2000b. *Overcoming Human Poverty, UNDP's Poverty Report 2000*. United Nations. Available at: www.undp.org/povertyreport.

World Bank 2000. *Attacking Poverty World Development Report 2000/2001*. Washington, DC: The World Bank. Available at: www.worldbank.org/poverty/wdrpoverty/report/index.htm.

Ziccardi, A., ed. 2001. *Pobreza, Desigualdad Social y Ciudadanía, los límites de las políticas sociales en América Latina*. (Poverty, Social Inequality and Citizenship, limits of social policies in Latin America). Buenos Aires: Consejo Latinoamericano de Ciencias Sociales.

References to Chapter 1

ALTERNATIVA (Fundación Alternativas para el Desarrollo) and PNUD (Programa de las Naciones Unidas para el Desarrollo). 1992. *Directorio de Organizaciones No Gubernamentales Dedicadas al Desarrollo en El Ecuador*. (Director of nongovernmental development organizations in Ecuador.) Quito, Ecuador: ALTERNATIVA and PNUD.

Altieri, M. 1995. *Agroecology: The Science of Sustainable Agriculture*. Boulder, CO: Westview.

Bebbington, A. 1993. "Modernization From Below: An Alternative Indigenous Development?" *Economic Geography* 69: 274–92.

————. 1996. "Organizations and Intensifications: Campesino Federation, Rural Livelihoods and Agricultural Technology in the Andes and Amazon." *World Development* 24(7): 1161–77.

Bebbington, A., H. Carrasco, L. Peralbo, G. Ramón, V. Torres, and J. Trujillo. 1993. "Fragile Lands, Fragile Organizations: Indian Organizations and the Politics of Sustainability in Ecuador." *Transactions of the Institute of British Geographers* 18: 170–96.

Breslin, P. 1987. *Development with Dignity: Grassroots Development and the Inter-American Foundation*. Rosslyn, VA: Inter-American Foundation.

Brown, L., J. Brea, and A. Goetz. 1988. "Policy Aspects of Development and Individual Mobility: Migration and Circulation from Ecuador's Rural Sierra." *Economic Geography* 64: 147–70.

Brysk, A. 2000. *From Tribal Village to Global Village: Indian Rights and International Relations in Latin America*. Stanford, CA: Stanford University Press.

Bunch, R. 1982. *Two Ears of Corn: A Guide to People-Centered Agricultural Improvement*. Oklahoma City, OK: World Neighbors.

Cadena, R. 1995. Assistant Director CARE Ecuador. Interview with author. Quito, Ecuador, July.

CARE (International). 2001. *CARE Annual Report*. Atlanta: CARE International.

CARE (Ecuador). 1995. *Proyectos en Ejecución* (Current Projects). Quito: CARE Ecuador.

Carpio, P. 2001. Director, Oficina de Investigaciones Sociales y del Desarrollo (Social Research and Development Office). Interview with author. Cuenca, Ecuador, August.

Carpio, R. 1994. Director, Agricultural Programs, Plan International—Cañar. Interview with author. Azogues, Ecuador, October.

———. 1995. Director, Agricultural Programs, Plan International—Cañar. Interview with author. Azogues, Ecuador, June.

———. 2001. Director (retired), Agricultural Programs, Plan International—Cañar. Interview with author. Cuenca, Ecuador, August.

Carroll, T. 1992. *Intermediary NGOs: The Supporting Link in Grassroots Development*. West Hartford, CT: Kumarian.

Clark, J. 1991. *Democratizing Development*. London: Earthscan.

Commander, S., and P. Peek. 1986. "Oil Exports, Agrarian Change and the Rural Labor Process: The Ecuadorian Sierra in the 1970s." *World Development* 14: 79–96.

Conway, G., and E. Barbier. 1988. "After the Green Revolution: Sustainable and Equitable Agricultural Development." *Futures* 20: 651–70.

Cordero, F. 2001. Program Director, Plan International Austro. Interview with author. Cuenca, Ecuador, August.

Fisher, J. 1993. *The Road from Rio: Sustainable Development and the Nongovernmental Movement in the Third World*. London: Praeger.

Freire, M. 2001. Director of Health Programs, Plan International Ecuador. Interview with author. Quito, Ecuador, August.

Gárate, J. 1995. Director, PROMUSTA–CARE. Interview with author. Cañar, Ecuador, June.

———. 2001. Director, PROMUSTA–CARE. Interview with author. Cañar, Ecuador, August.

Hulme, D., and M. Edwards, eds. 1997. *NGOs, States and Donors: Too Close for Comfort?* New York: St. Martin's Press.

Instituto Nacional de Estadística y Censos (INEC). (National Statistics and Census Institute). 1990. *Análisis de los Resultados Definitivos del V Censo de Población y IV de Vivienda* (Analysis of Final Results of the Fifth Population Census and Fourth Housing Census). Quito, Ecuador: INEC.

Instituto Internacional de Reconstrucción Rural (IIRR) 1996. *Manual de Prácticas Agroecológicas de los Andes Ecuatorianos* (Manual of Ecudorian Andes Agroecological practices). Quito, Ecuador: IIRR.

Jokisch, B. 2001. Assistant Professor, Ohio University. Interview with author. Cañar, Ecuador, August.

Kaimowitz, D. 1993. "The Role of Nongovernmental Organizations in Agricultural Research and Technology Transfer in Latin America." *World Development* 21: 1139–50.

Keese, J. 1998. "International NGOs and Land Use Change in a Southern Highland Region of Ecuador." *Human Ecology: An Interdisciplinary Journal* 26 (3): 451–68.

———. 2001. "International NGOs and Sustainable Agricultural Development: A Methodological Approach with Examples from Highland Ecuador." *Ecuadorian Studies/Estudios Ecuatorianos* 1 (on-line). Available at: yachana.org/ecuatorianistas/journal/journal.html.

Knapp, G. 1991. *Andean Ecology: Adaptive Dynamics in Ecuador*. Dellplain Latin American Studies No. 27. Boulder, CO: Westview.

Lawson, V. 1988. "Government Policy Biases and Ecuadorian Agricultural Change." *Annals of the Association of American Geographers* 78: 433–52.

Mathewson, K. 1984. *Irrigation Horticulture in Highland Guatemala: The Tablón System of Panajachel*. Boulder, CO: Westview.

Mehra, R. 1997. "Women, Empowerment, and Economic Development." *Annals of the American Association of Political and Social Sciences* 55(4): 136–49.

Nietschmann, B. 1973. *Between Land and Water: The Subsistence Ecology of the Miskito Indians, Eastern Nicaragua.* New York: Seminar Press.

Paguay, J. 2001. Program Unit Director, Plan International Cañar. Interview with author. Cuenca, Ecuador, August.

Peet, R., and M. Watts. 1993. "Introduction: Development Theory and Environment in an Age of Market Triumphalism." *Economic Geography* 69: 227–53.

Plan International. 2001. *Worldwide Annual Report.* London: Plan International.

Plan Ecuador. 1994. Evaluación del Programa de Desarrollo Agropecuario de la Oficina de Campo Cañar Azuay (Agricultural Development Program Evaluation, Cañar Azuay Field Office). *Report.*

———. 2000. *Guía de Oficina de País* (Country Office Guide). Quito, Ecuador: Plan International.

Population Reference Bureau Inc. (PRB). 2001. *World Population Data Sheet.* Washington, DC: PRB.

PROMUSTA (Proyecto Manejo del Uso Sostenible de Tierras Andinas del Ecuador) (Sustainable Use of Ecuadorian Andean Lands Project). 1995. Metodología de Extensión. *Report.*

———. 1997. Consolidación y Retiro Proyecto Manejo del Uso Sostenible de Tierras Andinas, PROMUSTA (Consolidation and Withdrawal, Sustainable Use of Andean Lands Project). *Report.*

Redclift, M., and D. Preston. 1980. "Agrarian Reform and Rural Change in Ecuador." In *Environment, Society, and Rural Change in Latin America.* ed., D. Preston, New York: Wiley and Sons.

Torres, F. 1994. Director, CREA-DRI. (Economic Revitalization Centre for Azuay, Cañar y Marona-Stantiago Centro de Reconversión Económica de Azuay, Cañar y Morona-Santiago; Programme de Desarrollo Rural Intergral/Integrated Rural Development Program). Interview with author. Cuenca, Ecuador, December.

Turner, B. II. 1989. "The Specialist-Synthesis Approach to the Revival of Geography: The Case of Cultural Ecology." *Annals of the Association of American Geographers* 79: 88–100.

Wilken, G. 1987. *Good Farmers: Traditional Agricultural Resource Management in Mexico and Central America.* Berkeley: University of California Press.

Zimmerer, K. 1991. "Wetland Production and Smallholder Persistence: Agricultural Change in a Highland Peruvian Region." *Annals of the Association of American Geographers* 81: 443–63.

References to Chapter 2

APRODEV (Association of World Council of Churches Related Development Organizations in Europe). 2000. Comments on the Commission Paper "The Commission and Non-Governmental Organisations: Building a Stronger Partnership." Unpublished document, Brussels.

CIDSE (International Cooperation for Development and Solidarity). 2001. *Strategic Plan for 2001–2004.* Unpublished document, Brussels.

Department for International Development. 2000. *White Paper on Globalization.* Unpublished document, London.

Development Initiatives. 2000. *Global Development Assistance: The Role of Non-Governmental Organisations and Other Charity Flows.* Unpublished document, London.

Doolan, C. 1992. "British Development NGOs and Advocacy in the 1990s." In *Making a Difference: NGOs and Development in a Changing World*, ed. M. Edwards and D. Hulme. London: Earthscan Publications.

Edwards, M., and D. Hulme. 1992. "Scaling-up the Development Impact of NGOs: Concepts and Experiences." In *Making a Difference: NGOs and Development in a Changing World*, ed. M. Edwards and D. Hulme. London: Earthscan Publications.

EURODAD. 2001. Country Profiles: Honduras. Unpublished internal document, Brussels.

Friedman, E.J., K. Hochstetler, and A.M. Clark. 2001. "Sovereign Limits and Regional Opportunities for Global Civil Society in Latin America," *Latin American Research Review* 36(3): 7–35.

Homeless International. 2000. "Partners." www.homeless-international.org/partners.

Interforos. 2000a. *Honduras Poverty Reduction Strategy Paper*. Unpublished document, Honduras.

————. 2000b. Second Anniversary of the Passing of Hurricane Mitch. Unpublished document/Honduras.

International Institute for Environment and Development (IIED). 2001. *Human Settlements*. www.iied.org/humanprojects (31 January 2001).

Government of Honduras. 2000. *Interim Poverty Reduction Strategy Paper.* Government of Honduras.

Grugel, J. 1999. "European NGOs and Democratisation in Latin America: Policy Networks and Transnational Ethical Networks." In *Democracy Without Borders*, ed. J. Grugel. Routledge: London.

Grugel, J. 2000. "Romancing Civil Society: European NGOs in Latin America." *Journal of Interamerican Studies and World Affairs* 42(2): 87–107.

Liaison Committee of the NGOs with the EU. 2001a. *Proposals from the Development NGOs on the Community Budget for 2002*. Unpublished document, Brussels.

Liaison Committee of the NGOs with the EU. 2001b. *Comments on the Conclusion of the EC Co-Financing Scheme (B7–6000) and Recommendations for Follow-Up.* Unpublished document, Brussels.

Mandelson, P. 1998. Forward, *Liberalising Trade in Services—A Consultative Document on the GATS 2000 Negotiations at the World Trade Organisation and Forthcoming Bilateral Negotiations.* Department for Trade and Industry, UK Government.

Moore, M., and J. Putzel. 2000. "Thinking Strategically about Politics and Poverty," *Working Paper No. 8*. Brighton, UK: Institute of Development Studies.

Oxfam International. 2000. *Letter to the IMF*. Unpublished document, Oxford, UK.

Oxfam UK. 2001. *Oxfam Country Reports Latin America and the Caribbean*. Oxfam: Oxford.

World Development Movement. 2001. *Stop the GATStrophe*. Unpublished document, London.

References to Chapter 3

Asociación Civil Don Jaime de Nevares (Quilmes). 2000. "La Consulta del Banco Mundial a la Sociedad Civil en la Argentina. Economía Política de la Participación." ("World Bank consultation with Civil Society in Argentina. Political Economy of Participation.") In *El Tercer Encuentro Nacional por un Nuevo Pensamiento, Movimiento social y Representación Política*, mimeograph, October. (Third National Conference for New Thinking, Social Movements and Political Representation.)

Asociación Civil Madre Tierra. Madre Tierra Civil Association. 2000. "La Memoria y el Aguante." "Memory and Aguante" Workshop: Caminando Juntos por la Dignidad (Walking together for dignity), Morón Municipality, Buenos Aires Province, November 18 and 19.

Banco Mundial (World Bank). 2000. "Un Pueblo Pobre en un Pais Rico." ("Poor people in a rich country.") Informe No. 19992– AR, Spanish version. Reducción de la Pobreza y Manejo Económico. Región de América Latina y el Caribe, Banco Mundial (Poverty Reduction and Economic Management. Latin American and Carribean Region, World Bank). March 23.

————. "Estrategia de Asistencia País. Respuesta al Proceso Consultivo con la Sociedad Civil" (Country Assistance Strategy. Response to the Civil Society Consultation Process). Document. Available on the Internet at www.bancomuncial.org.ar/sco_civ.htm/newsnetwork.

Basualdo, E. 2001. "La crisis de la convertibilidad en la Argentina" ("The convertibility crisis in Argentina"). Red Nacional y Popular de Noticias (National People's News Network). Buenos Aires, August.

Beccaría, L. 1992. "Cambios en la estructura distributiva 1975–1990" ("Changes in the distribution structure 1975–1990"). In Cuesta Abajo. Los Nuevos Pobres: Efectos de la Crisis en la Sociedad Argentina (Going Downhill, The New Poor: Effects of the Crisis on Argentinean Society). UNICEF/Editorial. Buenos Aires: Losada.

Cesilini, S. 1999. "Prólogo." In Ciudadanía y Sociedad Civil en la Ciudad de Buenos Aires. Repertorio de Organizaciones No Gubernamentales (Citizenship and Civil Society in the City of Buenos Aires. Listing of Non-Governmental Organizations), Banco Mundial y Gobierno de la Ciudad de Buenos Aires (World Bank and Buenos Aires City Government).

Feliu, P. 2000. Las Voces de los Pobres (The Voices of the Poor). Banco Mundial: Buenos Aires.

Filmus, D. 1997. El Perfil de las Ongs en la Argentina (Profile of NGOs in Argentina). FLACSO-Banco Mundial: Buenos Aires.

INDEC (National Statistics and Census Institute–Instituto Nacional de Estadísticas y Censos). 2001. "Encuesta Permanente de Hogares, Gran Buenos Aires." "Household Survey May of 2001, for Greater Buenos Aires."

Lozano, C. 1996. "Crisis del Estado-Providente y reestructuración de la intervención pública." ("Crisis of the Provider State and Restructuring of Public Intervention."). In Desempleo estructural, pobreza y precariedad (Structural Unemployment, Poverty and Precariousness) ed. S. Peñalva and A. Rofman. Buenos Aires: Nueva Visión.

Luna, E. 2000. "Mapa institucional" ("Institutional Map"). In Con fines Sociales. Organizaciones de la Sociedad Civil de Promoción y Desarrollo de Argentina (With Social Aims: Civil Social Development Organizations in Argentina). Buenos Aires: PNUD-GADIS.

Petras, J. 1997. "Imperialism and NGOs in Latin America." Monthly Review 49(7)10–26.

PNUD-GADIS (United Nations Development Programme, Grupo de análisis y desarrollo institucional y social) (Analysis and Social and Institutional Development Group) 2000. Con fines sociales. Organizaciones de la Sociedad Civil de Promoción y Desarrollo de Argentina. Buenos Aires: PNUD-GADIS.

References to Chapter 4

Aguilar, M.A. 1993. "Decentralización y Gobiernos Municipales: Limitaciones y Posibilidades." ("Decentralization and Municipal Governments: Limitations and Possibilities.") Paper presented at a seminar on "La cuidad y la calidad de vida: El rol del municipio," ("City and quality of life: the role of the municipality"). Organized by the Consejo de Investigación, Universidad Nacional de Salta, October.

Comaroff, J., and J. Comaroff. 1992. *Ethnography and the Historical Imagination.* Boulder, CO: Westview Press.

Crush, J., ed. 1995. *Power of Development.* New York: Routledge.

Escobar, A. 1995. *Encountering Development: The Making and Unmaking of the Third World.* Princeton, NJ: Princeton University Press.

Fundapaz. 1988. Fundapaz Annual Report. 1988/89. Buenos Aires: Fundapaz.

Jelin, E. 1994. "The Politics of Memory: The Human Rights Movement and the Construction of Democracy in Argentina." *Latin American Perspectives* 81(21), 2: 38–58.

Occhipinti, L. 2000. "Global Visions, Local Voices: Religious NGOs and Development in Rural Argentina." Ph.D. diss., McGill University, Montreal, Canada.

Olmedo, J.R.1990. *Puna, Zafra y Socavón: Homenaje al pueblo Colla.* Madrid: Editorial Popular.

Pigg, S.L. 1992. "Inventing Social Categories Through Place: Social Representations and Development in Nepal." *Comparative Studies in Society and History* 34: 491–513.

Scott, J.C. 1998. *Seeing Like a State.* New Haven, CT: Yale University Press.

References to Chapter 5

Bebbington, A., et al. 1993. *Non-Governmental Organizations and the State in Latin America.* London and New York: Routledge.

Boserup, E. 1970. *Women's Role in Economic Development.* New York: St. Martin's Press.

Braidotti, R., et al. 1994. *Women, the Environment and Sustainable Development: Towards a Theoretical Synthesis.* London: Zed Books.

Chaterjee, P. 1989. "Colonialism, Nationalism, and Colonized Women: The Contest in India." *American Ethnologist* 16(4): 622–33.

———. 1993. *The Nation and Its Fragments: Colonial and Postcolonial Histories.* Princeton, NJ: Princeton University Press.

Chowdhry, Geeta. 1995. "Engendering Development? Women in Development (WID) in International Development Regimes." In *Feminism/Postmodernism/Development*, ed. M. Marchand and J. Parpart. London: Routledge.

Conklin, B., and L. Graham. 1995. "The Shifting Middle Ground: Amazonian Indians and Eco-politics." *American Anthropologist* 97(4): 695–710.

Colloredo-Mansfeld, R. 1999. *The Native Leisure Class: Consumption and Cultural Creativity in the Andes.* Chicago: University of Chicago Press.

Fisher, W.F. 1997. "Doing Good? The Politics and Antipolitics of NGO Practices." *Annual Review of Anthropology* 26: 439–64.

Healy, K. 1992. "Back to the Future: Ethnodevelopment Among the Jalq'a of Bolivia." *Grassroots Development* 16(2): 22–34.

Hirshman, M. 1995. "Women and Development: A Critique." In *Feminism/ Postmodernism/Development*, ed. M. Marchand and J. Parpart. London: Routledge.

Kleymeyer, C. 1992. "Cultural Energy and Grassroots Development." *Grassroots Development* 16(1): 22–31.

Mohanty, C. 1991. "Under Western Eyes: Feminist Scholarship and Colonial Discourses." In *Third World Women and the Politics of Feminism*, ed. A. Russo, L. Torres, and C. Mohanty. Bloomington: Indiana University Press.

Nash, J. 1993. "Introduction: Traditional Arts and Changing Markets in Middle America." In *Crafts in the World Market: The Impact of Global Exchange on Middle American Artisans*, ed. J. Nash. Albany: State University of New York Press.

Orlove, B., and S. Brush. 1996. "Anthropology and the Conservation of Biodiversity." *Annual Review of Anthropology* 25: 329–52.

Porter, M. 1999. "Introduction: Caught in the Web? Feminists Doing Development." In *Feminists Doing Development: A Practical Critique*, ed. M. Porter and E. Judd. London: Zed Books.

Ramos, A. 1998. *Indigenism: Ethnic Politics in Brazil*. Madison: University of Wisconsin Press.

Razavi, S., and C. Miller. 1995. *From WID to GAD: Conceptual Shifts in the Women and Development Discourse*. Geneva: United Nations Research Institute for Social Development.

Reyna, S. 1997. "The Dating Game: 'Romancing' Development Knowledge and the National Bourgeois Among the Desert Palms of Mauritania." *Urban Anthropology* 26(3–4): 331–67.

Scott, C. 1995. *Gender and Development: Rethinking Modernization and Dependency Theory*. Boulder, CO: Lynn Rienner Publishers.

Shiguango, J., et al. 1993. "An Experiment in Rainforest Conservation: Project PUMAREN in Ecuador Demonstrates that Forest Management can Support Indigenous Territorial Claims." *Cultural Survival Quarterly*. 17(1): 56–59.

Sinchi Sacha. 1996. *Programa Huacamayo Urcu I: Aprovechamiento y manejo sustentable del Bosque de los Huacamayos* (Huacamayo Urcu I Program: Sustainable Use of Huacamayos Forest). Quito: Fundación Sinchi Sacha.

———. 1997. Report. "Cerámica: Fusion Hombre-Naturaleza-Hombre, Experiencia sustentable para el Desarrollo" ("Ceramics: Connections between Man and Nature: A Sustainable Development Experience"). Quito: Sinchi Sacha Foundation archives.

Smith, C. 1991. "Maya Nationalism." North American Congress on Latin America (*NACLA*) 25(3): 29–34.

Smyth, Ines. 1999. "NGOs in a Post-Feminist Era." In *Feminists Doing Development: A Practical Critique*, ed. M. Porter and E. Judd. London: Zed Books.

Stearman, A. 1994. " 'Only Slaves Climb Trees': Revisiting the Myth of the Ecologically Noble Savage in Amazonia." *Human Nature* 5(4): 339–57.

Stephen, L. 1993. "Weaving in the Fast Lane: Class, Ethnicity, and Gender in Zapotec Craft Commercialization." In *Crafts in the World Market: The Impact of Global Exchange on Middle American Artisans*, ed. J. Nash. Albany: State University of New York Press.

Whitten, D., and N. Whitten. 1985. *Art, Knowledge, and Health: Development and Assessment of a Collaborative, Auto-Financed Organization in Eastern Ecuador*. Occasional Paper #17. Cambridge, MA: Cultural Survival.

———. 1987. *Arte, cultura y poder de los Canelos Quichua de la Amazonia*

Ecuatoriana (Art, culture, and power of the Canelos Quichua of the Ecuadorian Amazon). Quito: Museo del Banco Central del Ecuador.

———. 1988. *From Myth to Creation: Art from Amazonian Ecuador*. Urbana: University of Illinois Press.

———. 1993. "Canelos Quichua: Culture, Ceramics and Continuity." *In Amazon Worlds: Peoples and Cultures of Ecuador's Amazon Region*, ed. N. Paymal and C. Sosa. Quito: Sinchi Sacha Foundation.

Wilson, P. 2003. "Ethnographic Museums and Cultural Commodification: Indigenous Organizations, NGOs, and Culture as a Resource in Amazonian Ecuador." *Latin American Perspectives* 30(1).

References to Chapter 7

Bussau, et al. 1999. Governance with Policy: A Resource Kit for Facilitators. Sydney: Governance Centre, Opportunity International Australia.

Christen R. 2000. *Commercialization and Mission Drift: The Transformation of Microfinance in Latin America*. Washington, DC: CGAP.

Getu, M. 1996. "The Dynamics of Micro Enterprise Development." In *Micro Enterprise Development in Theory and Pactice*, ed. M. Getu. Melbourne: Frank Daniels Pty. Ltd.

Horn, N. et al. 1997. *Transformation Case Studies: Ghana, Indonesia, Russia and Colombia*. Oak Brook, IL: Opportunity International.

IDH. 2000. *Transformation Plan: Trust Bank Program*. Tegucigalpa, Honduras.

Katalysis Partnership. 2001. *Market Survey of the Microcredit Environment in Central America*. Los Angeles: Katalysis Partnership.

LARO (Latin America Regional Office). 2000. *"The Group of Twelve": Leadership Development for Boards of Directors*. Bogota, Colombia: LARO.

OCTS (Opportunity Center for Transformation Studies). 2000. *Measuring Transformation: Conceptual Framework and Indicators*. Oxford, UK: OCTS.

Opportunity International (OI). 1998. *A 5-Year Vision Statement for the Opportunity International Network*. Network Office. Oak Brook, IL: Opportunity International.

———. 2000a. *The Next Decade of Opportunity: Executive Summary*. Network Office. Oak Brook, IL: Opportunity International.

———. 2000b. *Annual Report 2000*. Network Office, Oak Brook, IL: Graphics Products.

———. 2001a. *Opportunity International Network Partner Reporting System*. Network Office, Oak Brook, IL: Opportunity International.

———. 2001b. *Opportunity International Commercial Plans*. Network Office, Oak Brook, IL: Opportunity International.

OI Canada. 1999. *Microenterprise in the Rural Communities Surrounding Tegucigalpa, Honduras: A Joint Project of CAUSE and Opportunity International Canada*. Toronto: OI Canada.

———. 2001. *CIDA Partnership Progress Report: Microenterprise Supporting Development in Danli Honduras*. Toronto: OI Canada.

OI United Kingdom. 2001. *National Lottery Grant Evaluation Report*. Oxford, UK: OIUK.

Olsen, A., and K. Lindgren. 2001. *Tool Kit for Training New Loan Officers: A Resource for Trust Bank Programs*. Oak Brook, IL: Women's Opportunity Fund.

Reed, R., and S. Cheston. 1999. "Measuring Transformation: Assessing and Improving the Impact of Microcredit." *The Journal of Microfinance* (Fall).

Sen, A. 1999. *Development as Freedom.* Oxford, UK: Oxford University Press.

SEEP. 1995. *Financial Ratio Analysis of Micro-Finance Institutions.* New York: Pact Publications.

Sherman, A.L. 1999. *The Soul of Development: Biblical Christianity and Economic Transformation in Guatemala.* New York: Oxford University Press.

Stickney, C. 2000. *Mid-Term Report to WOF: IDH Transformation Project.* Tegucigalpa, Honduras: IDH.

Verhagen, K. 2000. *The Pitfalls of Microfinance and Its Underlying Philosophy.* Grand Rapids, MI: Calvin College.

United Nations Development Program (UNDP). 2000. *Human Development Report 2000.* New York: United Nations.

Women's Opportunity Fund (WOF). 1998. *Trust Bank Manual.* Oak Brook, IL: Women's Opportunity Fund.

References to Chapter 9

Appadurai, A. 1991. "Global Ethnoscapes: Notes and Queries for a Transnational Anthropology." In *Recapturing Anthropology. Working in the Present,* ed. R.G. Fox, School of American Research Advanced Seminar Series. Santa Fe: School of American Research Press.

———. 1996. *Modernity at Large: Cultural Dimensions of Globalization.* Vol. 1. Minneapolis and London: University of Minnesota Press.

Auge, M. 1995. *Non-places: Introduction to an Anthropology of Supermodernity.* Trans. J. Howe. London and New York: Verso.

Boli, J., and G.M. Thomas, eds. 1999. *Constructing World Culture: International Nongovernmental Organizations Since 1875.* Stanford, CA: Stanford University Press.

Brosius, J.P. 1999. "Analyses and Interventions: Anthropological Engagements with Environmentalism." *Current Anthropology* 40(3): 277–309.

Cabrera, C.A., and E.P. Vallejo. 1997. *El Mito al Debate: Las ONG en Ecuador.* Quito: Abya-Yala.

Cleary, D. 1991. "The 'Greening' of the Amazon." In *Environment and Development in Latin America: The Politics of Sustainability,* ed. D. Goodman and M. Redclift. Issues in Environmental Politics. Manchester, UK and New York: Manchester University Press.

Clifford, J. 1997. *Routes: Travel and Translation in the Late Twentieth Century.* Cambridge, MA and London: Harvard University Press.

Conklin, B.A., and L.R. Graham. 1995. "The Shifting Middle Ground: Amazonian Indians and Eco-Politics." *American Anthropologist* 97(4): 695–710.

Cresswell, T. 1996. *In Place/Out of Place: Geography, Ideology, and Transgression.* Minneapolis and London: University of Minnesota Press.

Dirlik, A. 2001. "Cultural Identity and the Politics of Place." In *Places and Politics in an Age of Globalization,* ed. R. Prazniak and A. Dirlik, Lanham, MD: Rowman & Littlefield.

Escobar, A. 1995. *Encountering Development: The Making and Unmaking of the Third World.* Princeton, NJ: Princeton University Press.

———. 2001. "Place, Economy and Culture in a Post-Development Era." In *Places and Politics in an Age of Globalization*, ed. R. Prazniak and A. Dirlik, Oxford, UK: Rowman & Littlefield.

Fisher, J. 1998. *Non-Governments: NGOs and the Political Development of the Third World*. West Hartford, CT: Kumarian Press.

Hannerz, U. 1996. *Transnational Connections: Culture, People, Places*. London and New York: Routledge.

Hecht, S., and A. Cockburn. 1990. *The Fate of the Forest: Developers, Destroyers and Defenders of the Amazon*. New York: Harper Perennial.

Hirsch, E., and M. O'Hanlon, eds. 1995. *The Anthropology of Landscape. Perspectives on Place and Space*. Oxford, UK: Clarendon Press.

Kane, J. 1995. *Savages*. New York: Knopf.

Kimerling, J. 1991. *Amazon Crude*. New York: Natural Resources Defense Council.

MacCannell, D. 1973. "Staged Authenticity: Arrangements of Social Space in Tourist Settings." *American Journal of Sociology* 79(3): 589–603.

Malpas, J.E. 1999. *Place and Experience. A Philosophical Topography*. Cambridge, UK: Cambridge University Press.

Marcus, G. 1998. *Ethnography Through Thick & Thin*. Princeton, NJ: Princeton University Press.

Markowitz, L. 2001. "Finding the Field: Notes on the Ethnography of NGOs." *Human Organization* 60(1): 40–46.

Nugent, S. 1993. *From "Green Hell" to "Green" Hell: Amazonia and the Sustainability Thesis*. Glasgow, Scotland: University of Glasgow, Institute of Latin American Studies.

Olwig, K.F., and Kirsten Hastrup, eds. 1997. *Siting Culture: The Shifting Anthropological Object*. London and New York: Routledge.

Patin, T. 1999. "Exhibitions and Empire: National Parks and the Performance of Manifest Destiny." *Journal of American Culture* 22(1): 41–59.

Peluso, D. 1993. "Conservation and Indigenismo." *Hemisphere* (Winter/Spring): 6–8.

Redford, K.H. 1990. "The Ecologically Noble Savage." *Orion Nature Quarterly* 9(3): 27–29.

Ruiz, L., ed. 1993. *Amazonia Escenarios y Conflictos (The Amazon, Scenes and Conflicts)*. Quito: CEDIME and Abya Yala.

Sack, R.D. 1997. *Homo Geographicus. A Framework for Action, Awareness, and Moral Concern*. Baltimore and London: Johns Hopkins University Press.

———. 1999. "A Sketch of a Geographic Theory of Morality." *Annals of the Association of American Geographers* 89(1): 26–44.

———. 2001a. "The Geographic Problematic: Empirical Issues." *Norwegian Journal of Geography* 55(3): 107–16.

———. 2001b. "The Geographic Problematic: Moral Issues." *Norwegian Journal of Geography* 55(3): 117–25.

Santos-Granero, ed. 1996. *Globalización y Cambio en la Amazonia Indígena (Globalization and Change in the Indigenous Amazon)*. Vol. 1. Quito, Euador: FLACSO and Abya-Yala.

Schmink, M., and C.H. Wood. 1992. *Contested Frontiers in Amazonia*. New York: Columbia University Press.

Segarra, M. 1997. *Embedding Political Identity: Professionalizing NGOs in Ecuador*. New York: Columbia University Institute of Latin American and Iberian Studies.

Slater, C. 1996. "Amazonia as Edenic Narrative." In *Uncommon Ground. Rethinking the Human Place in Nature*, ed. W. Cronon, New York and London: W.W. Norton.

Smith, R. 1993. *Crisis Under the Canopy: Tourism and Other Problems Facing the Present Day Huaorani.* Quito, Ecuador: Abya-Yala.

Sponsel, L.E., ed. 1995. *Indigenous Peoples and the Future of Amazonia.* Tucson and London: University of Arizona Press.

Tsing, A. 2000. "The Global Situation." *Cultural Anthropology* 15(3): 327–60.

Tulchin, J.S., and R.H. Espach, eds. 2001. *Latin America in the New International System.* Boulder, CO and London: Lynne Rienner Publishers.

Vickers, W.T. 1984. "Indian Policy in Amazonian Ecuador." In *Frontier Expansion in Amazonia,* ed. M. Schmink and C.H. Wood. Gainesville: University of Florida Press.

Wesche, R., and A. Drumm. 1999. *Defending Our Rainforest: A Guide to Community-Based Ecotourism in the Ecuadorian Amazon.* Quito, Ecuador: Acción Amazónica.

Wood, M.E. 1998. *Meeting the Global Challenge of Community Participation in Ecotourism: Case Studies and Lessons from Ecuador.* Washington, DC: USAID and The Nature Conservancy.

References to Chapter 10

Aubry, A. 2002. "Chiapas: de República Bananera a República Maquiladora." (Chiapas: From Banana Republic to Maquila Republic) *La Jornada,* January 6.

Bauzon, K.E. 1992. *Development and Democratization in the Third World: Myths, Hopes, and Realities.* Washington, DC: Crane Russack.

Black, J.K. 1999. *Development in Theory and Practice: Paradigms and Paradoxes.* 2d ed. Boulder, CO: Westview Press.

Briggs, C. 1986. *Learning How to Ask.* New York: Cambridge University Press.

Burgerman, S.D. 1998. "Mobilizing Principles: The Role of Transnational Activists in Promoting Human Rights Principles." *Human Rights Quarterly* 20: 905–23.

Castellanos, R. 1988. *A Rosario Castellanos Reader: An Anthology of Her Poetry, Short Fiction, Essays, and Drama,* ed. M. Ahern. Austin: University of Texas Press.

Coordinadora [de los Altos]. 2001. "A Summary of the Ley Indígena." Personal communication.

Duffield, M. 1997. "The Symphony of the Damned: Racial Discourse, Complex Political Emergencies and Humanitarian Aid." *Disasters* 20: 173–93.

Duran Duran, C. 2001. "Trabajando Con Comunidades Diversos" (Working with Diverse Communities). Paper presented at the Annual Meeting of the Society for Applied Anthropology, Mérida, Mexico, March.

Earle, D. 1984. "Cultural Logic and Ecology in Community Development: Failure and Success Cases Among the Highland Maya." Ph.D. diss., Department of Anthropology, State University of New York at Albany.

———. 1994. "Indigenous Identity at the Margin." *Cultural Survival* (Spring): 26–30.

Earle, D., and J. Simonelli. 2000. "Help Without Hurt: Community Goals, NGO Interventions and Lasting Aid Lessons in Chiapas, Mexico." *Urban Anthropology* 29(2): 97–144.

Eber, C. 2001. "Cracking the Vessel of Oppression: Women and Change in San Pedro Chenalhó, Chiapas, Mexico." Paper presented at the 2001 meeting of the Latin American Studies Association, Washington, DC, September.

Edwards, M., and D. Hulme. 1996. "Too Close For Comfort? The Impact of Official Aid on Nongovernmental Organizations." *World Development* 24: 961–73.

Ervin, A. 2000. *Applied Anthropology: Tools and Perspectives for Contemporary Practice.* Boston: Allyn and Bacon.

Escobar, A. 1998. "Conclusion: Imagining a Postdevelopment Era." In *Crossing Currents: Continuity and Change in Latin America,* ed. M.B. Whiteford and S. Whiteford. Englewood Cliffs, NJ: Prentice Hall.

Freire, P. 1970. *Pedagogy of the Oppressed.* New York: Continuum Publishing.

Gardner, K., and D. Lewis. 1996. *Anthropology, Development and the Post-Modern Challenge.* London: Pluto Press.

Gezon, L. 2000. "The Changing Face of NGOs: Structure and Communitas in Conservation and Development in Madagascar." *Urban Anthropology* 29(2): 181–215.

Hackenberg, R.A. 1999. "Victims of Globalization: Is Economics the Instrument Needed to Provide Them a Share of Wealth?" *Human Organization* 58(4): 439–42.

Hines, C. 2000. *Localization: A Global Manifesto.* London: Earthscan Publications.

IDEFEM. 1998. Informe Sobre Las Actividades Principales (Activity Report for 1997). Realizadas Durante 1997. Unpublished manuscript in author's possession.

Loker, W.M. 2000. "Sowing Discord, Planting Doubts: Rhetoric and Reality in an Environment and Development Project in Honduras." *Human Organization* 59(3): 300–10.

Long, N. 1992. "Introduction." In *Battlefields of Knowledge: The Interlocking of Theory and Practice in Social Research and Development,* ed. N. Long and A. Long. London: Routledge.

Mama Maquin-CIAM. 1994. "From Refugees to Returnees." Chiapas, Mexico: Mama Maquin-CIAM.

Melel. 2000a. "ONG's Anuncian Jornada de Consulta Para Formular Propuestas de Gobierno" ("NGOs Announce Consultation on Government Proposals"). Melel Xojobal, Jueves, 14 de septiembre de 2000.

———. 2000b. "Fox Pretende Impulsar La Participacion de las ONG's en Política Publica" ("Fox Encourages NGO Participation in Public Policy"). Melel Xojobal. Lunes, 18 de septiembre, 2000.

Nash, J.C. 2001. *Mayan Visions: The Quest for Autonomy in an Age of Globalization.* New York: Routledge.

Orlove, B. 1999. "Working in the Field: Perspectives on Globalization in Latin America." In *Globalization and the Rural Poor in Latin America,* ed. W.M. Loker. Boulder, CO: Lynne Riener Publishers.

Powers, N.R. 2001. *Grassroots Expectations of Democracy and Economy.* Pittsburgh: University of Pittsburgh Press.

Rew, A. 1997. "The Donor's Discourse: Official Social Development Knowledge in the 1980s." In *Discourses of Development: Anthropological Perspectives,* ed. R.D. Grillo and R.L. Stirrat. New York: Berg Publishers.

Roberts, B. 2000. "NGO Leadership, Success, and Growth in Senegal: Lessons From Ground Level." *Urban Anthropology* 29(2): 143–80.

Ross, J. 2000. *The War Against Oblivion: The Zapatista Chronicles 1994–2000.* Monroe, ME: Common Courage.

———. 1995. *Rebellion From the Roots:Indian Uprising in Chiapas.* Monroe, ME: Common Courage.

Schensul, S.L. 2000. "Commando Research: A Rapid Applied Anthropology Technique." In *Classics of Practicing Anthropology 1978–1998,* ed. P.J. Higgins and J.A. Paredes. Oklahoma City, OK: Society for Applied Anthropology (SfAA).

Sillitoe, P. 1998. "The Development of Indigenous Knowledge: A New Applied Anthropology." *Current Anthropology* 39(2): 223–35.

Simonelli, J. 2002. "The Scent of Change in Chiapas." In *Personal Encounters: A Reader in Cultural Anthropology*, ed. L.S. Walbridge and A.K. Sievert. New York: McGraw-Hill.

SfAA (Society for Applied Anthropology). 2000. Working With NGOs: Navigating and Negotiating the Personal, the Local and the Global. Panel organized by J. Simonelli. Papers: "Development Debacles as Lessons," D. Earle. "Who Do You Represent? Neutrality, Resistance and Community Projects," J. Simonelli. Annual Meeting of the Society for Applied Anthropology, San Francisco, March 2000.

SfAA. 2001. Workshop and Conversation: Building a Network of Cooperation for Chiapas. Panel organized by J. Simonelli. Papers: "Theory, Application, and Value: Using Chiapas Community Development to Discuss Lasting Ideas," D. Earle; "Bottom-Up, Top-Down, Inside-Out: Community Development in Chiapas," J. Simonelli. Annual Meeting of the Society for Applied Anthropology, Mérida, Mexico, March 2001.

Speed, S., and J. Collier. 2000. "Limited Indigenous Autonomy in Chiapas, Mexico. The State Government's Use of Human Rights." *Human Rights Quarterly* 22: 877–905.

United Nations High Commission for Refugees (UNHCR). 2001. Mission Statement. Available at: www.unhrc.ch/un&ref/mission/ms1.htm.

Verillo, E., and D. Earle. 1993. "The Guatemalan Refugee Crafts Project: Artisan Production in Times of Crisis." In *Crafts in the World Market*, ed. J. Nash, Albany, NY: SUNY Press.

Wake Forest University. 2000. Video Conference Between the World Bank Artisan's Research Unit and Members of Jolom Mayaetik Cooperative. Organized and moderated by J. Simonelli. Unpublished transcript in author's possession. Wake Forest University, April 15.

Warren, K.B. 1998. *Indigenous Movements and Their Critics*. Princeton, NJ: Princeton University Press.

World Bank/NGOs. 2000. "The World Bank Group: Nongovernmental Organizations and Civil Society." Available at: wbln0018.worldbank.org/essd/essd.nsf/NGOs/home.

World Bank/Participation. 2001. "The World Bank Group: The World Bank Participation Sourcebook." Available at: wbln0018.worldbank.org/wbi/sourcebook/sba211.htm.

About the Editor and Contributors

Ana María Condori is founder and president of the Uñatatawi Foundation, a small NGO in La Paz, Bolivia. She is from the highland Aymara community of Choquecota in the department of Oruro, and is the author of the book, *Mi Despertar/Nayan Uñatatawi* (My Awakening), an autobiographical "testimonial of a woman who has lived in different worlds." Starting from her longstanding involvement with the El Ceibo Cocoa Cooperative, Condori has worked extensively with grassroots Bolivian organizations, particularly women's groups, and has been closely involved with the work of the Cooperative's Technical and Social Promotion Committee. She also has over twenty years' experience encouraging business startup in poor Bolivian communities in partnership with the New York–based Trickle Up Program.

Duncan Earle, Ph.D., is an applied cultural anthropologist, currently associate professor of Anthropology and Chicano Studies, University of Texas El Paso. As codirector of the Maya Study program, he is also adjunct associate professor at Wake Forest University. He received graduate degrees in anthropology from the State University of New York–Albany. With over twenty-five years of field experience in research and community development in Chiapas, Guatemala, and on the U.S.–Mexican border, he has published extensively, including: "Help Without Hurt: Community Goals, NGO Interventions and Lasting Aid Lessons in Chiapas, Mexico," in *Urban Anthropology* (2000); "Mayas Aiding Mayas: Guatemalan Refugees in Chiapas, Mexico," in *Harvest of Violence: The Maya Indians and the Guatemalan Crisis*, edited by R.M. Carmack, University of Okalahoma Press (1988); "Indigenous Identity at the Margin," *Cultural Survival* (1994); "The Guatemalan Refugee Crafts Project: Artisan Production in Times of Crisis," in *Crafts in the World Market*, edited by J. Nash, SUNY Press (1993); and "The Highland Maya in the Lowlands; A Case of Self-Development" in *Mesoamerica* (1983), as well as various other publications. In addition to Spanish, Earle is fluent in two Maya languages. He was a past Mellon Fellow at Vanderbilt University.

Robyn Eversole is research fellow with the Centre for Regional Development and Research at Edith Cowan University's Faculty of Regional Professional Studies in southwestern Australia. She formerly worked as program officer for the Americas with the Trickle Up Program, an international NGO, and has conducted research in Bolivia since 1994 on issues including microenterprise development, NGOs, and grassroots organizations, with funding from the U.S. Fulbright Foundation, McGill University, and elsewhere. She is originally from West Virginia and holds a Ph.D in anthropology from McGill University, Montreal, where she specialized in the anthropology of development. She is also the author of several articles on development issues and five books for children, including *Red Berry Wool* (Albert Whitman 1999) and *The Flute Player/La Flautista* (Orchard Books 1995).

Patricia Feliu is a sociologist, professor, and researcher at the University of Buenos Aires, Argentina. She has worked as a consultant for the International Migration Organisation, the World Bank, and other international and national organizations, on themes of social policy, local development, and social program evaluation. Recent studies include: "Diagnóstico y mapeo de la actividad de agricultura urbana, Ciudad de Buenos Aires y conurbano bonarerense" (Diagnostic and Mapping of Urban Agriculture Activity in the City of Buenos Aires and Surrounding Area); "Elaboración de mapas, técnica para trabajar en grupos de discusión" (Mapmaking: A Technique for Discussion Groups); "Informes nacional de la Consulta con los pobres en Argentina" (National Report on the Consultation with the Poor in Argentina); and "Una experiencia en cultura de la salud. Municipio de José C. Paz" (An Experience of Health Culture in José C. Paz Municipality). *Las voces de los pobres, Argentina* (*Voices of the Poor, Argentina*) was published by the World Bank, Buenos Aires, in November 2000.

Makonen Getu holds a Ph.D. in economics and economic history from the University of Stockholm. His career in international development has included work as a program officer in Lesotho with the United Nations Development Program, as a research officer with the Swedish Agency for Research Co-operation with Developing Countries, and as a deputy country director for World Vision International (Zambia). He is currently director of Opportunity International's Opportunity Centre for Transformation Studies in Oxford, England. Getu is the author of two books: *Socialism, Participation and Agricultural Development in Ethiopia* and *Microenterprise Development in Theory and Practice*, as well as numerous articles on issues related to development and microcredit.

Jean Grugel, Ph.D., is senior lecturer in politics at the University of Sheffield. She has been visiting professor at the Instituto Ortega y Gasset (Universidad Complutense de Madrid, Spain), Universidad Central de Caracas, Venezuela, and Universidad de Salvador, Buenos Aires, Argentina. She is currently cochair of the Latin America–Europe section of the Latin America Studies Association (LASA). She has written *Politics and Development in the Caribbean Basin: Central America and the Caribbean in the New World Order*, Macmillan/the University of Indiana Press, 1995; *Franco's Spain* (with T. Rees), Edward Arnold, 1997; *Regionalism Across the North-South Divide* (edited with W. Hout), Routledge, 1998; *Democracy Without Borders: Transnational and Non-State Actors in Eastern Europe, Africa and Latin America*, Routledge, 1999; and *Democratization*, Palgrave, 2002. She is currently working on a twentieth-century history of Latin America and beginning a project on the new political economy of aid.

Frank Hutchins received a Ph.D. in cultural anthropology from the University of Wisconsin–Madison. He has been a Fulbright Fellow, an Inter-American Foundation Fellow, and a W.K. Kellogg Fellow. His dissertation was on "The Cultural Impacts of Ecotourism in Ecuador's Amazon"; recently he has presented papers based on his research to the American Anthropological Association, the Latin American Studies Association, the Conference of Latin Americanist Geographers, and the Twentieth Midwest Conference on Andean and Amazonian Archaeology and Ethnohistory. He currently teaches at Drake University. His previous work was in journalism, including holding the position of city editor at the *Charleston Daily Mail*, Charleston, West Virginia.

James R. Keese holds a Ph.D. from the University of Arizona and is a geography lecturer in the Social Sciences Department at California Polytechnic State University. His research interests include smallholder agriculture, sustainable development, and nongovernmental organizations in Latin America and the Andes, and he has conducted field research in Ecuador, Bolivia, and Mexico. Publications include various articles for the *Encyclopedia of World Geography* (2001), as well as "International NGOs and Land Use Change in a Southern Highland Region of Ecuador" in *Human Ecology: An Interdisci-*

plinary Journal (1998); "El Proyecto Ligmate: Modelo de Cooperación Interinstitucional en El Cañar" (The Ligmate Project: A Model of Inter-Institutional Cooperation in El Cañar) in *Cántaro: Cuestiones Sobre Desarrollo En El Austro* (1995); and "International NGOs and Sustainable Agricultural Development: A Methodological Analysis with Examples from Highland Ecuador" recently accepted for publication in *Ecuadorian Studies/Estudios Ecuatorianos.*

Ana Mayta is the founder and director of Acción Creadora (Creative Action) (ACRE), an NGO in El Alto, Bolivia, that works to improve technical quality and market links for textiles produced by women in outlying migrant settlements. She is a Bolivian business professional with several years of experience working with the NGO and international cooperation sector in La Paz.

Laurie Occhipinti has been doing anthropological research in northwestern Argentina since 1996. She received her Ph.D. in anthropology in 2000 from McGill University, Montreal, and currently lectures at Northeastern University in Boston. Her dissertation research examined the role of Catholic NGOs in economic development in indigenous communities. Her current research interests continue to focus on religious NGOs to develop a better understanding of ideas of development based on notions of social justice. She also continues to work in the Wichí communities of the Argentine Chaco in order to help formulate strategies for land use, economic sustainability, and indigenous rights in the region.

Jeanne Simonelli, Ph.D., is an applied cultural anthropologist and writer; she is currently professor and chair of anthropology at Wake Forest University. She received graduate degrees in public health and anthropology from the University of Okalahoma. Her field experiences are united by the broad theme of change and choice in difficult situations and have resulted in three books, *Crossing Between Worlds: The Navajos of Canyon de Chelly* (1997), *Too Wet To Plow: The Family Farm in Transition* (1992), and *Two Boys, A Girl, and Enough!* (1986). She is currently doing fieldwork on development and conflict resolution in Chiapas, Mexico. Recent publications and presentations resulting from that work include "Help Without Hurt: Community Goals, NGO Interventions and Lasting Aid Lessons in Chiapas, Mexico" with Duncan Earle in *Urban Anthropology* (2000) and two sessions at professional meetings, "Alternate Visions: Understanding Conflict and Conflicting Understanding in Chiapas: Presentations in Honor of June Nash" at the annual meetings of the American Anthropological Association, San Francisco, November

2000, and "Workshop and Conversation: Building a Network of Cooperation for Chiapas," at the annual meeting of the Society for Applied Anthropology, Merida, Mexico, March 2001. She received the 2000 prize for poetry from the American Anthropological Association, for her series of poems titled *Conflict Zone: Expressions of Fieldwork in Chiapas.* Current fieldwork is supported by grants from the Archie Fund, Wake Forest University, and the Carr Foundation, Oneonta, NY. She is co-director of the Maya Study Program at Wake Forest University.

Patrick C. Wilson received his Ph.D. from the University of Pittsburgh in 2002. He conducted fieldwork in 1995 and again between 1997 and 1999 on indigenous organizing and development in Ecuador's Amazon basin with funding from the Fulbright Institute of International Education, the National Security Education Program, and the University of Pittsburgh's Center for Latin American Studies. His dissertation, "Indigenous Federations, NGOs, and the State: Development and the Politics of Culture in Ecuador's Amazon," studies the history of indigenous ethnic organizing in Ecuador's Amazon basin, and its constant but nebulous articulation with the Ecuadorian state with international and national development NGOs, and with oil, mining, and timber companies.

Index